John Devoy's *Catalpa* Expedition

John Devoy's
Catalpa Expedition

Edited by
Philip Fennell and Marie King

NEW YORK UNIVERSITY PRESS
New York and London

NEW YORK UNIVERSITY PRESS
New York and London
www.nyupress.org

© 2006 by New York University
All rights reserved

Library of Congress Cataloging-in-Publication Data
Devoy, John, 1842–1928.
John Devoy's Catalpa expedition / Philip Fennell and
Marie King, editors.
p.   cm. — (Ireland House series)
Includes bibliographical references and index.
ISBN-13: 978-0-8147-2748-5 (cloth : alk. paper)
ISBN-10: 0-8147-2748-4 (cloth : alk. paper)
1. Fremantle (W.A.)—History. 2. Irish—Australia—Fremantle
(W.A.)—History—19th century. 3. Escapes—Australia—Fremantle
(W.A.)—History—19th century. 4. Political prisoners—
Australia—Fremantle (W.A.) 5. Penal colonies—Australia—
Fremantle (W.A.) 6. Catalpa (Bark) 7. Fenians.
I. Title: Catalpa expedition. II. Fennell, Philip. III. King, Marie.
IV. Title. V. Series.
DU380.F8D48 2006
994.1′1—dc22   2005024874

New York University Press books are printed on acid-free paper,
and their binding materials are chosen for strength and durability.

Manufactured in the United States of America
10 9 8 7 6 5 4 3 2 1

For George W. King
who sailed the seven seas
for forty years

CONTENTS

Foreword by Martín Kevin Cusack	*ix*
Introduction by Terry Golway	1
Acknowledgments	11
Abbreviations	13
Editors' Prologue	15
Editors' Note	26
I Cruise of a New Bedford Whaler That Brought Humiliation to England—Irish Skill and Yankee Grit Combined—Six Irish Military Prisoners Taken from an English Prison in Western Australia by The Clan-na-Gael—How and Why the Work Was Done	27
II Seven Thousand Men Knew of the Expedition, but There Was No Traitor—Discussed from Maine To California—Yet the Blow Fell on England Like a Bolt from the Blue—How the Work Was Started —The Committee in Charge	38
III John Mitchel Knew of the Project and Helped to Raise Funds —A Characteristic Letter	47
IV Official Report of the Work Done Presented to a Convention in 1876—The Arduous Work of Raising the Money—How John Boyle O'Reilly Got a United States Naval Engineer to Inspect the Vessel	54
V [No heading in the original account. The chapter describes the final preparations and departure of the *Catalpa*.]	63
VI How John J. Breslin and Thomas Desmond of San Francisco Were Selected to Do the Work—An Appointment by James Stephens	72
VII Auspicious Beginning of the Expedition by Captain Anthony Succoring a Ship in Distress—Caught Whale in the North Atlantic —John Breslin's Official Report of the Enterprise—Anxiously Waiting for Ship's Arrival	78

Contents

VIII John J. Breslin's Graphic Account of the Escape of the Six Prisoners, the Dash for the Boat, the Long and Weary Pull for the Ship, the Arrival on Board in the Nick of Time, and the Sharp Parley With the "*Georgette*"—The Victory Won   88

IX Breslin's Difficulties with the Men on the Homeward Voyage— Complained of Food and Treatment and Were Discontented— Demanded to Be Put Ashore and Forced a Change in the Plans— Arrived in New York   109

X Unexpected Arrival of the Vessel in New York Creates Many Difficulties—Factional Attempt to "Capture" The Men from the Committee Foiled by Patrick Lennon's Quiet Threat to Use Force —Work of Providing for the Soldiers   123

XI Work of Raising Funds for the Rescued Men and the Winding Up of the Expedition—The Slander-Monger at Work—Financial Statement of the Enterprise   130

XII The Expedition Wound Up After Many Difficulties—John King's Narrative of His Part in the Work—The Fenians in Australia Had a Rescue Project of Their Own—Meeting with Breslin—How He Ran the Quarantine   139

XIII John King Continues His Narrative of His Personal Part in the Enterprise—Meeting with the Two Men Sent From the Other Side of the Atlantic on the Same Errand—The Two Parties Arrange to Cooperate   150

XIV Conclusion of John King's Narrative of His Share in the Splendid Work—The Severe Ordeal in the Open Boat and the Race for the Ship Facing British Guns—Safe in the Land of the Free   159

Editors' Epilogue   167

Appendix A: Letters from James Wilson   *185*
Appendix B: From the Report of the Eighth Annual [Clan-na-Gael]
    Convention, Cleveland, Ohio, September 4, 1877   *194*
Appendix C: Dramatis Personae   *211*
Sources   *213*
Index   *219*
About the Editors   *225*

FOREWORD

Martín Kevin Cusack

The story of this daring and noble historical event has been told before. Other historians over the years, sensing its importance as a reflection of the burning desire of the Irish for freedom, have published it or alluded to it many times in articles, in books, and even as an Australian radio drama. This book, by Philip Fennell and Marie King, descendants of pardoned Fenian prisoner Thomas McCarthy Fennell, brings us a first-hand primary source account of the episode written by men more personally and directly involved in the episode than previous historians.

This is the work of one of the Irish-born American Fenians, John Devoy, who shouldered much of the responsibility for planning the daring enterprise and moving it forward. His was the onerous task of raising funds to purchase, fit out, and man the whaling ship *Catalpa*. The task was made even more difficult by both skepticism about the success of the venture and suspicions of dishonesty engendered by the need for absolute secrecy about details, which need required that specifics be withheld from nearly seven thousand American Fenians from whom subscriptions for funds were sought.

Though it has been told before, and though it narrates an event that occurred more than 125 years ago, this story is timely today because it causes us to reflect upon fundamental values that are basic to a civilized free society. These men, in most cases with the support of their families, succeeded in this enterprise because they were imbued with a strong sense of sacrifice, loyalty to their comrades, and dedication to the principles of justice and freedom.

It is not just a story of the Irish desire for freedom from British rule. It is about America and the American spirit of liberty. The Fenians, known as the Irish Republican Brotherhood in Ireland and later as the Clan-na-Gael in the United States, and their predecessor organization, the Young Irelanders, all upheld America as a role model. Our Fenian antecedents in their memoirs, poetry, and diaries frequently extolled the American achievement as an inspiration as they strove to free Ireland from British

Foreword by Martin Kevin Cusack

rule. References to America, sometimes called "Columbia," are to be found in the diaries and letters of my forebear, John Sarsfield Casey ("The Galtee Boy"), and Denis B. Cashman, as well as in the memoir of Thomas McCarthy Fennell and the literature of John Boyle O'Reilly.

Those four Fenians, who earlier had written of their experiences, as well as the six who were freed by the *Catalpa* rescue, shared the hardships of transportation to Australia aboard the *Hougoumont,* the last of the convict ships, and incarceration in Fremantle Prison. Upon release, most of those who were civilians with shorter sentences made their way to America, but they never forgot their left-behind comrades, who, as British military men, did not benefit from the amnesty granted the civilians.

In America, over the 150 years prior to the War of Independence, an American culture of *e pluribus unum* (one out of many) had evolved. Of that culture were Captain George Anthony, his cousins, his forebears, and his associates, as well as the millions of assimilated immigrants who followed in the nineteenth-century. The unique American culture also called for embracing the idea of individual self-reliance—a kind of personal independence enjoyed by citizens of the now independent, free country. They lived in an atmosphere that was ideally suited for the conception of grand ventures of this kind.

Having achieved independence, the new country's leaders had the wisdom to adopt that truly revolutionary document, the United States Constitution, which established the severely limited form of self-government that enabled liberty to thrive and a great nation to emerge. The newly founded American country gave its citizens a maximum of privacy and freedom from *their own* government. Americans of that period were free to succeed or fail in life. They did not ask what their government could do for them—that was the thinking of peoples content to live under monarchs or socialism.

The seemingly impossible goal of first freeing men from a remote prison and then rescuing them from a foreign land more than fourteen thousand miles distant called for imaginative planning and daring execution. The undertaking, of necessity, brought together elements of the American culture in the "Yankee Grit" of Captain George Anthony and the characteristic raw courage of the heretofore failed (and jailed) revolutionaries—the newly exiled-to-America Irish Fenians.

Some of the latter (even Devoy, initially) offered plans that were wholly impractical, such as forming an armed band of men to free the prisoners by an assault on Fremantle Prison. Though well-intentioned, their ideas

Foreword by Martin Kevin Cusack

were similar to the thinking of earlier American Fenians who had hatched such harebrained, doomed-to-failure schemes as invading Canada to trade captured Canadian territory for Ireland's freedom from Britain.

Fortunately, there were among the planners exiled Irish Fenians in America who had absorbed the American culture and brought sensible ideas as well as courage ("Irish Skill") to the fore: workable plans that ultimately led to success when joined in brilliant execution with "Yankee Grit." ("Irish Skill" and "Yankee Grit" are from the title of Devoy's first chapter.) These were men like Thomas McCarthy Fennell, Denis B. Cashman, and, of course, John Boyle O'Reilly and John Devoy. Fennell was the first to propose a practical plan: send a ship in the guise of a grain or cargo carrier that would earn revenue to offset some of the burdensome costs of the venture. As it turned out, the plan finally settled upon by O'Reilly and others, a whaling expedition that included revenue-earning expectations, had its roots in the plan Fennell had first proposed.

Devoy maintains the first-hand telling of the story by incorporating a full report by John J. Breslin and a detailed narrative written by John King, both of whom were directly involved and "on the ground" at the actual rescue.

This is an exciting, suspenseful story of a venture of daunting complexity—one that I'm proud to introduce, having had two granduncles, James J. Ryan and Captain (Union Army) William Cusack who, as Irish-born American Fenians, were strong behind-the-scenes supporters of the *Catalpa* rescue.

INTRODUCTION

Terry Golway

He was born in County Kildare before the Famine and he lived to see the founding of the Irish Free State. One of the hardiest of Fenians, he served as an organizer for James Stephens in 1865 and as an ally of Michael Collins in 1922. He feuded bitterly with Jeremiah O'Donovan Rossa and with Eamon de Valera. He traveled to Ireland as a fugitive in 1879 to meet with Charles Stewart Parnell; he returned a hero in 1924, at the invitation of William Butler Yeats.

John Devoy was one of the most formidable Irish patriots of the nineteenth and early twentieth centuries, a determined, passionate, and single-minded advocate for Ireland's freedom. He spent most of his long life in New York, but he never truly assimilated and did not regret it. John Devoy was not an immigrant. He was an exile.

He also was a writer, and in that capacity he became the unofficial historian of a movement he served for more than sixty years. The book you are holding is his account of one of the most remarkable (and most successful) ventures he undertook in the name of Irish freedom: the rescue of a half-dozen imprisoned Irish rebels who were wasting away in the prison colony of Western Australia in 1876. Devoy wrote this long and valuable recollection of that episode in 1904, when he was editor of his own newspaper, the New York–based *Gaelic American.*

Who was this extraordinary man, and how did he emerge as the voice of Irish nationalism in America? Why did such diverse figures as Parnell, Michael Davitt, John Boyle O'Reilly, James Connolly, Padraig Pearse, and Yeats seek him out?

It was not necessarily because John Devoy was a charming, amiable fellow. Hard men rarely are, and John Devoy was a hard man indeed. He lashed out at critics, and sometimes even at allies. He did not make friends; he created alliances. He never married and spent many years living in cheap hotel rooms. Although an accomplished journalist who rose to become foreign editor of the *New York Herald* in the late 1870s, he sacrificed a promising career in newspapers so he could better devote himself to organizing

Introduction by Terry Golway

revolution in Ireland. His writing is filled with passionate fury and devoid of ironic detachment. He had dark eyes and a deep voice, a barrel chest and a flowing beard. He was a serious man, engaged in a serious business.

A British spy who infiltrated the Irish Republican movement in America named Thomas Beach once described Devoy as

a man of weighty influence. Forbidding of aspect, with a perpetual scowl upon his face, he immediately conveyed the idea of being a quarrelsome man, an idea sustained and strengthened by both his manner of speech and gruffness of voice. . . . [His] friendships were few and far between, and had it not been for his undoubted ability . . . he could never have reached the prominent place which he subsequently attained in the Fenian organization.[1]

Beach, who insinuated himself into Devoy's confidence in the 1880s while posing as a doctor and Irish sympathizer named Henri Le Caron, was not particularly generous in his assessment of Devoy's personality. However, he did identify exactly what it was that made this man so important: his undoubted ability. John Devoy knew how to organize. He knew how to agitate. Though he had pledged his loyalty to a nonexistent Irish Republic, he had little tolerance for romantic dreamers and even less for those who valued the fireworks of gesture more than the hard work of organization. This hard-headed, steely-eyed approach was not, suffice it to say, a hallmark of the Irish-American movement prior to Devoy's arrival in 1871. Once Devoy took control of revolutionary activities in the United States in the mid-1870s, Irish America became, in essence, a second front in the struggle to win Ireland's freedom.

John Devoy was born in the townland of Kill in County Kildare on September 3, 1842, the third of eight children born to William and Elizabeth (Dunne) Devoy. The Devoy and Dunne families, long-time farmers in Kildare, had been involved in Ireland's struggle for decades. Devoy's paternal grandfather, also named John, was a member of the Society of United Irishmen, founded in the 1790s by Theobald Wolfe Tone. His maternal grandfather, Johnny Dunne, fought with the United Irishmen in 1798, the Year of the French. The spirit of rebellion was alive in young John Devoy's home. His father, William, and his uncles were active in Daniel O'Connell's mass movement against the Act of Union, which had united Great Britain and Ireland in 1801. William Devoy was a repeal warden in O'Connell's organization—the rough equivalent of being a block captain in the American urban political machine of the early twentieth century.

Introduction by Terry Golway

William and Elizabeth Devoy and their children lived in a small cabin just off the Dublin road. Their farm was just half an acre, hardly enough to ward off starvation, so William Devoy earned extra money by working as a laborer. The Devoys were literate, comparatively prosperous, and definitely pious. In his later years, William Devoy described his Sunday routine in a letter to John: "I rise at six o'clock on Sunday and go to seven o'clock mass . . . and wait for the eight o'clock mass . . . go to breakfast, then the 11:30 and 12 o'clock masses, and on to the park. . . . Sometimes I sleep . . . then on to vespers at 7:30 and that ends the day's amusements."[2]

It was not religion but politics that young John absorbed at the crowded Devoy dinner table. His father and uncles talked excitedly about O'Connell's repeal movement, and they told family legends about the Devoys and Dunnes who did their part for Ireland in the days of Wolfe Tone. Young John kept himself awake at night, listening to his father read aloud from the nationalist newspaper, *The Nation*.

With their tiny farm supplying strawberries, cabbage, and, of course, potatoes, and with William Devoy apparently never lacking for work, the Devoys were not hungry in the mid-1840s. Elsewhere in Ireland, however, the potato crop was in ruins, and Irish families were starving, dying, or leaving. Famine, or more precisely, the ruin of Ireland's potato crop, would lead to the death of a million Irish people and the emigration of another million or more. The Great Famine, which began in 1845 and lasted until about 1851, was the defining moment for a generation of Irish people, an enduring symbol of Britain's neglect and misrule. In County Kerry, Devoy's future friend and antagonist, Jeremiah O'Donovan Rossa, suffered terribly. At one point during the Hunger, Rossa heard his parents quietly discussing the disappearance of a donkey from their farm. They soon realized, to their horror, that somebody had killed and eaten the animal. Months later, Rossa watched his father slowly starve to death. That terrible experience turned the young boy into one of Ireland's most ferocious nationalists.

The Devoys were spared suffering and tragedy, but their lives changed as the Famine neared its end. John's father, William, lost his job and they simply couldn't survive on the small plot of land they farmed. So, they packed their belongings into a cart and set out for Dublin, twelve miles away. Within a few months, on August 14, 1849, John's oldest sibling was dead of cholera. James Devoy, who was just fourteen years old, was one of eleven thousand Dubliners who died of the disease during the Famine. Every night the family knelt together on the floor of their new home and prayed for the repose of James's soul. In his old age, John Devoy would

Introduction by Terry Golway

remember the welts he developed on his knees from those long, grief-stricken sessions.

When John was about ten years old, he engaged in his first public act of rebellion. This glimpse of a future life of agitation took place in a primary school on Dublin's Marlborough Street. Young John decided one morning that he would not participate in the daily singing of "God Save the Queen," the national anthem of the United Kingdom—a nation that, according to the Act of Union, included Ireland. John's scandalized teacher immediately sent for the school's superintendent, a man named Sheehy.

"Sing, sir," Sheehy commanded. John refused, and Sheehy responded by cracking the student's skull with a piece of slate. John missed several days of school because of what he called a "lightness in the head," and when he returned to class without a parent to explain his absence, Sheehy was waiting for him. Armed with a cane, he was ready to teach John another lesson in obedience, that is, until the young boy took matters into his own hands. He rammed Sheehy at thigh-level, knocking him off balance, and then administered a kick to the superintendent's shins. John was immediately expelled, but he had struck his first blows against oppressive authority.

The attack on Sheehy did not end John Devoy's formal education. His parents found another school for him, and he continued to educate himself in Irish history. He became friendly with another young man by the name of James J. O'Kelly, the son of a Dublin blacksmith. Together, in 1861, the eighteen-year-old Devoy and his friend O'Kelly were inducted into a shadowy organization called the Irish Republican Brotherhood (IRB), run by a dreamy nationalist named James Stephens. John Devoy was now a Fenian.

The Fenians pledged themselves to an Irish Republic that existed in their minds, but nowhere else. To help prepare himself for the coming struggle on the Republic's behalf, Devoy ran away from home and joined the French Foreign Legion several weeks after joining the IRB. It was an ironic decision: in his zeal to learn the military skills needed to overthrow British rule in Ireland, Devoy found himself part of a French garrison in Algeria. The would-be freedom fighter was part of an occupying army.

His North African adventure lasted about a year, and Devoy would later recall that he fired his weapon so infrequently it began to rust. Suffice it to say, if he had been looking to test his courage and skill under fire, he was in the wrong place at the wrong time. Nevertheless, when he returned to Ireland and the IRB in 1862, Devoy was no longer considered an inexperienced youth, but a military veteran. James Stephens, the IRB's chief, assigned Devoy the important task of recruiting new Fenians in County

Introduction by Terry Golway

Kildare. Devoy did his job well, enough to earn Stephens's full confidence. In late 1865, Devoy was given the highly sensitive task of recruiting Irish-born British soldiers into the Fenian movement. In other words, he was in charge of fomenting treason in the armed forces. The IRB hoped that when the time came to rise, the British army in Ireland would be so subverted that troops would switch sides en masse, and fight not for the queen but for the Republic.

Devoy went about his task with energy, passion, and courage; he at one point disguised himself as a British soldier in order to gain admission to a garrison where soldiers-turned-Fenians were getting ready to launch a rebellion on their own. All the while, James Stephens kept postponing the planned revolt, and then it was too late. The British realized, to their horror, just how successful Devoy's efforts had been, and they quickly rounded up as many Fenians as they could. Devoy himself was arrested in February 1867, not long after paying a visit to his new fiancée, Eliza Kenny of County Kildare. The rebellion he helped plan took place several weeks after his arrest. It was crushed in no time.

In the dark cells of places like Millbank and Dartmoor Prisons, Devoy met other jailed Fenians, including Jeremiah O'Donovan Rossa. There, they continued to resist British authority, with Rossa creating an international incident by smuggling out word of conditions in the prisons.

In 1871, Devoy, Rossa, and several other Irish prisoners were released on condition that they never return to Ireland. There was little question about their next destination—they sailed to New York, where they would continue to work for Ireland, far from the prying eyes of British authorities.

Devoy's arrival in New York harbor in January 1871 marked a turning point in Irish-American history. The Famine generation and its children were gathered in America's cities in numbers too great for any political organization to ignore. In New York, a city of one million people in 1870, some 20 percent were Irish born and another 37 percent had at least one Irish-born parent. By contrast, there were only about three thousand Italians in the city at the time, and about eighty thousand Jews.

What's more, New York had emerged as the capital of an Irish Republic in exile during and just after the Civil War. The American equivalent of the IRB, the Fenian Brotherhood, was headquartered in the city and openly recruited Union Army veterans into a self-styled army of the Irish Republic. Tammany Hall, shrewd as ever, had detected change in the air and was actively courting the Irish-American vote—in fact, Tammany

Introduction by Terry Golway

sent a delegation of Democrats to greet Devoy, Rossa, and their comrades when they arrived in New York harbor. Local Republicans had the same plan, though, and the result was a first-class brawl aboard the vessel that brought the Irish prisoners across the Atlantic.

Even as the Irish were becoming the dominant ethnic group in many American cities, Irish-American political exiles were something of a national joke. The Fenian Brotherhood had broken up in dissension, with two competing groups claiming to speak for Irish-American exiles. Three times since the end of the Civil War, an army of Irish-American Fenians had marched on British-ruled Canada in hopes of provoking war between the United States and Britain, a war that they believed could lead to Ireland's freedom. The first invasion, launched in 1867, actually succeeded for several days and was cheered by newspapers like the *New York Herald,* which believed that Britain was pro-Confederate during the Civil War. Some fifteen hundred Irish-Americans, many of them Union Army veterans, fought a skirmish with Canadian militia before being driven back across the border. Subsequent invasions, however, were miserable failures, and the press turned on these Irish-American exiles who seemed better at talking than at fighting. The Fenian Brotherhood, which had seemed a formidable force on paper, was reduced to a laughingstock.

John Devoy changed all of that, and he did it by purchasing a ship called the *Catalpa* and organizing an improbable rescue mission involving careful coordination, thousands of dollars, and breathtaking audacity.

The story of how that rescue unfolded is told in Devoy's words in the following pages and needs no elaboration here. However, a few words about John Devoy and his place in Irish America in 1876 are in order.

In a measure of his strength of personality and his abilities, he quickly became a dominant force in the Irish-American exile movement. He paid his bills by working for the *New York Herald,* an institution that employed more than a few Fenians, including Devoy's friend and fellow exile James J. O'Kelly, who was the paper's chief drama critic. (The literary talents and interests of the Fenian leaders never cease to amaze.) Devoy joined a fledgling organization called Clan-na-Gael, founded by yet another Irish-American nationalist on the *New York Herald*'s staff, Jerome Collins; he was the paper's meteorologist. As the Fenian Brotherhood collapsed amid dissension and incompetence, the Clan-na-Gael took its place as the voice of Irish nationalism in America. As a young newcomer Devoy saw in the Clan the foundation for a new, competent, and effective revolutionary organization for Ireland's exiles in America.

Introduction by Terry Golway

What the Clan, what Devoy, and what Irish America needed was a victory of some sort, something that would wipe away the bitter memories of the Fenian Brotherhood's internal squabbles and the ill-fated Canadian adventures.

The opportunity soon presented itself; in late 1873 or early 1874, Devoy received a letter from an Irishman named James Wilson. Devoy had sworn Wilson, then a soldier in the British army, into the IRB during Devoy's younger days. Wilson had been arrested, charged with treason, and, along with several others like him, transported to the prison colony of Western Australia. The prisoners had heard about the release of Devoy, Rossa, and their colleagues, but what about the men who remained in prison? "Dear friend," Wilson wrote, "remember this is a voice from the tomb." Wilson asked Devoy to help them somehow "with your tongue and pen, with your brain and intellect, with your ability and influence. We think if you forsake us, then we are friendless indeed."[3]

This was the beginning of the audacious enterprise that became known as the *Catalpa* rescue.

Wilson's letter was more than just a plea for help. It struck a personal chord with Devoy. He, after all, was the man responsible for Wilson's plight. He had recruited Wilson into the IRB, and now Wilson was rotting away in Western Australia because he had taken the oath pledging his allegiance to the Irish Republic.

Devoy was determined to do something to rescue the forgotten rebels of Western Australia. But his colleagues in Clan-na-Gael did not share his determination, at least not at first. And who could blame them? Australia was a world away. A rescue operation seemed a fool's errand, a fantastic adventure worthy of a dreamer but not of a hard-headed pragmatist like John Devoy.

After the Clan's leadership turned down Devoy's outrageous suggestion, Devoy himself took over the Clan. And, as the following pages will explain, he set out on a mission to bring home the rebels from Australia.

The ensuing rescue—a complex, expensive and audacious scheme— was a milestone in Irish-American nationalist history. The rescue retrieved not just the prisoners but the very credibility of the Irish-American exile movement. Devoy showed just how effective these exiles could be—that Irish America had left behind mere rhetoric and farcical adventures to become a force in Anglo-Irish, and Anglo-American, affairs.

What is striking in Devoy's narrative is the extent to which the Irish exile movement had spread to so many segments of the community. His advisors, colleagues, and co-conspirators included a medical doctor (and, let it be noted, a Presbyterian) named William Carroll of Philadelphia; his friend O'Kelly, the drama critic of the *New York Herald*; the poet and author John Boyle O'Reilly of Boston; and even a United States senator, S. B. Conover—of Florida, no less. Conover's involvement, according to Devoy's plan, was critical. The *Catalpa*'s crew, once it plucked the prisoners from Australia, was ordered to set sail for Florida, where the state's distinguished senator was to arrange for the ship's secret arrival. The senator was the grandson of Irish Presbyterian rebels who fought, like Devoy's family, in the rebellion of 1798. Conover himself was a member of Clan-na-Gael.

Also noteworthy during the 1870s was the very public nature of Irish-American agitation, much to the anger of Great Britain—and of Devoy, a born conspirator. Even as Devoy was launching the top-secret rescue mission, his fellow Fenian and exile Jeremiah O'Donovan Rossa had announced in the *Irish World* newspaper that he would begin collecting money for what he called a "skirmishing fund." Money collected from the Irish-American community, he said, would go towards weapons for the Irish at home to use against Britain. "England will not know where or how she is to be struck," Rossa wrote in announcing the fund.[4]

Devoy was livid when he read Rossa's words. Just as the top-secret *Catalpa* mission was about to reach its climax, here was Rossa drawing attention to Irish revolutionary activities in America. Devoy had no objections to using Irish-American money for weapons; he just didn't think it was wise to call attention to such activities. "We don't see why on earth we should announce our intentions to the world," Devoy wrote to a fellow Clan-na-Gael member. And, in a clear reference to the *Catalpa* mission, he wrote, "We have one 'skirmish' [underway] now. If that succeeds, it will give us an immense lift and we can then tackle the same job in England."[5]

Devoy clearly saw that the *Catalpa* mission would electrify Irish America and would bring Clan-na-Gael new recruits, more money, and worldwide publicity.

It did all that, all right. The *Catalpa* rescue was an astonishing success, and it achieved all that Devoy hoped it would. Devoy and Clan-na-Gael showed that Irish America was more than overheated rhetoric and political pandering. After the mission's success, Great Britain could not afford to ignore the exiles who were plotting in America, far beyond its reach.

The *Catalpa* mission also marked John Devoy as the most important and most effective leader of the Irish-American exile movement. He would hold that title for decades to come.

Introduction by Terry Golway

The story of the *Catalpa* mission ends in 1876, but John Devoy's work truly was just beginning. His activities in future years would make him one of Ireland greatest, though often-neglected, patriots. Devoy also demonstrated a philosophical flexibility that speaks to political changes underway in the north of Ireland in recent years. For example, he quickly understood the potential for genuine political and land reform when Charles Stewart Parnell rallied Irish public opinion in the 1880s. As a sworn Fenian, he was pledged to fight for Irish freedom, not for mere political reform and certainly not for social changes like land reform. But, in a break with the Irish republican movement, Devoy aligned Clan-na-Gael with Parnell and the Fenian-turned-social-reformer Michael Davitt in the early 1880s. The linking of Irish revolutionaries with Parnell and Davitt foreshadowed a similar alliance more than a century later, when Gerry Adams of Sinn Fein, John Hume of the Social Democratic and Labor Party, and Irish prime minister Albert Reynolds moved the republican movement into mainstream politics.

Even after Parnell's collapse, Devoy persisted in the face of internal dissension within the Irish-American movement. In 1903, he put his journalistic skills back to work by founding a weekly newspaper called the *Gaelic American*. (Devoy had briefly published another weekly, the *Irish Nation,* in the 1880s.) The newspaper served as the voice of Clan-na-Gael, and Devoy rallied Irish-American activists with his frequent and first-hand histories of Ireland's national struggle, which explains his multipart series recounting the *Catalpa* rescue. The message to twentieth-century readers was clear: Irish America could, and would, play a role in winning Irish freedom.

Of course, Devoy was doing more than simply recording memories and chronicling current events. He continued to organize Clan-na-Gael activities, preparing for a day he knew could come. Through the early years of the century nearly every Irish patriot of note stopped by his cramped offices in downtown Manhattan to seek his advice or ask for introductions to other prominent Irish Americans. His contacts ranged from James Connolly to Yeats to Joseph McBride to Padraig Pearse. In the years leading to World War I, he became the IRB's envoy to the German consulate in New York, where he laid the groundwork for the arms shipment that never reached the Easter rebels in 1916.

After the rebellion, as both his sight and hearing began to betray him, he remained tireless on Ireland's behalf. So, when Eamon de Valera came to New York to raise money for the realization of the Republic of Ireland, he naturally sought Devoy's help and advice. To hear Devoy tell it,

9

Introduction by Terry Golway

however, de Valera was less interested in the latter and far more interested in the former. The two men wound up despising each other and fought a war of words on American soil even as the climactic battle for Irish freedom was underway back home.

Devoy sided with Michael Collins after the treaty, regarding partition and the oath to Britain's monarch as compromises on the road to full freedom for all Ireland. By then, he was well into his eighties, a living link between the Irish Republican Army of 1922 and the Irish Republican Brotherhood of 1865.

In 1924 Devoy returned to Ireland a hero as a private visit home turned into a state occasion for the greatest of Fenians. The journey also led to a surprise: Devoy, a lifelong bachelor, saw the woman he had left behind when he was arrested in 1867. Eliza Kenny was an aging widow who had married another man after she failed to hear from Devoy once he sailed to New York in 1871. The two had a touching reunion, and legend has it that Devoy offered to make good on his offer of decades earlier. She declined, or so the story goes, and Devoy went back to New York. He nearly returned to Ireland one more time, in 1927, but he canceled the trip when he learned that his old love, Eliza, had died.

Devoy himself died in Atlantic City, New Jersey, on September 29, 1928. His body was returned to Ireland, and he received a state funeral culminating in burial in Glasnevin Cemetery.

He left behind a legacy of determination. He also left behind his words and his memories.

Enjoy them.

NOTES

1. William O'Brien and Desmond Ryan, eds., *Devoy's Post Bag.* 2 vols. (Dublin: Fallon, 1948, 1953), 2:47.

2. Terry Golway, *Irish Rebel: John Devoy and America's Fight for Ireland's Freedom* (New York: St. Martin's Griffin, 1998); 23–24.

3. Seán Ó Lúing, *The Catalpa Rescue* (Tralee, Ireland: Anvil Books, 1965), 57.

4. *Irish World,* March 4, 1876.

5. William O'Brien and Desmond Ryan, eds., *Devoy's Post Bag.* 2 vols. (Dublin: Fallon, 1948, 1953), 1:142–43.

ACKNOWLEDGMENTS

We are indebted to Kevin Cusack for his significant support and guidance over the years. H. A. Willis has encouraged, supported, cajoled, occasionally admonished, and otherwise helped us through this project. Walter McGrath has enthusiastically supported our work and provided material, including his own writings on the *Catalpa*. David Sheehy, a descendant of Fenian Denis Cashman (who played a part in this story), and his wife Mary unhesitatingly shared material about Denis and his life in Boston.

We especially thank Professor Marion Casey for her knowledge and confidence that this manuscript would be published, along with Professors J. J. Lee and Eileen Reilly, all of New York University's Glucksman Ireland House, whose commitment assured the project's completion. Despina Papazoglou Gimbel and the staff of NYU Press patiently guided us through the publishing process.

Our research brought us into contact with many fine institutions and people: Laura Pereira at the Kendall Institute, New Bedford Whaling Museum, who has been a seemingly endless source for information; Timothy Meagher and Patrick Cullom at The American Catholic History Research Center and University Archives of Catholic University of America; and the many librarians and pages at the New York Public Library. The Mid-Hudson Library System, Adriance Public Library (N.Y.), and Patti Haar and the entire staff of the Patterson Library Association (N.Y.) patiently accommodated a remarkable number of interlibrary loan requests. We also benefited from collections and services at the New Bedford Public Library, the San Francisco History Center of the San Francisco Public Library, the Elmer Holmes Bobst Library and the Institute of Fine Arts of New York University, the Free Library of Philadelphia, the New York Genealogical and Biographical Society, the Boston Public Library, the Chicago Public Library, the Thomas P. O'Neill Jr. and John J. Burns Libraries of Boston College, the Raynor Memorial Libraries of Marquette University, the Hesburgh Library of Notre Dame University, the John Hay Library of Brown University, the O'Malley Library of Manhattan College, the National Army

Acknowledgments

Museum (UK), the Vassar College libraries, the Research Library of the Rhode Island Historical Society, the National Archives and Records Administration (New York Region), the Manuscript Division of the Library of Congress, the Central Park Conservancy, the Philadelphia Police Museum, and the Rush Rhees Library of the University of Rochester.

Questions to the Down County Museum (Northern Ireland) and the Old Drogheda Society (Ireland) yielded helpful answers; Paul Anzalc, an archivist with the Roman Catholic Diocese of St. Paul, Minnesota, provided information on Father Patrick McCabe, and Peter Bridge of Hesperian Press, Western Australia, provided a number of old newspaper accounts related to this work. Matthew Bermingham, Paddy Waldron, Patrick McCarthy, and Rob Besford also responded to overseas inquires, as did Noel Kissane and the staff of the National Library of Ireland and Sister Marie Therese Foale, RSJ, Adelaide Archdiocesan Archives. William Cobert again welcomed us to the American Irish Historical Society's headquarters and guided us through the library holdings. Jack Wemp shared not only his artistic depiction of the *Catalpa* and *Georgette* confrontation but also his research on the subject. Brian and Daniel (Jr.) Fennell extended their respective areas of expertise to solve some otherwise frustrating research issues. We have appreciated the advice of Robert Levy, Nerou (Neil) Cheng, and C. P. Crow and the help of Peter and Priscilla Laubenstein. Nancy Tanner of the Book Cove in Pawling, New York, has been a supporter of this and our other efforts over the years.

ABBREVIATIONS

In the footnotes, the following abbreviations are used for the following sources.

Catalpa Log   *Logbook of Bark Catalpa of New Bedford, Mass., April 29, 1875 to August 23, 1876.* Captain George S. Anthony, The Kendall Institute and New Bedford Whaling Museum: microform, Log #557; #283/397-488.

FO   Foreign Office (U.K.)

FSLDS   Family Search site of the Church of Jesus Christ of Latter-Day Saints

GA   *Gaelic American*

IA   *Irish American*

IW   *Irish World*

NA   National Archives

NYT   *New York Times*

O.E.D.   *Oxford English Dictionary,* 2nd edition

PRO   Public Records Office (U.K.)

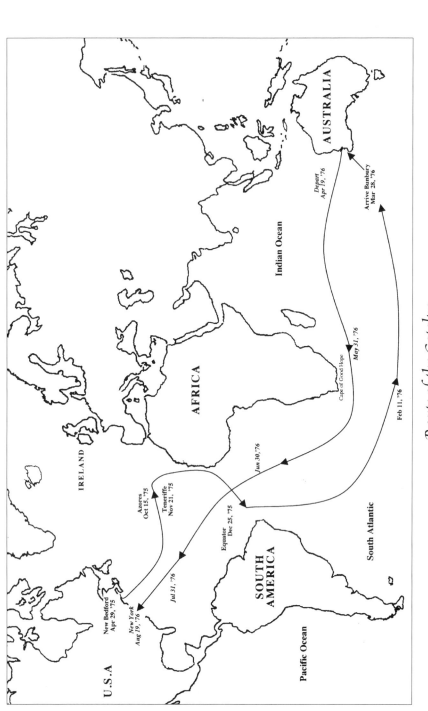

EDITORS' PROLOGUE

This day commences with Light breeses from the SE.
and Clear weather—at 9 AM took our anchors and
stood to sea—at 11:30 the Captian [*sic*] came On board
with officers—Crew all on board.
— *Catalpa Log,* Thursday, April 29, 1875[1]

There was nothing unusual about the bark *Catalpa* working its way out to sea that afternoon. For years whalers departing from New Bedford had followed this route through Buzzards Bay. As was customary, the local papers had listed the ship's crew and stated its destination (accurately) as being the Atlantic and Indian Oceans.[2]

Originally built as a merchant ship, the *Catalpa* had been converted to a whaler and then, nearly two decades later, it reverted back to its original form. When purchased by new owners in 1875, it was again made a whaler.[3] The wisdom of that decision had raised a few eyebrows among the whaling merchants of New Bedford.[4]

The American whaling industry was in decline, the golden age of whaling having long passed. In 1846, 735 American whalers produced over three hundred thousand barrels of oil. Thirty years later, there were only

---

1. The daily log entry recorded information from noon to noon. The date of the entry was the date at the *end* of the period. In this entry, there was nothing recorded (the voyage had not commenced) for the first part of the 24-hour period that started at noon on April 28. Not until the following morning (29th) does the entry start. Any events recorded for the afternoon of the 29th appear in the next day's entry, dated April 30, and so on and so forth. The chief mate was responsible to the owners for keeping the log. *Captain George S. Anthony, Logbook of Bark Catalpa of New Bedford, Mass., April 29, 1875 to August 23, 1876.* The Kendall Institute, New Bedford Whaling Museum: microform, Log #557; #283/397-488; R. H. Dana, Jr., *Two Years Before the Mast and Twenty-four Years After,* 61st printing (New York: Collier, 1937), 16.

2. "Crew List," [New Bedford] *Evening Standard,* April 29, 1875.

3. The ship had returned to the United States from Surinam in 1874. "Marine Intelligence," *New York Times* (hereafter *NYT*), August 21, 1874, 8.

4. "The Escaped Fenians," *New-York Daily Tribune,* August 21, 1876, 5.

169 ships, and they produced less than seventy-three thousand barrels.[5] Nantucket had some years earlier ceded its dominance in the industry to New Bedford,[6] and New Bedford had flown the banner well. The elegant houses of owners, agents, and captains lining the streets attested to its success and wealth as well as the overall vibrancy of the city. Sailors from ports around the world were visible in all quarters.

But the 1859 discovery of petroleum in Pennsylvania foretold the end of the demand for whale oil. No longer would small ships need to undertake expensive and dangerous voyages throughout the seven seas. The Civil War also took its toll on the industry, particularly when Confederate cruisers, built in Britain during the war, destroyed American whalers as distant as Australia. New Bedford even prepared for an attack by these rebel cruisers.[7] While the "*Alabama* claims" addressed this issue and were eventually settled in America's favor after the war, bitterness about the destruction, the complicity of the British government, and that government's arrogant response to negotiations lingered. The fleet had also been pruned during the war when the Navy Department purchased a dozen or so of the older whalers to join the Union's "Stone Fleet." (These ships were filled with stone and sunk at southern harbor entrances to help enforce blockades.)[8]

Then, in 1871, thirty-three whalers were destroyed in the Arctic, trapped by ice. Miraculously, not one of the twelve hundred people aboard was killed, but New Bedford's share of the lost oil and ships was significant. The local natives had warned the captains of the danger, but their advice was ignored, and the unheralded explorers of the oceans learned a devastating lesson. Those ships would never be replaced.[9]

The past successes, or excesses, of the industry had forced whalers to go farther and farther for their prey, making the average journey last three

---

5. Elmo Hohman, *The American Whaleman: A Study of Life and Labor in the Whaling Industry* (Clifton, NJ: Augustus M. Kelley, 1972), 302.

6. Edouard A. Stackpole, *The Sea-Hunters: The New England Whaleman during Two Centuries, 1635–1835* (Philadelphia: Lippincott, [1953]), 454.

7. Leonard Bolles Ellis, *History of New Bedford and Its Vicinity, 1602–1892* (Syracuse, NY: D. Mason, 1892), 320–21.

8. The warships *Alabama, Florida,* and *Shenandoah* were built or refitted near Liverpool during the Civil War. Despite the protests of the United States, the British allowed them to be delivered to the Confederacy, where they proceeded to do considerable damage to U.S. commercial shipping, particularly whalers. In 1872, the British finally settled U.S. claims in the amount of $15.5 million. Granville Allen Mawer, *Ahab's Trade: The Saga of South Seas Whaling* (St. Leonards, N.S.W.: Allen and Unwin, 1999), 267, 272; Samuel Eliot Morison, *The Oxford History of the American People* (New York: Oxford University Press, 1965), 726–29; *Story of Yankee Whaling* (New York: American Heritage Publishing, 1959), 83–84.

9. "Polar Sea Perils," *NYT,* November 14, 1871, 2; Albert Cook Church, *Whale Ships and Whaling* (New York: Norton, 1960), 18.

Editors' Prologue

to four years.[10] Long gone were the days of shore whaling, a common sight on the east coast into the eighteenth century. In 1870, New Bedford's industrial base began to shift to cotton manufacturing and flour mills. Firms such as Wamsutta brought a new vitality to the community. Opportunities for those who previously enjoyed careers at sea now abounded on land.[11]

The nation, indeed all of North America, was in the midst of a depression that had started with the Panic of 1873 and would last five years. (The onset was so severe that the New York Stock Exchange closed for the first time in its history.) Railroad building virtually ceased, other industries suffered, and mercantile failures were numerous. The steep decline of the entire U.S. merchant fleet that started during the Civil War continued. Unemployment was high, and most of those who did find work labored for only part of the year. Labor unrest was widespread and violent, one example being the strikes organized by a secret society in Pennsylvania, the Molly Maguires.[12]

The new owners of the *Catalpa* were obviously risking a great deal. While whaling would continue through the end of the century, the profit and availability of the product diminished annually. There were many more prudent opportunities available to investors. One owner was John T. Richardson, an established local agent and owner of other vessels who presumably knew what he was doing. The other owner of record, unknown in New Bedford, was businessman James Reynolds of New Haven, Connecticut. They selected a local man as master of the ship: George Smith Anthony, Richardson's son-in-law.

The captain descended from one of America's first families that is believed to have arrived from England in the 1630s. George's branch moved from Rhode Island to Massachusetts,[13] eventually settling in Dartmouth. New Bedford, originally part of Dartmouth, was set off in 1787.

Humphrey Anthony, a mariner, married Phebe Thornton Smith and lived in New Bedford.[14] Their son George was born August 23, 1843,[15] the

---

10. Sperm whaling cruises were longer than others. Mawer, xiv; Hohman, 84–85.

11. Ellis, 376–84.

12. "A Review of the Panic," *NYT*, August 22, 1873, 1; *Encyclopedia Britannica*, 1993, 29, 242–44; Morison, 745–47; Sean Dennis Cashman, *America in the Gilded Age*, 3rd edition (New York: New York University Press, 1993), 107–11.

13. Charles L. Anthony, *Genealogy of the Anthony Family from 1495 to 1904* (Sterling, IL: Charles L. Anthony, 1904), 23–24, 110.

14. Charles L. Anthony, 117.

15. *Vital Records of New Bedford, Massachusetts to the Year 1850*. Volume—Births (Boston: New England Historic Genealogical Society, 1932).

Editors' Prologue

fifth of seven children. On March 21, 1852, tragedy struck the family when Humphrey, captain of the New Bedford schooner *Henry Curtis,* drowned at sea.[16] He reportedly missed his reckoning and the ship went ashore at Noman's Land (about three miles southwest of Martha's Vineyard). He followed the fate of his brother, who had also died at sea.[17] He was fifty years old, and George was only nine. Phebe raised the family in New Bedford where uncles, aunts, and other relatives were close by.

George attended local schools. When he was fifteen, he pledged himself to the sea, not uncommon for a young man raised in the whaling culture.[18] Virtually everyone and every business in town were connected to this industry: the crew, their families, the ship agents, the suppliers, and the manufacturers. Some boys accompanied their fathers on the ever-lengthening voyages, and some as young as ten served as cabin boys. Signs of a declining industry did not deter Anthony, and he pursued whaling with great vigor. The New Bedford Port Society Records show that he sailed on the *Draco* in 1862 and 1868 (where he was first mate) and the *Cohannet* (where again he was first mate) in 1872.

He then married Emma Richardson, daughter of John T. and Sophia Wrisley Richardson, in 1874.[19] Promising Emma to stay at home, he took a mechanic's position at a local manufacturing company.[20] Sophie, the first of two children, was born in January 1875. But when the call came to return to his previous vocation, he did not hesitate. This was not only about the lure of the sea, of course, and his prompt response was probably based on several other factors.

The prestige and authority inherent in the captain's position was very appealing. Here, a young man could assume extraordinary responsibility.[21] Economically, the captain of a whaler could do quite well with his lay (the share of compensation paid the officers and crew at the end of a voyage). After the owners took their share of the profits, the balance was divided,

16. "Disaster to the Schooner *Henry Curtis* and Loss of the Captain and Cook," [New Bedford] *Republican Standard,* March 25, 1852.

17. Charles L. Anthony, 117.

18. Z. W. Pease, *The Catalpa Expedition* (New Bedford, MA: George S. Anthony, 1897), 72.

19. Charles L. Anthony, 117–18.

20. Pease, *Catalpa,* 72. The manufacturer was the Morse Twist Drill and Machine Company, which was established in New Bedford in 1864. By the 1870s it was a successful provider of precision tools. Zephaniah W. Pease, ed., *History of New Bedford* (New York: Lewis Historical Publishing, 1918), 1, 253–54.

21. "The captain, in the first place, is lord paramount. He stands no watch, comes and goes when he pleases, and is accountable to no one, and must be obeyed in everything, without a question, even from his chief officer." Dana, 16.

New Bedford Wharf, 1870 (Courtesy New Bedford Whaling Museum)

with the largest amount, expressed in fractions, going to the captain and the smallest to the cabin boy. The rule of thumb worked out to be about one-third each for the ship's outfit, crew, and owner.[22]

Another influence on George may have been his ancestral roots and contemporary relations—his blood, as it were. The Anthonys of America were participants—not spectators—in the development of their country. George's relatives included Susan B. Anthony, the great suffragette; Henry Bowen Anthony, a governor of Rhode Island and four-term U.S. senator; George Tobey Anthony, governor of Kansas; and William Arnold Anthony, a pioneer scientific inventor.

Regardless of how much George knew of his relatives, he shared their boldness and determination. In his book on the *Catalpa,* Zephaniah Pease wrote, "I have always suspected that Devoy and his friends must have aroused the sympathy of Captain Anthony and awakened within him a

22. Mawer, 111.

Editors' Prologue

personal interest in the men whose zeal for patriotism had placed them in an unfortunate position."[23]

Although most of those watching the *Catalpa*'s departure did not know it, this was to be no ordinary whaling expedition. Anthony was one of only two aboard who knew the real objective, and it was to remain confidential for as long as possible. The other man was Denis Duggan, who filled the ship's cooper/carpenter position. He was an Irishman placed on board by the owners. In the interim, the twenty-four officers and crew members[24] of the *Catalpa* were to do what everyone expected: hunt for whales.

The *Catalpa* made its way to the whaling grounds of the north Atlantic, and for five and a half months seemingly meandered until reaching its first port of call, the Azores,[25] a distance of about twenty-three hundred miles from New Bedford.[26] In that long stretch of landless latitudes, the ship was actively whaling.[27] While many types were observed, only the "aristocrat of whales," the sperm, was being sought. The whale's head contained a large quantity of spermaceti, high-quality oil. It was the one whale to produce ambergris, a valuable ingredient for perfumes.[28] Generally, its overall yield exceeded the then industry average of forty-five barrels per whale.[29] Its length ranged up to sixty feet and its weight, up to one hundred thousand pounds, and while being pursued, it achieved speeds up to twenty-seven miles per hour.

Successful sperm kills occurred in May, June, August, and September.[30] July seems to have been a frustrating month, with log entries such as "So ends another day in a gale—nothing but gales and no whales."[31] In fact,

---

23. Pease, *Catalpa*, 76. (Zephaniah W. Pease (1861–1933) was a well-known journalist and writer in New Bedford. He was associated with the [New Bedford] *Morning Mercury* for over fifty years and also served as the collector of the Port of New Bedford in the 1890s. "Z. W. Pease Dead," *NYT*, June 25, 1933, 22.)

24. "List of Persons Composing the Crew," *Catalpa Log*.

25. An Atlantic archipelago located approximately eight hundred miles east of Portugal, of which it is part. "Azores," *Britannica*, 1, 757.

26. Anthony apparently was handicapped throughout the voyage by defective chronometers. The one he left New Bedford with was consistently off and a replacement he obtained at Flores was not much better. Pease, *Catalpa*, 83, 88, 90. (The device is used to determine longitude.) Only one reference to this matter is found in the log. On January 13, it is simply noted that one chronometer had stopped. *Catalpa Log*.

27. Captains followed their prey's well-known migratory patterns. Patricia C. McKissack and Fredrick L. McKissack, *Black Hands, White Sails: The Story of African-American Whalers* (New York: Scholastic Press, 1999), 100.

28. Stackpole, 27–29, 48.

29. *Story of Yankee Whaling*, 38.

30. *Catalpa Log*, May 6, 13, June 13, August 25, 27, September 19, 1875.

31. Ibid., July 15, 1875.

there was a seven-week gap between hunts. Twenty-two-year-old boat-steerer Robert Kanaka died of consumption on August 22 and was buried at sea.[32]

One relief from the tedium between hunts was the gams with other whalers. This custom of socializing was engaged in as often as possible. When two or more ships met, they stopped and visited, perhaps as long as overnight. The captain of the guest ship would go aboard the host, the host's mate would go aboard the guest, and the crews would visit as permitted (a precaution in case whales were sighted). The opportunity to talk with new men, compare notes on the hunt, and obtain news, any news, no matter how old, was relished by officers and crew alike.[33] In all, the *Catalpa* had sixteen gams between July and October, all with American whalers. The frequency can be attributed to the location of the ships that were following normal whaling routes from New England to the Azores or the Cape Verde islands.[34] Even ships destined for the Pacific by way of Cape Horn would generally pass these islands.

The *Catalpa* arrived at Flores on October 14[35] and later went on to Fayal, spending three weeks in the Azores. Anthony had to deal with a variety of matters, not the least of which concerned the crew. Captains expected a high crew turnover during these voyages.[36] Whenever the anchor dropped, men would jump ship for any number of reasons—even the great writer Herman Melville deserted his whaleship in the Pacific. The first reason was economic—the ordinary crew member's lay was a poor incentive to remain on board. After expenses were deducted from the lay, there was often only a paltry sum in the end. It was even possible for crew members to end up owing money, particularly if the voyage had been unsuccessful. Another reason for not staying aboard was the captain being a brutal or unfair man. (There is no evidence that Anthony was such a person.) And if the cook was not very good, a crew jumping ship could be guaranteed. (The cook had a particularly thankless job. Shortly after leaving port, the fresh provisions would be exhausted, leaving only preserved food.) To limit desertions, captains sometimes would not permit shore leave, in which case a determined man simply jumped overboard and

32. Ibid., August 22, 1875.

33. Mawer, 99–100.

34. Cape Verde lies 385 miles off the west coast of Africa. It consists of ten islands and belonged to Portugal. *Britannica,* 2, 826–27.

35. *Catalpa Log.*

36. This was considered one of the industry's most intractable problems. Mawer, 129. "Three out of every ten men deserted on average." Hohman, 69.

Editors' Prologue

swam ashore. But generally the port authorities cooperated in returning such men to the ship.[37]

In an ominous sign for the future, the log recorded that the carpenter/cooper, Denis Duggan, and two others returned to the ship drunk from a binge on their first night in Flores.[38] When confronted by the captain, Duggan was very insolent. Because he was the other member of the ship's company who knew of the *Catalpa*'s true mission, Anthony let it pass, but it left him increasingly uncomfortable about the mission's outcome.[39] Anthony decided to tell his first mate, Samuel Smith, the true purpose of the mission. While Smith may have been surprised, he remained loyal throughout the voyage.[40]

Seven crewmen were lost at Fayal. Four deserted and three were "discarded" for health reasons.[41] Five replacements were recruited to fill the ranks, Anthony no doubt planning to add more at Tenerife as necessary.[42] Just over two hundred barrels of sperm oil were transferred to a lighter (to be shipped home) on October 28,[43] and fresh water and food were taken on over a period of days.

The *Catalpa* next put in at Santa Cruz, Tenerife, in the Canary Islands,[44] on November 20. The two crew members who had been returned by the Azorean authorities literally jumped ship again the following day. A boat was lowered and they were brought back. This time the captain put them in irons and sent them to steerage. One, Keill, said "he was no calf" and

---

37. The "Whaleman's Shipping Paper," signed by crew members, was a legal contract that a captain could cite when requesting the assistance of the authorities. Hohman, 67. (The standard "Whaleman's Shipping Paper" of the period, the agreement among owner, master, seamen, and mariners, also prohibited liquor on board, except for medicinal purposes. All parties to the contract had pledged to abide by this and drunkenness was also prohibited.)

38. *Catalpa Log,* October 16, 1875.

39. *Report of the Eighth Annual Convention,* "V.C." [Clan-na-Gael], Cleveland, Ohio, September 4–8, 1877, 55, "The Fenian Brotherhood Records and O'Donovan Rossa Personal Papers," The American Catholic History Research Center and University Archives, Catholic University of America, Washington, DC.

40. This occurred somewhere between Fayal and Tenerife. Pease, *Catalpa,* 93–95.

41. The local American consul would become responsible for the welfare of discarded crew members. Frequently, the foreign port assessed the ship a fee for all discharged crew members, thereby discouraging the practice. Hohman, 111.

42. Pease described another problem Anthony encountered at Fayal. Apparently, the *Catalpa* had caught a large quantity of albacores right before entering port. The customs authorities insisted that duty be paid on the fish or that they be disposed of. Anthony got rid of the lot. No mention of this is made in the ship's log. Pease, *Catalpa,* 88–89.

43. Pease, *Catalpa,* 89; *Catalpa Log.*

44. The Canary Islands are an Atlantic Ocean archipelago, belonging to Spain, about sixty miles west of the African coast. Tenerife is the largest of the islands. "Canary Islands," *Britannica,* 2, 793.

Editors' Prologue

"sassed" the captain. Over the next few days he complained he could "not make water." The condition necessitated a doctor coming aboard and treating Keill, who then returned to duty.[45] (Also, according to Pease, Anthony had to seek the assistance of the United States consul in documenting the replacement crew members whom he had taken on in the Azores. The Tenerife authorities had faulted the ship's papers and insisted they be put in order.)[46] Three more men were recruited.

After taking on more provisions, the *Catalpa* continued on its mission on November 26, heading south. It crossed the Tropic of Cancer at the end of November and passed the Cape Verde Islands around December 6. While these islands were a frequent port of call, it was not surprising that the *Catalpa* passed them by. Stopping at Tenerife had satisfied the ship's needs, and Captain Anthony did not want to lose any more crew members.

There was very little whaling over the next three and a half months that it took the *Catalpa* to reach its destination. A pod was sighted in mid-December with a successful chase, but another sighting didn't occur until mid-February and was fruitless.[47] The endless routines of repairing and maintaining the ship occupied the crew's time.

On February 16, one unusual event reportedly occurred. The *Catalpa* encountered the *Ocean Beauty*, bound from London to New Zealand. Several accounts claim that the captain of that ship (without providing his name) had been the captain of the prison ship *Hougoumont* on its 1867 voyage to Western Australia, and he offered Captain Anthony charts of the area.[48] The ship had transported, among others, sixty-two Irish political prisoners[49] to Western Australia. The irony of the encounter was that six of those prisoners were still at Fremantle Prison, and that was why Anthony was going there.

* * *

45. *Catalpa Log,* November 21–26, 1875.

46. Pease, *Catalpa,* 96–97.

47. *Catalpa Log,* December 20, 1875, February 6, 1876.

48. The captain of the 1867–68 *Hougoumont* voyage was William Cozens. However, Lloyd's Register lists a Pearce as the captain of the *Ocean Beauty* during this encounter with the *Catalpa*. A W. C. Cuzens is listed as master of the *Peep O'Day. Lloyd's Register of British and Foreign Shipping,* July 1, 1875–June 30, 1876 (London: Wyman and Sons, 1875); *Catalpa Log,* February 16, 1876. Pease described the encounter between Anthony and Cozens in chapter 15 of his book. Pease, *Catalpa,* 103–6.

49. Most accounts give sixty-two as the number of Fenians aboard; some, however, give sixty-three.

Editors' Prologue

This day commences with Light breeses from the S SW and clear pleasant weather
—Steering in toward the Land—At 2 pm of Cape Naturaliste and then Rept. Her off
down along the Land—At 5 pm passed vasse—at 7 pm came to anchor in ten fathoms of water—give her thirty fathoms of chain and furled the Sails and set Officers
watches for this night—Middle and Latter part Light breeses from the W—At 5 am
got under way and steered down along the Land towards Bunbury—At 10 am came
to anchor off Bunbury in 7 fathoms of water—gave her 45 fathoms of chain and furl
the Sails—So ends this day.

—Catalpa Log, Tuesday, March 28, 1876

Eleven months after leaving New Bedford, the *Catalpa* arrived at her destination: Western Australia.

The last of the world's continents to be discovered, Australia is com-
prised of nearly three million square miles. It was first surveyed by the
famous British explorer, Captain James Cook, in 1770, but was ignored by
his government until the disposition of convicts became a priority in the
next decade. Then, according to historian Robert Hughes, "Australia . . .
began as a continent of sin, the dump for English criminals."[50] The British
dispatched its first fleet of convicts in 1788 to Botany Bay, on the east coast.
Over the next eighty years, 160,000 men, women, and children would be
transported on 825 ships to various locations. Western Australia was colo-
nized in 1829. Comprising over 975,000 square miles, it was initially to
be free of convicts. But during the next twenty years the colony was stag-
nant and the frustrated colonists petitioned for convicts, believing that
free labor would provide the necessary seed for growth. (The petition
came at the same time the other colonies were withdrawing from this type
of labor.)[51]

From 1850 to 1868, almost ten thousand male prisoners were sent to the
colony. They were incarcerated at Fremantle, where a massive prison,
termed the "establishment" by the locals, dominated the town. Later, some
were sent out in work gangs to nearby areas. Those who conducted themselves properly were released on a "ticket-of-leave." This entitled them to
some freedom, but they were required to find work, stay employed, and be
on good behavior. If they completed this stage satisfactorily, freedom was
forthcoming. But work was dependent on the free settlers, and as one con-

---

50. Robert Hughes, "The Real Australia," *Time,* September 11, 2000, 99.

51. Robert Hughes, *The Fatal Shore: The Epic of Australia's Founding* (New York: Knopf, 1987), 143, 573–
77; convict transportation stopped in New South Wales in 1840 and Tasmania in 1853. Hughes,
588–90.

Editors' Prologue

vict recalled, "The crying evil of the [legal] code was the power it gave these settlers to take from the prison as many men as they chose and work them as slaves on their clearings. While so employed, the very lives of these convicts were at the mercy of their taskmasters, who possessed over them all the power of prison officers."[52]

Putting aside any moral issue of convict labor, its material benefits to the state were substantial in the areas of public works, communications, and shipping.[53] However, responding to pressure from the other colonies and domestic concern about its cost and brutality, the British government discontinued all convict transport with the last ship, the *Hougoumont,* sailing from Portland in October 1867. The *Hougoumont* made its 89-day voyage with 280 prisoners, including the group of Fenians. Nine years later, there remained at Fremantle a small group of those Fenians who had not been freed. At the time the *Catalpa* arrived at Western Australia, its population was just over twenty-seven thousand, of which only a small portion were still prisoners.[54]

52. Keith Amos, *The Fenians in Australia, 1865–1880* (Kensington, N.S.W.: New South Wales University Press, 1988), 123; John Boyle O'Reilly, *Moondyne Joe: A Story from the Underworld* (New York: P. J. Kenedy and Sons, 1879) 13; C. M. H. Clark, ed., *Select Documents in Australian History, 1851–1900* (Sydney: Angus and Robertson, 1969), 282; *Britannica,* 14, 406, 485.

53. J. S. Battye, *Western Australia: A History from Its Discovery to the Inauguration of the Commonwealth* (Nedlands, W.A.: University of Western Australia Press [facsimile edition], 1978), 255–56.

54. Ibid., appendix 4.

EDITORS' NOTE

Each installment of John Devoy's *Catalpa* account has been transcribed in its entirety, starting with chapter 1. Devoy included correspondence, diary entries, and reports of others, including John J. Breslin and John King, which have been formatted differently to distinguish them from Devoy's words but are in the same order as they appeared originally. Information from two other sources has been inserted in chapters 8 and 9, set off by brackets. They are portions of an Australian newspaper report and a Clanna-Gael annual report, both of which shed further light on events but were not part of Devoy's original work.

Devoy's punctuation and spelling have been left intact. He used American spelling and conventions of the day. Some of the spelling may be inconsistent or wrong, but is recognizable and no changes have been made. In the rare instance when a clarification has been necessary, an editorial note, in brackets, will be found. The chapter titles in the table of contents and at the beginning of each chapter are the subtitles as they appeared for each installment in the newspaper.

The editors have also cited and quoted from the *Catalpa* log, retaining the original spelling ("Captain," for instance, is spelled "Captian"). To provide for smoother reading, dashes and periods have been added since very little punctuation was discernible within the original text. This retention of original style also applies to quotations from newspaper accounts.

[I]

CRUISE OF A NEW BEDFORD WHALER

That Brought Humiliation to England—Irish Skill and Yankee Grit
Combined—Six Irish Military Prisoners Taken from an English
Prison in Western Australia by The Clan-na-Gael—
How and Why the Work Was Done

The unveiling of a monument to James Reynolds[55] in New Haven on July 3 last [1904] by the Irish Nationalists of Connecticut, recalls an event in recent Irish history in which he played a prominent and very creditable part. It is twenty-eight years since the whaling bark *Catalpa* landed in New York six Irish soldiers of the British army, who had been tried by court martial in 1866 for connection with the Fenian movement in Ireland and sentenced to penal servitude for life. They had been taken from a British prison at Fremantle, Western Australia, four months before by an expedition under command of John J. Breslin, sent from the United States by the Clan-na-Gael for that purpose and put aboard the *Catalpa*, commanded by Captain George S. Anthony, of New Bedford, Mass., who had been commissioned by the Clan-na-Gael to carry them to the land of the free. The expedition from first to last was a combination of Irish skill and pluck and Yankee grit which may safely be made a model for many other enterprises in the future.

James Reynolds was the "Managing Owner" of the *Catalpa*, holding seven-eighths of her value, the other eighth being held by Captain Anthony's father-in-law, John T. Richardson, of New Bedford, who was the shipping agent who fitted out the vessel. Mr. Richardson was fully aware

---

55. James Reynolds (1831–1897) was born in County Cavan and sent to America by his father in the 1840s. He established himself in New Haven, CT, as a glass founder. Because of his willingness to take a significant financial risk in the rescue venture, he was known as "Catalpa Jim" for many years after. "James Reynolds' Monument Unveiled," *Gaelic American* [hereafter *GA*], July 9, 1904, 1.

Cruise of a New Bedford Whaler

Bark *Catalpa* of New Bedford (E. N. Russell, Library of Congress, Prints and Photographs Division)

of the object of the expedition and went into it fully understanding all the risks involved. Both Anthony and Richardson were recommended for the work by Captain Henry C. Hathaway, then "Captain of the Night Watch" in New Bedford, who had been introduced to me, the agent of the Clan-na-Gael, by John Boyle O'Reilly.[56] Hathaway was third mate of the American whaling bark *Gazelle,* on which O'Reilly had escaped from prison in Western Australia in 1869 and the final success of that escape was mainly due to the skill and devotion which the mate had displayed at a most trying moment. Neither Hathaway, Anthony nor Richardson, who are all alive today, have, so far as they know, a drop of Irish blood in their veins, but each undertook the work they were asked to perform as readily as if they had been sworn Fenians, and right well did they perform it.

56. John Boyle O'Reilly (1844–1890) was born in County Meath. He became a trooper in the British army's Tenth Hussars and joined the Fenian movement. Eventually betrayed, he was court-martialed and sent to Australia on the last prison ship *Hougoumont* in 1867. He escaped from Australia in 1869 aboard a New Bedford whaler, the *Gazelle,* and made his way to the United States. William O'Brien and Desmond Ryan, eds., *Devoy's Post Bag, 1871–1928,* 1 (Dublin: C. J. Fallon, 1948), 14–15.

Cruise of a New Bedford Whaler

DOCUMENTS ATTESTING TO REYNOLDS' WORK

Two documents now in my possession make up the public record of Reynolds' connection with the bark *Catalpa,*—a bill of sale and a note for $4,000. The bill of sale is dated April 27, 1875, and has the signature of James C. Hitch, Register of Sales and Transfers at the Custom House in New Bedford and Justice of the Peace. It records the purchase of the vessel by John T. Richardson from F. W. Homan, of Gloucester, Mass., gives her dimensions and recites the fact that she was built at Medford in 1844, with other interesting details.[57] The transfer to James Reynolds is stated thus quaintly:

To have and to hold the said seven-eighths Bark Catalpa and appurtenances thereunto belonging unto him, the said James Reynolds, his executors, administrators and assigns, to the sole and only proper use, benefit and behoof of him, the said James Reynolds, his executors, administrators and assigns, forever, and I, the said John T. Richardson have, and by these presents do promise, covenant and agree, for myself and my heirs, executors and administrators, to and with the said James Reynolds, his heirs, executors, administrators and assigns, to warrant and defend the said seven-eighths of said Bark Catalpa and all the other before-mentioned appurtenances against all and every person and persons whomsoever.

The note showed what a self-sacrificing man James Reynolds was. It read as follows:

New Bedford, April 27, 1875.

$4,000.
Thirty days after date I promise to pay to the order of John T. Richardson at the Mechanic's National Bank, Four Thousand Dollars, Value Received.

James Reynolds

On the back of the note are recorded payments beginning April 29, and ending May 24, 1875, amounting in the aggregate to $4,364.41. It was necessary to secure immediate possession of the vessel and commence fitting her out, and, as the funds were not on hand Reynolds secured Richardson

---

57. The *Catalpa,* named for a type of American tree, was built in Medford, MA, in 1844. It was registered in New Bedford in 1852 to Mandell/Robinson/I. Howland and Co. Specifications: 90' × 25' × 12.2'; 202.05 tons (new measurement). It also served as a merchant vessel. *Ship Registers of New Bedford, Massachusetts,* 3 (Boston: National Archive Project, 1940); Pease, *Catalpa,* 77; *Catalpa* File Notes, New Bedford Whaling Museum library, October 2001.

29

Cruise of a New Bedford Whaler

by his note. Had it gone to protest all he had in the world would have been sacrificed, but the Clan-na-Gael was at work from Maine to California and the note was redeemed within thirty days.

FENIANISM IN THE BRITISH ARMY

Why was this expedition, reaching half way around the world, and requiring two years for its accomplishment, undertaken? A generation has nearly gone by since it was brought to a close and the young men who now fill the ranks of the National movement have only a vague idea of how it all came to pass. It is about time the chief incidents in the story were told.

In 1871 the last batch of Fenian prisoners tried in the civil courts from 1865 to 1867 were released on condition of residing out of Ireland. They included the men who, under James Stephens had been instrumental in organizing a strong section of the Fenian organization in the British army, but the soldiers whom they had induced to join were still held prisoners. Seven[58] of these were at Fremantle, Western Australia, and three[59] in England, the rest were either out on "ticket of leave" in Australia or had died. Gladstone, who was Premier of England at the time, had yielded to a strong pressure of public opinion, brought about by the Amnesty agitation led by Isaac Butt,[60] George Henry Moore[61] and John Nolan,[62] and wanted to release all the prisoners, but a characteristic English reason prevented it. The Duke of Cambridge, Commander-in-Chief of the British army, interposed an objection against all the military prisoners and his word was law with his august cousin, Queen Victoria. Releasing these Fenian soldiers, he said, would be subversive of discipline in the army, and as

58. Thomas Darragh, Thomas Henry Hassett, Michael Harrington, James Wilson, Robert Cranston, Martin Hogan, and James Keilley. Keilley had been transported in 1867 to Australia at the same time as the other prisoners aboard the convict ship *Hougoumont.* However, his peers believed he had tried to curry favor with the Crown prosecutor during his trial. This was never forgotten, and he would not be included in the escape plans. John Devoy, *Recollections of an Irish Rebel* (New York: Chas. D. Young, 1929), 257; Amos, 230–31.

59. Charles McCarthy, Thomas Chambers, and John Patrick O'Brien. These three military Fenians were released in 1878. O'Brien and Ryan, 1, 304.

60. Isaac Butt (1813–1879) was a lawyer, member of Parliament, defender of Fenians, founder of the home rule movement, and president of the Amnesty Association. S. J. Connolly, ed., *The Oxford Companion to Irish History* (New York: Oxford University Press, 1998), 65.

61. George Henry Moore was a member of Parliament from Mayo and active in the Amnesty Association. Devoy wrote of Moore being frequently consulted by the IRB, though he was not a member. Amos, 188; Devoy, 322.

62. "Amnesty John" Nolan founded the very successful Amnesty Association in 1868. Devoy, 366.

Cruise of a New Bedford Whaler

the duke was a great soldier, as soldiers go near the top of the army in England, that settled it. His Royal Highness had won distinction in the Crimea by promptly falling from his horse at the opening of the battle of the Alma and had to nurse a dislocated shoulder at home in England during the balance of the war. But he knew all about discipline and red tape and he was quite sure it would have a bad effect on the army to let those Fenian fellows out.

15,000 UNIFORMED FENIANS

There were 15,000 Fenians in the British army in 1865. Of these 8,000 were stationed in Ireland and if a Fenian had charge of the war office he could not have placed the disaffected regiments in England in better positions for effective work in case the Fenian leaders knew their business. But one half the Fenians in America were too busy planning an absurd invasion of Canada,[63] and the other half too busy fighting for existence to have any time to spare for thought about conditions in Ireland, while the leaders at home lacked the clearness of view and the decision which would have enabled them to see a great opportunity which might never come again. At that time more than half the British army was Irish. The fact was not recorded in the army lists, which merely gave the birthplace of the soldiers, and many thousands of men born in England, Scotland or Wales, of

---

63. A militant Fenian faction, led by William Roberts, sought to seize Canadian territory and force the British into negotiations for Ireland's independence. Incursions by small groups of Fenians occurred in 1866 until President Andrew Johnson announced that U.S. neutrality laws were being violated by the Fenians. One unintended result of those raids was that Canadians finally unified under the threat, and the Dominion of Canada was created. Another "invasion" was launched in 1870 but was easily rebuffed by the authorities on both sides of the border, with President U. S. Grant issuing a proclamation against the Fenians. G. Smith, "Fenian Invasions of Canada," *Military History,* February 2000, 50; Morison, 727. As a reporter for the Boston *Pilot,* John Boyle O'Reilly observed this last attempt from Vermont, and, for a brief moment, participated. The experience caused him to rethink his support of the Fenian movement, and soon after, he resigned from the Brotherhood and the Clan-na-Gael, though he continued to support the cause of Irish independence and never forgot his Fenian comrades. A. G. Evans, *Fanatic Heart: A Life of John Boyle O'Reilly* (Boston: Northeastern University Press, 1997), 180–81. In 1870, Hamilton Fish, U.S. Secretary of State, suggested to Lord Derby, Britain's foreign minister, that in light of the friction created between the United States and Britain by Canadian problems with Fenians and others (Indians, settlers, and the like), Britain should consider withdrawing from Canada. Fish was confident this would eliminate any problems between the two great powers. Lord Derby did not think it possible. This was in fact a long-held U.S. view of Canada. In the previous century, Benjamin Franklin expressed the country's position that a divided North America was "unnatural." William D'Arcy, *The Fenian Movement in the United States: 1858–1886* (New York: Russell and Russell, 1971), 344; Morison, 727.

Irish parents, were just as amenable to the work of the Fenian organizer as those born in Ireland. In 1865 there were about 26,000 British soldiers in Ireland and more than half of them were Irish, although only 8,000 were sworn Fenians. One of the most strongly Fenian regiments, the 87th Foot —the old Fag-a-ballaghs—was stationed in one of the forts at Portsmouth [England] and the men were ready to seize a steamer at short notice and start for Ireland. Twenty men of the regiment, hearing rumors from friends at home of an intended rising, grew impatient towards the close of 1865 and started for Ireland. They got a thirty days' furlough, and out of the thirty shillings' pay in advance given them, paid ten shillings a man for their passage to Dublin. On the expiration of their furlough they got civilian clothes and remained until all were arrested. Only two were convicted for Fenianism, William Curry[64] and Patrick Tierney,[65] because there was no informer among the twenty, and the rest could be only punished for desertion. Curry was convicted on the testimony of spies belonging to other regiments, got two years' imprisonment and fifty lashes, and Tierney was convicted for an attempt to kill Warner,[66] the informer. A monument in the form of a Celtic cross is erected to Tierney's memory in the same cemetery where lie the remains of James Reynolds in New Haven.

ORGANIZATION BROKEN IN 1866

The story of Fenianism in the British army will be told at another time. It is enough now to say that the military organization remained intact until many months after the real crisis of the Fenian movement, the arrest and trial of leading lieutenants of James Stephens[67] which followed the sei-

64. William Curry was described by Devoy as "the most useful and efficient man I had" when they were recruiting military Fenians. He was arrested and publicly flogged (fifty lashes) in Dublin. O'Brien and Ryan, 1, 106–9. Timothy Daniel Sullivan honored the event in his poem, "The Flogging of Private Curry," *Poems* (Dublin, [190?]), 103–4.

65. Patrick Tierney, alias Edward O'Connor, from Clare, was a corporal in the 87th. He served twelve years under very harsh conditions, first at Mountjoy Prison and then at Spike Island. Under a conditional pardon, he came to America in 1878. Devoy, 148–49; "A Banished Fenian," *Tribune,* December 13, 1878, 5.

66. John Warner was a B (captain) in the Fenians and betrayed the organization in Cork. Among others, he testified against Darragh at his trial. Leon Ó Broin, *Fenian Fever: An Anglo American Dilemma* (New York: New York University Press, 1971), 12; Pease, *Catalpa,* 17–19.

67. James Stephens (1824–1901) was born in Kilkenny and joined the Young Ireland 1848 uprising. He escaped to France and eventually returned secretly to Ireland. He founded the Irish Republican Brotherhood in 1858 and became "Chief Organizer of the Irish Republic." Considered an extraordinary organizer, he inexplicably was unable to order a well-planned uprising in 1865

Cruise of a New Bedford Whaler

zure and suppression of the Dublin *Irish People,* in September, 1865. Had the projected insurrection taken place in 1865, as originally announced by Stephens, it would have found 8,000 men in the ranks of the British garrison ready to join it and more than 3,000 others in the regiments in England which would naturally be among the first sent as reinforcements to Ireland. Some of these regiments were actually sent among the reinforcements to Ireland in the end of 1865 or the beginning of 1866, while no regiment was sent out of Ireland until all chance of a formidable uprising had disappeared. The British government had only the vaguest kind of knowledge as to the work done in the army and did not fully realize the danger until the spring of 1866, when a number of soldiers were arrested. They were tried by court martial in the Royal Barracks in Dublin in the summer of 1866 and sentenced to various terms of imprisonment.

The story of the trials must also wait. It is enough to say here that while there was a large number of informers, it is a wonder there were not more under the circumstances. Owing to the split in America and the wholesale arrests in Ireland there was not a penny to defend the military prisoners, and it appeared to them that the organization was entirely broken up and that the promises made to them were mere idle boasts. Besides that, an Irish "officer and gentleman," one Captain Whelan, went from man to man in the cells at Arbor Hill military prison and told each that the man in the next cell had turned informer, and that the civilian organizers had regularly turned in to the Castle[68] the names of all soldiers sworn in. Yet nine-tenths of the men remained true and few of those who gave evidence told all they knew. Most of the informers told barely enough to clear themselves, and their evidence had to be extracted from them by long and painful cross-examination and much suggestion.

A Voice from the Dungeon

When the last batch of Fenian prisoners arrived in New York in January, 1871,[69] they found the Fenian organization shattered by the split, with the

---

and again in 1866. After that, he faded rapidly from the movement except briefly during the 1880s when his business brought him to the United States. Devoy, 272–80.

68. From the thirteenth century through 1922, Dublin Castle was the seat of British authority in Ireland. Connolly, 163.

69. Two batches came from England in January. The first was aboard the Cunard steamship *Cuba* and included O'Donovan Rossa, Charles Underwood O'Connell, John Devoy, John McClure, and Harry S. Mulleda. They were known as the *"Cuba* Five." The second arrived aboard the Cunard ship *Russia* and included nine men: Thomas Francis Bourke, Edmund Power, Edward Pilsworth St.

Irish Exiles, "The *Cuba* Five." John Devoy, far left, shortly after his 1871 arrival in the United States (Library of Congress)

Canadian wing broken up and the O'Mahony[70] section fast dwindling into decrepitude. The Clan-na-Gael had been organized four years and was steadily making headway, but was not then fitted for any kind of active operations. Some months after their arrival news of the public reception given them in New York found its way into the prison at Fremantle, with

---

Clair, Patrick Lennon, William Francis Roantree, Patrick Walsh, Peter Maughan, Denis Dowling Mulcahy, and George Brown. The second round of pardons for the nonmilitary Fenians incarcerated in Australia did not become effective until the spring of 1871, and those who chose to leave did not arrive in the United States until the summer. O'Brien and Ryan, 1, 2; Amos, 188–90.

70. John O'Mahony (1819–1877) was a native of County Cork. He was a Young Irelander who escaped to France during the 1848 Uprising. He came to America and was a principal founder of the Fenian Brotherhood in 1858, becoming its Head Center. During the American Civil War, he organized the New York National Guard's Ninety-Ninth Regiment, composed mostly of Fenians. Despite these significant contributions, he was not considered a particularly good leader and was unable to prevent the Brotherhood's split in 1865. He continued to be active in the movement until his death. O'Brien and Ryan, 1, 78–80.

Cruise of a New Bedford Whaler

the mention of the address of Peter Curran,[71] a man in whose house in Dublin a picked body of the soldiers had been brought to meet the famous Captain McCafferty,[72] with a view to organizing a cavalry corps under his command. The result was the receipt by Curran of the following letter, signed by Martin Hogan, but not in his handwriting:

"Perth, Western Australia

"May 20th, 1871.

"My Dear Friend: In order that you may recollect who it is that addresses you, you will remember the night of the 17th of January, 1866, some of the Fifth Dragoon Guards being in the old house in Clare Lane with John Devoy and Captain McCafferty. I am one of that unfortunate band and am now under sentence of life penal servitude in one of the darkest corners of the earth, and as far as we can learn from any small news that chances to reach us, we appear to be forgotten, with no prospect before us but to be left in hopeless slavery to the tender mercies of the Norman wolf.

"But, my dear friend, it is not my hard fate I deplore, for I willingly bear it for the cause of dear old Ireland, but I must feel sad at the thought of being forgotten and neglected by those more fortunate companions in enterprise who have succeeded in eluding the grasp of the oppressor. If I had the means I could get away from here any time. I therefore address you in the hope that you will endeavour to procure and send me pecuniary help for that purpose and I will soon be with you.

"Give my love and regards to all old friends—Roantree,[73] Devoy, Burke (General),[74] McCafferty, Captain Holden,[75] O'Donovan Rossa,[76] St. Clair[77] and others,

---

71. Peter Curran's house was a primary meeting place for Fenians, particularly military members, during the period 1865–1866. A Dublin vintner, Curran later emigrated to America, where he was Devoy's initial correspondence link to the military Fenians still imprisoned at Fremantle, W.A. O'Brien and Ryan, 1, 83; Seán Ó Lúing, *Fremantle Mission* (Tralee: Anvil Books, 1965), 1–2.

72. Born in America, John McCafferty served in the Confederate Army during the American Civil War. He joined the Fenians and journeyed to Ireland several times intending to fight for independence. He planned the Chester Castle attack that did not occur due to an informer. He was arrested, tried, and sentenced to death. His was one of the cases in which the U.S. government intervened by expressing strong concern for its citizens. As a result, his sentence was reduced to life; he was released in 1871 and returned to the United States. O'Brien and Ryan, 1, 36–37; Ó Broin, 126–29, 177–79.

73. William Francis Roantree (1829–1918) was born in County Kildare. He came to America and served in the U.S. navy. He returned to Ireland in 1861 and organized Fenians in the British army. Arrested and sentenced to ten years, he was pardoned in 1871 and returned to America on the *Russia*. He eventually went back and died in Dublin. O'Brien and Ryan, 1, 29.

74. There were two Burkes/Bourkes. General (Fenian Army) Thomas F. Bourke (1840–1889) was born in Tipperary, emigrated to America, and served as a private in the Confederate Army (with John Mitchel) during the Civil War. Afterward, he joined the Fenians. He returned to Ireland to lead the Tipperary forces, fought at Ballyhurst Fort, and was arrested and initially

Cruise of a New Bedford Whaler

not forgetting yourself and Mrs., and believe me that, even should it be my fate to perish in this villainous dungeon of the world, the last pulse of my heart shall beat 'God Save Ireland.'

"Direct your letter to Rev. Father McCabe,[78] Fremantle. Do not put my name on the outside of the letter. I remain

"Yours truly,

"Martin J. Hogan."

"Erin go brágh!"

This letter was at once given to me, and I promptly answered it. I had nothing to do with starting the organization in the army; that work was begun by "Pagan" O'Leary,[79] and continued after his arrest and

---

sentenced to death. Amnestied in 1871, he returned to the United States aboard the *Russia*. Thereafter he was active in the Clan and helped carry the resolution authorizing the *Catalpa* rescue, approved at their 1874 convention. General (Union Army) Denis F. Burke (1841–1893) was born in Ireland and came to the United States in the 1850s. Following distinguished service in the Irish Brigade, he returned to Ireland in 1867, was arrested, and was released on the appeal of the U.S. government. He returned to New York where he lived the rest of his life. O'Brien and Ryan, 1, 27–28; T. D. Sullivan, A. M. Sullivan, D. B. Sullivan, eds., *Speeches from the Dock; or, Protests from the Dock* (Providence, RI: Murphy and McCarthy, 1881), 193–94; O'Brien and Ryan, 1, 27–28; "General Thomas Francis Bourke," *NYT,* November 12, 1889, 5; "Passing of Judge John W. Goff," *GA,* November 22, 1924, 1; "Death of Gen. Denis F. Burke," *NYT,* October 20, 1893, 1.

75. Thomas M. Holden was born in Dublin c. 1835. During the American Civil War he served in a New York unit. He was sworn into the Fenian Brotherhood in 1865 and in 1866 was arrested in Dublin. Michael H. Kane, "American Soldiers in Ireland, 1865–1867," *Irish Sword* 90 (2002).

76. Jeremiah O'Donovan Rossa (1831–1915) was born in County Cork. He was a grocer who became associated with the Fenian movement at its inception. He was first arrested in 1858 for his part in the Phoenix conspiracy and was held for six months. Upon his release, he became a major organizer traveling through England, Ireland, Scotland, and America. Arrested again in 1865, he was sentenced to life imprisonment. His particularly brutal prison life drew international attention, during which he was elected a member of Parliament for Tipperary. He was amnestied in 1871 and came to America (aboard the *Cuba*), where he very forcefully championed Irish independence for the rest of his life. O'Brien and Ryan, 1, 10–12; Sullivan et al., 171.

77. Edward Pilsworth St. Clair was a military Fenian. St. Clair was particularly successful in recruiting others in the British army. Following his arrest, imprisonment, and conditional pardon, he came to America in 1871 on the *Russia.* O'Brien and Ryan, 1, 14.

78. Reverend Patrick McCabe (1828–1899) was a Roman Catholic priest. Born in County Cavan, he was ordained and went to Australia in 1859. He was very sympathetic to the Fenian prisoners. John Boyle O'Reilly's successful 1869 escape was due in large part to McCabe's help. He also served as an intermediary for prisoner mail, which otherwise would have been subject to inspection by the authorities. For this reason, the authorities removed him in 1870 from ministering at Fremantle. Amos, 154, 155, 208; Peggy O'Reilly, "Fr. Patrick McCabe," *Journal of the Old Drogheda Society* (2000): 206–12; Geraldine Byrne, *A Basilica in the Making: The Centenary of St. Patrick's, Fremantle* (Fremantle, W.A.: Mazenod Press, [2000]), 20–21; D. F. Bourke, *The History of the Catholic Church in Western Australia* (Perth, W.A.: Archdiocese of Perth, 1979), 72, 93.

79. Patrick O'Leary was born in the 1820s in Cork. He went to America to study for the priesthood. The outbreak of the Mexican-American War in 1846 led him to change vocations, and he joined the U.S. army. He subsequently developed a myriad of spiritual beliefs, hence the nickname

Cruise of a New Bedford Whaler

conviction in 1864 by William F. Roantree, with James Rynd,[80] Thomas Baines[81] and others assisting him; but after these men had been either arrested or forced to remain "on their keeping," and when a warrant was out for my own arrest, Stephens appointed me "Chief Organizer for the British Army." Most of the evidence on which the soldiers were convicted related to meetings with me, and I therefore felt that I, more than any man then living, ought to do my utmost for these Fenian soldiers. But at that time nothing could be done except in the way of influencing opinion in favor of some plan to effect their release and most men considered the task of getting them out impossible of accomplishment.

In a few months another letter came from Hogan, this time in his own handwriting, and later one from James Wilson[82] (of the same regiment), containing more accurate and detailed descriptions of the situation of the men, but the plans suggested were wholly impracticable. Thomas McCarthy Fennell,[83] now of Elmira, N.Y., who had been released from Australia with the civilian prisoners, was the first man in America to propose a practical plan, which was to send an American vessel loaded with grain, or some other cargo, but there was no money to carry it out. A proposition that the organization undertake the rescue of the prisoners was laid by me in 1872 and 1873 before the then heads of the Clan-na-Gael, but they could not see their way to undertaking the work and doubted their ability to raise the funds. So matters drifted until 1874, when a convention held in Baltimore, decided to undertake the work, and appointed a committee to carry it out, on the understanding that the necessary funds should be raised by voluntary contributions.

"Pagan." He returned to Ireland and became a successful Fenian recruiter from the military ranks until his arrest in 1864. He was amnestied in 1871 and returned to the United States, where he died many years later. Ó Lúing, 17–18; O'Brien and Ryan, 1, 65–66.

80. James Rynd was a Kerryman who had served in the Irish Papal Brigade. Though arrested in 1865, more for his associations with Roantree and others than for specific acts, he was released without charges and emigrated to America where he settled in Boston. Devoy, 142–44

81. A Sligo native, Thomas Baines recruited Fenians in the British army. Arrested and convicted for treason, he was transported to Australia aboard the *Hougoumont* in 1867. Upon his release from Fremantle Prison, he came to America. O'Brien and Ryan, 1, 154; Amos, 289.

82. The full text of Wilson's letter may be found in *Devoy's Post Bag*, 2.

83. Thomas McCarthy Fennell (1841–1914) was born in Clare. One of the first from that area to join the Fenians, he became a successful recruiter for the movement. Active in the 1867 uprising, he was wounded, imprisoned, and transported aboard the *Hougoumont*. Pardoned and released in 1871, he settled in America. Thomas McCarthy Fennell, *Voyage of the Hougoumont and Life at Fremantle* (Philadelphia: Xlibris, 2000), 27, 31–32, 275–76, 278.

[II]

Seven Thousand Men Knew of the Expedition,

but There Was No Traitor—Discussed from Maine To California—
Yet the Blow Fell on England Like a Bolt from the Blue—
How the Work Was Started—The Committee in Charge

It will not be necessary to refer to the convention which decided to undertake the rescue of the Fenian military prisoners in Western Australia, except in so far as its proceedings concern that undertaking. I proposed the resolution with a full sense of the risk involved in entrusting the knowledge to such a gathering and the necessity of later on making it known in a more guarded way to the whole membership of the organization.

That risk had to be run or the money could not be raised. There was not a dollar available for such a purpose. Owing to the recent experience of Fenianism all funds, after providing for mere running expenses, were held by the branches—and very carefully guarded there—subject only to the final call for Irish revolution.[84] In other words, the funds were only available when actual fighting was to take place in Ireland. Up to then no call had ever been made to help the men in Ireland to prepare for such an eventuality. Through this policy a little over $42,000 had been accumulated in seven years, and was held by the local branches.

No Traitor in the Fold

There were sixty-one delegates present and they were not all, in the beginning at least, favorable to the proposition or friendly to the proposer. They

---

84. In 1874, the first secretary of the Clan, W. J. Nicholson, was expelled due to misuse of funds. While it seemed more poor judgment than anything else, others did not forget the matter for some time. O'Brien and Ryan, 1, 74.

had to be taken into confidence, so far as the actual purpose of the project was concerned, and to be given such information as to existing conditions in Western Australia as would enable them to judge what the chances of success might be. One letter only was read to them—that from Martin Hogan, already quoted—but his name was withheld and no mention was made of Father McCabe. A committee, of which I was chairman, and of which P. K. Walsh[85] of Cleveland, Patrick O'Connor[86] of New Haven (former "centre" of Galway), James O'Neill of Chicago (formerly of Leixlip, County Kildare), and P. O'Malley (I think of Louisville), were the other members, had previously considered the project and recommended, in guarded language, that it should be undertaken, but it was later found necessary to state plainly to the whole convention the nature of the undertaking in order to secure a favorable vote. The risk was taken and the result showed that there was no traitor among those sixty-one delegates.

The convention assembled in Baltimore on July 15, 1874, and lasted until late on the night of July 22. Jeremiah Kavanagh,[87] of Louisville, Ky., one of the American delegates sent with the remains of Terence Bellew McManus[88] to Ireland in 1861, and who delivered the funeral oration over his grave in Glasnevin, was chairman; a young lawyer named Loughlin, from Lowell, was vice-chairman, and Richard Casey, of Lawrence, Mass., was secretary.

RANK AND FILE ALL KNEW IT

There were then 6,317 members in the eighty-six branches of the organization, of whom 4,808 were in good standing. A report of the proceedings,

85. Patrick K. Walsh (probably the same Patrick Walsh who arrived on the *Russia* in 1871) was a leading nationalist whose active support of the Land League and other causes brought him into conflict with the Roman Catholic Church. He died in 1886. "Under the Ban of the Church," *NYT*, August 2, 1886, 1.

86. Patrick O'Connor ran a gun shop and had been a "centre" for Galway at the time of the Uprising. He came to the United States, settled in New Haven, married the daughter of James Reynolds, and remained active in the movement. Henry to Jeremiah O'Donovan Rossa, February 4, 1871, handwritten, "The O'Donovan Rossa Papers," The Catholic University of America Archives; "Monument Unveiled," *GA* (supra note 55).

87. In the 1860s, Jeremiah Kavanagh (1830–1921) was active with the Pacific coast Fenians operating from San Francisco. He eventually settled in Louisville and was an active Fenian organizer and, later, Clan supporter. D'Arcy, 20, 28; "Jeremiah Kavanagh, Old Fenian, Dies in Louisville, Aged 91 Years," *GA*, December 3, 1921, 1.

88. A Young Irelander from Monaghan, Terence Bellew McManus was imprisoned and transported to Van Dieman's Land, from which he escaped in 1853. He lived in San Francisco, CA, until his death in 1861. His funeral in Dublin was attended by thousands and became a significant rallying point for nationalists and the Fenians. Devoy, 22.

including a copy of Hogan's letter and the resolution to undertake the rescue, was printed and sent to the eighty-six branches then existing, and later to others which came into existence, and there can be no doubt that the great majority of these 4,808 members heard this report read. Those who did not hear it read learned the main fact that the work was about to be undertaken. During the twelve months that followed, at the end of which the membership had increased to 7,437, there were several circulars issued in which mention was made of the rescue project and a printed copy of a letter from Wilson, one of the prisoners, was sent round in order to allay doubts as to the possibility of success. So suspicious were some men of a fraud being practised upon them that they questioned the genuineness of this letter, and were only convinced when the envelope with the cancelled stamp and Australian postmarks were shown them. The work of collecting money went on in every branch, necessitating appeals, explanations, discussions, and sometimes quarrels; another convention of seventy-five delegates was held in 1875, and the accounts up to date audited, and so it went on until April, 1876, when the rescue was effected, and there were fully 7,000 men in the United States aware of the work in hand. The proof that there was then no informer or spy in the organization is made clear by the fact that the British Government took absolutely no precaution against a rescue and that the blow fell on them like "a bolt from the blue."[89] It may be proper to mention here that Le Caron[90] did not get into the organization until more than two years after the rescue was effected.

89. While it is true that the American Fenians managed to keep the information from reaching the British, the IRB was less successful. By January 1876, the British government was aware of an IRB plan to free the Fremantle military prisoners. That month, Lord Carnarvon warned the governor of Western Australia (Robinson) that some agents had sailed to Australia to carry out the plan. Amos, 225.

90. Major Henry Le Caron was born Thomas Willis Beach (1841–1894). A native of Ireland, Le Caron started spying on the Fenians for the British in 1865. Devoy referred to him as "The Prince of Spies," for he infiltrated the movement successfully for a period of years. (Le Caron never returned the compliment. In his book, his description of Devoy starts with, "[he had a] perpetual scowl upon his face" and goes downhill from there.) In 1890, he testified publicly in England and later wrote his memoirs. While a spy, he enjoyed gratuitous recognition in various quarters, an example being the following news note: "Dr. Le Caron, of Braidwood, Ill., although a Frenchman, is a very good *Irishman*. He took an active part in Fenianism and is as enthusiastically a worker today as ever." "Personal," [New York] *Irish Nation,* February 4, 1882, 4. Le Caron later wrote that he didn't join the Clan in the early years because of his other pursuits (e.g., medical school), and he thought it prudent to take a break after being so active in the Canadian incursions in which he served as a senior Fenian officer. Henri Le Caron, *Twenty-five Years in the Secret Service: The Recollections of a Spy* (London: Heinemann, 1892), 117, 103; John Devoy, "Story of the Clan-na-Gael," [I], GA, November 29, 1924; O'Brien and Ryan, 2, 46–51.

Seven Thousand Men Knew of the Expedition

The Committee in Charge

This open method of working, made necessary by the unfortunate experiences of Fenianism, could not be tried twice. Its chief chance of success lay in the fact that the British Government considered Fenianism to have been crushed and looked with contempt on the capacity for practical work of any remnant of it that might still hold together. It is the habitual attitude of British statesmen to regard every "redress of grievances" as a "final settlement" of the Irish difficulty, and Gladstone's disestablishment of the Irish Protestant Church and the Land Act of 1870 had been so recently heralded to the world as the beginning of "a new era of justice to Ireland," during which Ireland was to be governed entirely "in accordance with Irish ideas," that no one in England dreamt of such a project being possible. Besides, the main details of the work were known only to less than ten men, and the full knowledge was confined to five.

The work was originally entrusted to ten men by the convention in Baltimore in 1874, and they were not all present. The original committee consisted of John Devoy, chairman; Patrick Mahon of Rochester, N.Y., treasurer; Michael W. Leahy, of Washington, D.C., secretary; John W. Goff, New York; James Reynolds, New Haven, Conn.; Michael C. Boland, of Wilmington, Del.; Jeremiah Kavanagh of Louisville, Ky.; Thomas Tallon of Omaha, Neb.; John C. Talbot of San Francisco, and Felix Callahan of Montreal. The latter, however, was never able to attend meetings and is now dead. Patrick Mahon was a member of a big dry goods firm, and was a man of remarkable financial ability and of very strong character. His commercial standing and capacity were of immense service to the undertakings from first to last, and his death in 1880 at the age of forty-three was a severe blow to the National cause.[91] John W. Goff, now the Recorder of New York, was then a clerk in A. T. Stewart's dry-goods establishment,[92] but was studying law and had either then been admitted to the bar or was admitted soon after.[93] James Reynolds was a brass founder, doing a good

---

91. Patrick Mahon died in 1881 in Rochester, New York. "Obituary Notes," *NYT,* February 3, 1881, 3.

92. An Irish-born American, Alexander Turney Stewart established one of the most successful retail businesses in New York City that had gross sales of $50 million by 1865. Kenneth T. Jackson, ed., *The Encyclopedia of New York City* (New Haven, CT: Yale University Press, 1995), 1123–24.

93. John Goff was a thorn in Devoy's side even before the *Catalpa* expedition. He was born in Wexford about 1842 and emigrated to America at an early age. A bright and ambitious fellow, he joined the Fenians early on and was very active. "Passing of Judge John W. Goff," *GA,* November 22, 1924.

Seven Thousand Men Knew of the Expedition

business, and was a clear-headed, quiet, but very firm and resolute man. Leahy was a clerk in the War Department, who worked very well for a year, but, owing to personal misfortunes dropped out of the movement. John C. Talbot was a San Francisco dry-goods merchant, whose ability, sound judgment and devotion contributed very materially to the success of the enterprise. His business brought him often enough to the East to keep him in personal touch with the work, and one most important portion of it, which had to be attended to on the Pacific Coast, was wholly in his hands. It was done without a hitch or a flaw. Michael C. Boland was a carriage manufacturer in Wilmington, a man of unusual intelligence, whose tact and judgment were instrumental in raising considerable money for the work in Pennsylvania, Delaware, Maryland and Washington. Jeremiah Kavanagh, of Louisville, and Thomas Tallon, of Omaha, were good men, with a long experience of Fenianism, but, owing to their distance from the Atlantic Coast, were only able to attend one meeting each. Felix Callahan was an old Canadian Fenian who had been specially honored by being named in D'Arcy McGee's[94] most virulent pamphlet attack on Fenianism.

For the practical conduct of the preparations five men were active—Reynolds, Mahon, Talbot, Goff and myself—and in the latter stages the number was reduced to four and Dr. William Carroll[95] of Philadelphia was added. For the execution of the preparatory plans Reynolds and I took responsibility. The first part of the practical work was to raise the money, and the necessary amount could not be determined until the plan of action was arranged. All that had been left to the committee. They first started to raise the money.

THE PRELIMINARY WORK

Not knowing how much money would be needed all that could be done at first was to issue the appeal and start the work of collection. The only part

---

94. Darcy McGee was a Young Irelander from Wexford. He came to America after the unsuccessful 1848 uprising. He worked as a journalist and then emigrated to Canada, where he became a prominent public figure holding a parliamentary seat. He also changed his views about Irish nationalism, becoming an outspoken opponent of Fenianism, for which, it is thought, he was assassinated in 1868. O'Brien and Ryan, 1, 301; "Thomas Darcy McGee," *NYT,* July 14, 1855, 2, and "Murder of Thomas Darcy McGee," April 8, 1868, 1.

95. Dr. William Carroll (1835–1926) was born in County Donegal into an Ulster Presbyterian family. His family emigrated to America when he was a child. He became a physician, saw service in the Union Army during the Civil War, and joined the Fenians. Later he was a leader of the Clan-na-Gael and worked closely with Devoy. O'Brien and Ryan, 1, 125–26.

Seven Thousand Men Knew of the Expedition

of the plan agreed on was that a ship should be sent to Australia, but whether one should be chartered or bought outright we had no idea, nor was there any knowledge of the probable cost. But we went to work, hammer and tongs, to get all the money we could and communicated by letter with those ex-prisoners who had personal knowledge of the situation in Western Australia. These were John Boyle O'Reilly and John Kenealy, of Los Angeles, Cal. Thomas McCarthy Fennell of Elmira had given me all the information he had and many valuable suggestions, both by letter and in personal talks, and Denis Cashman had done the same. John B. Walsh,[96] of San Francisco, was frequently in receipt of letters from the military prisoners, and these were promptly sent on when there was anything of moment in them. But O'Reilly and Kenealy[97] were in close touch with the committee and giving valuable aid from the very conception of the project to its successful termination.

As to the man who was to take charge of the work and the number of men at his command, there was the same uncertainty. I had set my heart on going personally to take charge of the work, because the men had been under my charge in Ireland and their conviction was secured through evidence of their having attended meetings with me. I am safe in saying that the general desire of the members of the committee coincided with my wish and that if it had come to a vote at any time I would certainly have been selected.[98] When John J. Breslin was later on chosen it was on my proposition, and I made it knowing that the man was fit for the work in every way and that the selection was necessary for the success of the expedition. My idea was that we should send from twelve to fifteen carefully selected men, fully armed, on a ship calling at an Australian port, get them ashore in some way unobserved after a man sent by steamer had perfected his plan of rescue, and take the prisoners off, by main force if necessary.

John W. Goff also wanted to go, but on the ship, and had no objection to my going ahead by steamer. Some half dozen men were sounded as to their willingness to take part, without formally selecting any of them. In forty-five years of connection with the Irish movement my invariable

96. O'Reilly, Kenealy, Fennell, Cashman, and Walsh were convicted Fenians who had all been transported to Australia aboard the *Hougoumont*. Amos, 289–90.

97. John Kenealy was a Cork Fenian leader who was convicted largely on the perjured testimony of the informer Warner. He was sentenced to ten years, and when conditionally pardoned in 1869 came to America, settling in Los Angeles, California. Walter McGrath, "The Fenians in Australia," *Journal of Cork Historical and Archaeological Society* 254 (1990): 165–67; O'Brien and Ryan, 1, 83.

98. At the time, John Boyle O'Reilly wrote Devoy urging him to be the one to go alone to Australia. O'Brien and Ryan, 1, 86.

Seven Thousand Men Knew of the Expedition

experience has been that there is no difficulty whatever in getting men to volunteer for work involving risk of life or imprisonment. There are always more volunteers than are wanted and the difficulty always lies in selecting the fittest men and in appeasing those who are left out. This was the case in the selection of the bodyguard for Stephens when John Breslin liberated him from Richmond Prison [Dublin] in 1865, and it was so with the Australian rescue. All the troubles that came later—and there was a whole peck—arose from this cause. There are so many men in the Irish movement who want to have a hand in any work involving danger that it will be impossible to satisfy them all until the day comes for a general movement against England. That will tax the intellect, as well as the financial resources of the race, but if these two requisites are forthcoming the fighting spirit will give a good account of itself.

Some Leaves from a Diary

After six months of collection it was determined to ascertain definitely what could be done, and I was sent to New Bedford. For some time I kept a diary, and I have preserved all the correspondence and papers in connection with the work, so that I am able to write after fortifying my memory. I left New York on Friday, January 29, 1875, and stopped in New Haven to have a consultation with Reynolds, remaining till Saturday night in the hope of being able to have him come with me. He could not come, however, so I started alone for Boston to see O'Reilly. The old Celtic Club,[99] now one of the strongest branches in America, was then a small, struggling body. I called on its officers, but did not mention my mission, and found that the less I said about calling on O'Reilly, the better. He, Dr. R. D. Joyce,[100] Patrick A. Collins[101] and John E. Fitzgerald[102] had a few years

---

99. This was the Boston branch of the Clan-na-Gael. Ó Lúing, 67.

100. Robert Dwyer Joyce (1830–1883) was born in Limerick, was trained as a doctor, and emigrated to America in 1866. He was known for his poetry and songs. "Robert Dwyer Joyce," Princess Grace Irish Library, Monaco [http://www.pgil-eirdata.org], January 2002.

101. A major Boston politician, Patrick Collins (1844–1905) served in a variety of elected posts, including those of congressman and mayor of Boston, and was later appointed consul general at London. He was active with the Fenians in the 1860s, serving as a bond agent and organizer. He also served as the first president of the Irish Land League of America. "Patrick Collins," *Biographical Directory of the U. S. Congress* [http://bioguide.congress.gov], January 2002; D'Arcy, 51, 81, 400.

102. John E. Fitzgerald (1845–1900) was Boston's first Irish fire commissioner. He also served in the local and state legislatures and was appointed collector of internal revenue in the 1880s. "John E. Fitzgerald Dead," *NYT,* March 6, 1900, 5, and "Another Democrat Happy," August 3, 1886, 3.

Seven Thousand Men Knew of the Expedition

before resigned from the Clan (it was said at the archbishop's[103] request), and there was strong feeling on the matter. More than twenty years later I was reproached by one of the then members of the club for keeping the members in ignorance of my mission while I told John Boyle O'Reilly all about it. That was precisely what I did. I find this note in my diary for Monday, February 1, 1875:

"Called on O'Reilly and Cashman[104] at Pilot[105] office. Told O'R. my business. He offered to come with me and introduce me to Hathaway if I would wait till Tuesday, Monday being his busy day. Gladly consented, knowing his influence with Hathaway. Spent evening at his house, talking over his escape, etc., Cashman with us."

For the next two days I find the following:

"Feb. 2—Called on O'R. at Pilot office. Found him in bad humor, owing to his having learned that an ex-prisoner to whom he had lent a large sum of money had 'burst up.' Said he could not come, but would write a strong letter. Started for New Bedford that evening."

"Feb. 3—Stopped at Parker House. Had some delay in finding Hathaway. When I gave him O'R.'s note I saw a good effect produced at once. It was in the police station. He is captain of night police. Told me quietly to follow him. Went into courthouse and locked door. Sat down and talked whole thing over. Entered warmly into project. Found he knew all about our men. Recommended strongly the buying of a vessel and gave solid reasons why any other course would not be safe. Showed how it could be made to pay expenses. Splendid physique; handsome, honest face; quite English-looking. Wears only side whiskers; very reserved in manner; speaks low and slowly, but every word fits. Never without a cigar in his mouth. Eighteen years to sea, whaling all the time."

---

103. John Joseph Williams (1822–1907) was the fourth Roman Catholic bishop and first archbishop of Boston. "Williams," *Catholic Encyclopedia* [http://www.newadvent.org/cathen/], October 2002.

104. Denis Bambrick Cashman (1842–1897) was born in Waterford City. He became a Dublin "centre" and was arrested, sentenced to seven years, and transported aboard the *Hougoumont*. Upon his conditional pardon, he came to America and settled in Boston. He was closely associated with John Boyle O'Reilly. O'Brien and Ryan, 2, 291; Amos, 289; George E. Ryan, "Dennis [*sic*] B. Cashman, Warmly Devoted to His Native Land," *Bulletin,* The Eire Society of Boston, March (1983).

105. An influential Catholic newspaper, the *Pilot* was founded by Patrick Donahoe in Boston in 1836. John Boyle O'Reilly was the paper's editor, and in 1876, with Archbishop Williams, he purchased it. The *Pilot* is still published, now by the Boston Archdiocese, making it America's oldest Catholic newspaper. "Patrick Donahoe: Famous U.S. Publisher," *Cornafean Online* [http://www.cornafean.com], October 2001.

Seven Thousand Men Knew of the Expedition

I remained in New Bedford and called on Hathaway every morning and evening to discuss the project, and wrote the substance of what he recommended to the other members of the committee.[106] I recommended a change in the original programme—half formed, as it was—and, as Hathaway's plan would require much more money than we were likely to get by voluntary subscription in any reasonable time, I recommended that we should ask clubs as had large funds to lend a portion of them. I had then no doubt we could pay back the loans by the profits of the whaling. The total amount raised by voluntary contribution was, I believe, about $7,000, but just how much of that had been turned in at that time I cannot now say.

Here we were at last face to face with a crisis. If Hathaway was right—and events proved he was—we must get the necessary funds by a kind of revolution. All the members of the committee consented to make the effort, and then came the long strain that tested the organization and at the end made it a real revolutionary machine.

106. "Hathaway's Timely Advice—At the start the committee miscalculated the amount necessary to carry the rescue through. They thought that about five or six thousand dollars would be enough, believing that a deal could be made with an American whaler to take the men off after having been rescued. They also thought they could send twelve or fifteen men armed with the best rifles and revolvers to take them after a fight with the Government police force. It was Captain Hathaway who convinced them of their error in the latter case. He said: 'You must get them out by stratagem and stealthily or not at all. The Australian police force, who are all old soldiers and mounted, could beat any little band of men you could send there, and you couldn't land Irishmen there without at once attracting attention and spoiling the whole game.'" "Captain Anthony of the 'Catalpa' Dead," *GA*, May 31, 1913, 1.

[III]

John Mitchel Knew of the Project
and Helped to Raise Funds—A Characteristic Letter

In our efforts to raise the necessary money we did not confine ourselves to asking for funds already in existence. The proceeds of public entertainments of various kinds were thrown in and there was no difficulty in getting local committees to vote them for the Rescue Fund, as we already called it. Among these public affairs was a lecture at the Cooper Institute[107] by John Mitchel[108] in the very early stages of the enterprise, and the object was confided to Mitchel.

Mitchel had returned to Ireland in July, 1874, on the invitation of the Nationalists of Cork City (then known as "rebel Cork") to contest the seat in Parliament. He went in defiance of the British Government, being an escaped political prisoner, and everyone concerned knew that, if elected, he would refuse to take the oath.[109] In those days it was a favorite practice among the Fenians in Ireland to elect to Parliament some uncompromising Nationalist, not to serve as a member, but for the special purpose of refusing to take the oath, or as a protest against England's treatment of

---

107. "The Great Hall of The Cooper Union has stood for more than a century as a bastion of free speech and a witness to the flow of American History and ideas. When the hall opened in 1858, more than a year in advance of the completion of the institution, it quickly became a mecca for all interested in serious discussion and debate of the vital issues of the day." "Main Page," Cooper Union website [http://www.cooper.edu/administration/about/Welcome.html], October 2002.

108. John Mitchel (1815–1875) was a Young Ireland leader convicted of treason. First transported to Bermuda, he was then transferred to Van Diemen's Land from where he escaped with his family in 1853 and came to America. He published the *Irish Citizen* in New York and was a major figure in the independence movement. Due to his proslavery views, he fought in the Confederate Army (as did his sons, two of whom were killed) during the Civil War. He was not a Fenian, but his writings strongly influenced nationalist thinking. Connolly, 361; O'Brien and Ryan, 1, 7; Terry Golway, *For the Cause of Liberty: A Thousand Years of Ireland's Heroes* (New York: Touchstone, 2000), 120, 138; Thomas Keneally, *The Great Shame and the Triumph of the Irish in the English-Speaking World* (New York: Nan A. Talese, 1999), 260–66.

109. The oath of allegiance to the crown. O'Brien and Ryan, 1, 312.

Irish political prisoners and to discredit English rule in every possible way. To those "practical" men who think such action to be waste of time it may be explained that the Fenians and their sympathizers understood perfectly well that such exhibitions of disloyalty were very useful in keeping up in the minds of England's enemies the knowledge that Ireland was a possible ally in case of war. This was the idea of the Cork Nationalists and later of the men of Tipperary, who succeeded in electing John Mitchel, the uncompromising foe of England.

Mitchel sailed, if I remember aright, on July 14, 1874. I was then a reporter on the *Herald,* and generally did whatever Irish work was on hand. Felix De Fontaine, the city editor, had been a major in the Confederate Army, knew Mitchel personally and admired him. He assigned me to the work of reporting the departure, and had told me to "give the grand old man a good show." I did, and it was the last work I did before starting for Baltimore. In those days the whole country looked to the *Herald* for news, and the paper paid special attention to Irish affairs because, unlike the yellows of to-day, its conductors were good judges of news and saw that the news was printed.

It was at the dock that we in New York first met Dr. Carroll, of Philadelphia, and learned the mettle he was made of. He had come to see Mitchel off, being an old friend, and had no intention of going further than the steamer. Mitchel said to him, half jokingly, "I wish you were coming with me, doctor." The doctor went to the nearest dry-goods store, bought a few necessary things, sent a telegram to a medical friend in Philadelphia to look after his patients, bought a ticket on the dock and sailed for Ireland with Mitchel. It was this chivalrous action that made us trust Dr. Carroll, and from then on he was "in the swim," although he had been for some time a member of the Clan.[110] We found that he was a Donegal Presbyterian, had been a surgeon-major in the Federal Army in the Civil War, and had a standing and connections which were afterwards made most useful to the national cause.

John Mitchel's Characteristic Letter

Mitchel was beaten in Cork after a gallant fight made for him by the Nationalists, because in "rebel Cork" there was then, as there is now, a very

---

110. Dr. Carroll named one of his children Mitchel. National Archives (hereafter NA), "Federal Population Census Schedules," 1910, Microform Series T624, Roll 1400, page 7.

John Mitchel Knew of the Project

strong "shoneen"[111] element, because the young men had no votes and because there was no secret ballot. The British Government, learning the shattered condition of Mitchel's health, made up its mind that he would speedily die in prison if he should be arrested, and determined not to add to its unpopularity in Ireland, so he was allowed to return in peace to the United States. A committee waited on him and asked him to lecture at the Cooper Institute, and he gladly consented. The title of the lecture was "Ireland Revisited," and it gave a most interesting sketch of his trip and his impressions of the old land after an absence of twenty-six years. After the lecture the committee sent him a check for $100, and he promptly returned it, with the following characteristic letter:

Brooklyn, 8th Dec., 1874

"Dear Friend:

"The good Irishmen who are interesting themselves in a good and sacred work —which I need not more particularly specify, but which calls forth all my sympathies—will certainly allow me to make my humble contribution towards the fund which is to go to that noble use. I think I said to you before, that I could not think of making profit of a lecture, the proceeds of which were to be devoted to such a cause. Take back, therefore, this checque for $100; I will not have it. When I myself was in Australian captivity I never could have dreamed of any possibility of escape, but for the means supplied for that purpose by our good countrymen.

"Who should sympathize with our countrymen in bondage if I did not?

"Therefore, my dear friend, just cancel this checque; for it would be far more grateful to me—if I were young enough—to take a part in the expedition which, no doubt, will be made, than to derive any sort of personal profit from the devoted zeal of my countrymen in such a cause—which is in fact my own cause.

"Very truly your friend,

"John Mitchel"

We got a number of copies of this letter printed and circulated them among our friends, and it had a considerable effect in stimulating the work. John Mitchel did not get along very well with the leaders of American Fenianism, but the rank and file looked up to him more than to any other man of the Young Ireland movement. Their gospel of Irish Nationality was the gospel preached by John Mitchel.

---

111. "Used to indicate a person's inclination towards English rather than Irish standards and attitudes in cultural life, sport, etc." *Oxford English Dictionary,* 2nd edition [hereafter *O.E.D.*] [http://www.bomc.com], November 2001.

John Mitchel Knew of the Project

MITCHEL GOES HOME TO DIE

The men in other cities, when they read this letter, recognized that a lecture by John Mitchel would be a good way of raising money, and invitations began to pour in. He had accepted an invitation to Baltimore and all the arrangements had been made when a vacancy occurred in Tipperary, and the Nationalists there cabled an invitation to him to go over and stand for the county. He at once cancelled his Baltimore appointment and prepared to start for Ireland. The men in Baltimore were in consternation. Their tickets were printed, posters were up and there was no time to call off the meeting. Coughlin,[112] a Cork '67 man, who was at Ballyknockeen with Mackey[113] and O'Brien,[114] wrote me, asking that we urge on Mitchel the necessity of postponing his departure for Ireland for a few days. I was in Boston again, and find this entry on my diary under date of February 16, 1875:

"Wrote to Mitchel to urge him to go to Baltimore, but when delegation from Baltimore waited on him they could not prevail on him to postpone his departure. He said: 'If an angel came down from heaven to ask me to go to Baltimore I will sail for Ireland to-morrow.' Tom Bourke went in his stead, and did all right."

He sailed for Ireland, was elected for Tipperary after a most exciting and memorable contest and died, Member for Tipperary, in the house in which he had spent his childhood, while the British Parliament was rushing through the annulment of his election. So that it can be truly said that John Mitchel died fighting and after having won a victory over England. But the victory really was won by physical force. The young manhood of the Premier County had no votes, so they exercised the only kind of pressure within their reach on the old and middle-aged men who had the franchise. Left to themselves, the majority of the electors would have voted for John Mitchel, but they were exhorted from the altar by the priests,

---

112. John Coughlin was an apprentice silversmith from Cork city. Wounded at Ballyknockane, he was captured and sentenced to five years. Walter McGrath, "The Fenian Rising in Cork," *Sword,* Winter (1968).

113. William Mackey Lomasney (1841–1884) was born in Ohio. He went to Ireland in 1865 to help with the uprising. He fought at Ballyknockane and continued to fight for a year after until his arrest. Amnestied in 1871, he settled in Detroit for a time and ran a bookstore. He would eventually give his life to the cause. O'Brien and Ryan, 2, 4–7; Le Caron, 101.

114. James F. X. O'Brien (1828–1905) of Cork was a principal letter writer to the [Dublin] *Irish People.* He was convicted for his activities in 1867. Eventually pardoned, he later served as member of Parliament for Mayo and Cork City. Devoy, 44; O'Brien and Ryan, 1, 166.

intimidated by the landlords and marched off in a body to the polling booths where they had to openly declare their votes in the presence of witnesses. When private pressure and remonstrance from the Nationalists failed, the young fellows used fists, sticks and stones; many of the bodies of marching voters were broken up and a sufficient number of weak-kneed men were kept away from the polls to give the victory to Mitchel. They got the choice of being denounced from the altar or of having their heads broken, and they preferred to take their chances of the former to the certainty of the latter.

MEMORIAL MEETING FOR MITCHEL

The news of John Mitchel's death came in the midst of our hardest work, and we had to take suitable action. We organized a great memorial demonstration at the Hippodrome, on the site of what is now Madison Square Garden, and it was a great success, but not without much trouble and tension. The Clan in those days was not equipped for such demonstrations and had never before held one. Rules had to be ridden over roughshod, and it was done with the consent of 99 per cent of the rank and file, but the differences the process of riding roughshod engendered left their mark and made the subsequent work, so far as New York was concerned, doubly hard. I will not go into these difficulties now further than to say that they mainly concerned the choice of the chairman and the orator for the meeting, and that my personal part in them consisted in rejecting an offer that I, an unknown man, should act as chairman and another unknown man as orator.[115] The English press would proclaim as hopelessly lost the cause for which John Mitchel had given his life if unknown men undertook to speak for him at such a meeting. I did my utmost to have the local committee (of which Judge James Fitzgerald[116] of the Supreme Court was secretary) select Richard O'Gorman[117] as the

115. John Goff. O'Brien and Ryan, 1, 99.

116. James Fitzgerald (1851–1922) was born in Ireland. After coming to the United States, he read the law, served in both houses of the New York State legislature, worked in the New York district attorney's office, and eventually became a judge. He was active in Democratic politics for many years. "James Fitzgerald," *NYT*, December 18, 1922, 17.

117. A Young Ireland leader, Richard O'Gorman (1821–1895) escaped to America, where he remained in New York. While active in politics, he was not so in the U.S. Fenian movement. When the "*Cuba* Five" arrived in New York in January 1871, he led the Tammany greeting party. He was a lawyer and became a municipal judge. Devoy, 11, 298; D'Arcy, 1; O'Brien and Ryan, 1, 7; "Richard O'Gorman Dead," *NYT*, March 2, 1895, 9.

orator, but his practical abandonment of the national movement made him very unpopular with our men, and I failed. Finally Thomas Francis Bourke, who had been sentenced to death in Tipperary in 1867, and whose speech in the dock is one of the gems of Irish oratory, was selected as chairman, and Thomas Clarke Luby[118] as orator. They made magnificent speeches and the demonstration was a fitting tribute to Mitchel and a vindication of his principles. The meeting was the first of a great series held by the Clan-na-Gael for the purpose of putting its principles before the public every year since.

Unless compelled to do so by sheer necessity I will go no further into the differences above referred to, and will only mention others growing out of them in so far as it may be necessary to clear up the actual facts of the rescue.

While on the subject of raising money I may as well mention another incident which occurred at this time—the very eve of buying the *Catalpa* and getting her ready to start. Colonel Ric. Burke,[119] had only a few months before arrived in the country from Ireland, where he had spent some months recuperating after his terrible experiences in Broadmoor [Convict Lunatic Asylum] prison. He had just started on a lecturing tour, and proved most useful in privately talking up the rescue project among the men. His first lecture was in New Haven, where the influence of James Reynolds, Captain Larry O'Brien[120] and Pat. O'Connor had got the men interested. On my way back from New Bedford I got to New Haven on February 17 to confer with Reynolds, and was in time for Ric. Burke's lecture and a speech by Tom Bourke. At the meeting of the committee next

118. Thomas Clarke Luby (1822–1901) was born in Dublin of Protestant parents; he became a Young Irelander. He was arrested, imprisoned, and amnestied. He came to America and was very active in the Clan. He later worked with Stephens and wrote for the [New York] *Irish Nation*. O'Brien and Ryan, 1, 119.

119. Ricard O'Sullivan Burke (1838–1922) was born in County Cork. He joined the Cork Militia at age fifteen and then went to sea at age eighteen. When the American Civil War erupted, he joined the Union Army, where he learned engineering and rose to the rank of colonel. He later became a Fenian and played a very active role in preparations for the Uprising. He oversaw the 1867 Manchester Rescue and soon after was arrested. The failed explosion at Clerkenwell prison was intended to rescue him. He was released in 1872 and returned to America, where he became prominent in the Clan. O'Brien and Ryan, 1, 35–36.

120. Lawrence O'Brien (1842–1923) was born in Tipperary and when a child emigrated to America. He grew up in Connecticut and served as an officer in a state volunteer regiment during the Civil War. He then went to Ireland and was arrested in 1867. He escaped from Clonmel jail and returned to the United States by way of France. He joined the successful family building business in New Haven and remained active in the Clan for many years. He was a close friend of James Reynolds. O'Brien and Ryan, 1, 203–4; Devoy, 221–22; "Capt. Larry O'Brien, Old Fenian, Dead," *GA*, January 13, 1923, 1.

John Mitchel Knew of the Project

evening Burke was handed $200 as a first instalment of the proceeds of the lecture, and he at once handed over $75 of it as a contribution to the Rescue Fund. He had arrived in America unheralded, no money had been given him, and he was making a new start in the world, but he insisted on making this contribution.

Dion Boucicault[121] contributed $25 to the fund through James J. O'Kelly,[122] who was then the dramatic critic of the *Herald,* but Boucicault did not know exactly how the money was to be applied to the benefit of the Fenian military prisoners. He merely knew it was to aid them in some way. It was turned in as part of the proceeds of the Mitchel lecture.

121. Dion Boucicault (1820–1890) was born and raised in Dublin. He was a prolific and well-known playwright, actor, and theater manager whose career took him to England, France, America, and Australia. He also had an interest in the Fenian prisoners. In 1876, he wrote England's Prime Minister Disraeli urging their release. (Later, he reportedly appeared at Disraeli's office on the day of the *Catalpa* escape.) When the released Fenians Edward O'Meagher Condon and Patrick Meledy arrived in New York in 1878, Boucicault contributed $500 for their benefit. David W. Dwyer, "Dion Boucicault: His Life and Times" [www.msu.edu], November 2001; "Great Britain," *NYT,* January 10, 1876, 1; "Sympathizing with the Fenians," *Tribune,* October 28, 1878, 8; "J. W. Goff as an Irishman," *Tribune,* October 30, 1890, 1.

122. James J. O'Kelly (1845–1916) was born in Dublin. Like many Fenians, he had a remarkable life. He served in the French Foreign Legion (as did Devoy) and later became a colonel in the regular French army. He did not directly participate in the 1867 Uprising but helped with the reorganization of the IRB. He was a successful American journalist and later held the North Roscommon seat in Parliament for many years. O'Brien and Ryan, 1, 59–60.

[IV]

OFFICIAL REPORT OF THE WORK DONE

Presented to a Convention in 1876 — The Arduous Work of Raising the Money — How John Boyle O'Reilly Got a United States Naval Engineer to Inspect the Vessel

The time had at last come for taking definite action. We appeared to have a good prospect of obtaining sufficient money and we must look out for a ship. Trustees had kicked and refused to draw funds which branches had voted and many most embarrassing delays had occurred in this way. Two very good old Fenians, now dead, who were trustees of my own branch, had refused to draw the $2,500 voted by an overwhelming majority, and had to be removed from office and replaced by others before the money could be obtained. Michael Boland,[123] of Louisville, was a trustee there and held up a large sum of money in the same way. But eventually we got all the money voted, and I will give the financial account of the transaction before I close.

In a report dated July 1, 1875, and issued by John W. Goff, who had worked very hard to raise the money in the district which included New York and New Jersey, and for which he was responsible, I find the amount was $8,379.10, and the following reference to the trouble in getting it:

"Now that we have succeeded as far as it is possible, we can afford to be charitable, but we must not be forgetful; and while we are ready, if ultimate success crown our efforts, to share our joy thereat with the whole Irish race, we cannot but remember the patriots who neglected or refused to lend a hand when help was sorely needed."

123. Devoy had few good words for this Boland. (Not to be confused with Michael C. Boland of Delaware.) He came from Waterford. During the Civil War, he served as an officer in the Union Army and later saw action in one of the Fenian Canadian incursions. It is thought by some that he was a British spy. John Devoy, "Story of the Clan-na-Gael," [IV], GA, December 20, 1924, 5.

54

Official Report of the Work Done

What followed can be best told by quoting a portion of the report presented by the committee to a convention held in Philadelphia in August, 1876, after the cable had reported the complete success of the expedition.

The Official Report

"Philadelphia, August 9, 1876[124]

"To the * * * *

"Brothers—The undersigned, appointed as the A. P. R.[125] Committee by the Convention held in Providence, R.I., in July last year, on resigning into your hands the trust reposed in them, have the honor to submit the following report:

"In the report submitted by the last Committee to the Providence Convention a request was made that, in consequence of the peculiarly delicate and difficult nature of the undertaking, which was then in progress, and the serious risks incurred by the agents sent to take charge of it, the full details of the plan, the names of the agents and the ship and other particulars of the affair might not be asked by the Convention. The Convention, recognizing the necessity for secrecy and the fact that when operations of such importance are undertaken by an organization like ours it is absolutely necessary *to trust some one* and confide the management to a small number of men, was satisfied that a full account of the financial transactions with proper vouchers should be laid before the Committee on * * * *. The latter Committee, after a close and careful scrutiny of the accounts and vouchers and a personal examination of the committee, who had till then acted as the agents of the organization in the matter, and who were, and are still, responsible for all the steps taken— the plan, the choice of the executive agents and the financial outlay—made a favorable report to the Convention, and no further information was asked. The undersigned were then named as the committee to take charge of the affair and to direct whatever further operations in connection with it remained to be performed.

"As the undertaking has, fortunately, been crowned with success, by the rescue of all the prisoners whom it was intended to wrest from the hands of the British jailers in Western Australia, and the men are daily expected to land on American soil, the time has come when all the details can be given to the organization. The Convention has a right to know the whole history of the undertaking from beginning to end, the difficulties that stood in the way and the means by which they were overcome, so that it may be able to act intelligently in providing for such emergencies in the future.

124. This report was delivered ten days prior to the arrival of the *Catalpa* in the United States.
125. Australian Prisoner Rescue.

55

Official Report of the Work Done

The Initial Difficulties

"Several letters, smuggled out of the prison, were received from two of the imprisoned soldiers, James Wilson and Martin Hogan, by a member of this committee, during the years '72, '73 and '74, pointing out how a rescue could be effected and making urgent appeals for assistance. After making several ineffectual attempts to raise money to undertake a rescue and obtaining from the ex-prisoners who had come to this country from Australia all the information as to the prison arrangements, stations, guards, police, ports, shipping and other things necessary to form an exact idea of the situation, one of Wilson's letters was forwarded to the governing body in 1873, with a request to undertake the work. That body had its hands full with its own troubles and declined to take any action. The Baltimore Convention was next applied to, and the result was that the next committee was empowered to raise the necessary funds and proceed to work. The committee decided at its first meeting to call on the members for voluntary contributions, and as soon as the then chairman judged that a sufficient amount had been collected he was instructed to call a meeting to decide on a plan. The subscriptions came in slowly and the project met with much opposition in many branches, but finally, when it was ascertained that from six to seven thousand dollars had been raised, a meeting of the committee was called, and the matter laid before it. Seeing there was not money enough to purchase and fit out a ship, it was thought that a bargain might be made with a whaler to call at a port agreed upon in Western Australia and take the men on board when agents sent by steamer beforehand should have effected a rescue. The difficulties in the way were clearly seen, and the danger of failing to connect with a ship which could be more profitably employed in whaling than in waiting for the chance of a successful rescue was a source of anxiety, but for want of funds no other plan seemed then feasible.

Hathaway's Recommendations

"The committee appointed two of its members a committee to go to New Bedford and enter into negotiations with Captain Henry C. Hathaway, who had been mainly instrumental in taking John Boyle O'Reilly from Western Australia, and to ascertain the probable cost and other necessary information. A letter from Mr. O'Reilly to Captain Hathaway was procured, which made him at once enter heartily into the project. Being an experienced whaler, with a thorough knowledge of Western Australia and the Indian Ocean, he was recommended as the most competent judge as to what was best to be done, though being captain of police and having a family he could not undertake the work himself. He recommended that a ship should be purchased, fitted out as a whaler, a trustworthy captain put on board and sent to

Official Report of the Work Done

Australia. He pointed out how such ship could be made to pay her own expenses and even clear a profit if whaling was very good. For a small ship he estimated the cost would be about $12,000 for one year's voyage. There was no ship to sail for those parts for several months, and in no instance could he guarantee the good faith or honesty of the captain. He also pointed out how a whaler is likely to change his course according to his success in whaling, and as the value of two good whales would be much more than the committee could then offer as a reward for the accomplishment of the work, the risk of trusting to a captain who might be tempted to abandon the whole enterprise for the sake of good whale fishing was too great.

How the Money was Obtained

"On the other hand, there were no funds to purchase and fit out a ship—to say nothing of the cost of sending agents by steamer, so what was the committee to do? They were pledged to make the attempt, the money had been subscribed for that purpose, and they would be relieved from office in one year from their election. The appeal for voluntary subscriptions had only brought in half the amount estimated by Captain Hathaway, and as it had already been urged as strongly as possible there was no hope of doubling the amount by a fresh appeal. More than that, Captain Hathaway did not make his estimate on a particular ship whose price he knew, but rather made a rough calculation on what it would take to fit out a ship costing about $4,000 for a voyage of twelve months only. After due consideration of the whole position, and the chances of clearing money enough by a whaling voyage to pay back a loan, the chairman decided to ask the committee to appeal to the organization for the necessary amount from the revolutionary fund, leaving it optional with branches to give the money or not, and if they voted any, leaving the amount to their own discretion. It was known that many were hostile to the project in any shape, and many others were inactive through want of confidence; therefore, any attempt to levy a pro rata assessment would not realize a sufficient sum of money.

"Too much risk had already been run by communicating the fact that such a project was on foot to such a large number of men, without any guarantee that our ranks were free from British spies, and another appeal for funds, no matter in what shape it was put, would naturally create more talk, and, consequently, increase the risk of bad or indiscreet men gaining more knowledge than was safe to give to any but the few in charge of the enterprise. Still the risk had either to be run or the project abandoned at once, and a great deal of allowance was made for the fact that the British government entertained a profound contempt for our ability to successfully carry out such an enterprise.

"Each member of the committee was communicated with and the facts of the case laid before him. After a short time favorable replies were received from all

Official Report of the Work Done

and circulars were at once issued asking for the necessary funds. The trouble and anxiety experienced by the members of the committee at this period, the uncertainty as to whether money enough to start the expedition would come in or not, the disappointments, the refusals, and the various other annoyances to which they were subjected can be better imagined than described.

To Provide the Ship

"In the month of February a letter was received from Captain Hathaway, who had been requested to look out for a suitable ship that might be for sale and to recommend a whaling agent who could be entrusted with the work, stating that a ship in every way suitable was then for sale, that she could probably be bought for $6,000, and fitted out for $6,000 more, or a little over, and giving an inventory of her. This was about the best chance we could get, but the required amount was not on hand. However, according as it came nearer to the month of May the prices of ships would be increasing, as the demand grows larger in the spring, and the longer we waited the more money it would cost. Captain Hathaway said he might be able to delay the sale for a few days to give us time, and as there was no time for delay the Chairman at once telegraphed him to try and do so till March 1st, writing at the same time by mail to say that parties empowered to act for us would go to New Bedford on that day, and if everything was found all right and the price reasonable the ship would be bought and half the amount paid in cash, the balance to be paid in as short time as might afterwards be agreed upon.

"The six members of the committee who resided near enough to attend meetings were at once telegraphed and written to, so that as many of them as possible might be present to take part in the purchase, and that those who could not go might empower the others to act for them or not as seemed right to them. None were able to go but the Chairman and the member for the New York District, but the others all consented to leave the matter in the hands of whatever members might be able to go, and empowered them to act for them. Finding that only two members of the committee could go to New Bedford, and the absence of the treasurer, from reasons which will be apparent to those who know him, placing those two members in a rather delicate position, they determined, with the consent of the other four who had been communicated with, to take with them some members of the organization outside of the committee whose standing in the organization seemed to them to fit them to act as witnesses in the transactions, so as to protect the two members in question from insinuations of dishonesty. After the exposures of the previous year no man's reputation was safe through whose hands the money of any Irish revolutionary organization passed, except he took care to place his acts in the clearest and most unequivocal light.

The Agents Selected

"It should be stated here that all the members of the committee had been consulted about the plan and had given those who lived near enough to be able to attend meetings full power to act for them. Ample proof can be brought forward to show even more—that the majority of the whole committee had given two members, viz., Devoy and Reynolds, full power to act for them in any matter requiring immediate attention.

"The members outside of the committee who were selected to accompany Devoy and Reynolds to New Bedford, were Messrs. Miles O'Brien,[126] who had been at the Baltimore Convention, and James Muldoon,[127] who had been elected by the officers of the New York District to act as one of the trustees to hold the A.P.R. funds of that district.

"They proceeded to New Bedford on March 31st, arriving there on the following morning. They were informed that the ship they came to buy had been sold for a little over $6,000 on March 30th. Captain Hathaway introduced them to John T. Richardson, a whaling agent, whom he had previously recommended as the best man to act as agent in this enterprise. After a consultation with Captain Hathaway and Mr. Richardson, the latter was informed that he had been appointed agent and asked to look out for a suitable ship, so that the work might be begun with as little delay as possible.

"The sum of $1,500 was deposited with him, and Miles O'Brien proposed that instead of a receipt he should give a note for that amount in favor of John Devoy. Both O'Brien and Muldoon, as well as John W. Goff, expressed themselves in the highest terms of praise of both Richardson and Hathaway, and had no fault whatever to find with anything in the arrangement made with Richardson. Messrs. Goff, O'Brien and Muldoon returned to New York the same evening and Devoy remained for the purpose of paying over to Richardson the money to be forwarded by the treasurer and seeing after the purchase of the ship. All moneys after the first payment came in the form of checks from the treasurer—the first being in favor of Henry C. Hathaway, who at once turned it over to Richardson—all the subsequent ones to John T. Richardson. As soon as the checks arrived they were handed

---

126. Miles Murrough O'Brien caused Devoy much trouble. He was closely allied with John Goff. When Devoy opposed Goff speaking at the Mitchel memorial in 1875, O'Brien sided with Goff, and thereafter sought to undermine Devoy at every turn. Soon after the *Catalpa* departed, O'Brien and Goff, anticipating the mission's success, sought to discredit Devoy by suggesting he was physically incapacitated. After the mission succeeded, O'Brien circulated (as did Goff) various unfounded charges about misappropriations and malfeasance on the part of those overseeing the mission. Even Le Caron described O'Brien as a renegade Clan member. O'Brien and Ryan, 1, 88, 101, 108; John Devoy, "The Story of the Clan-na-Gael," [III], *GA*, December 13, 1924, 5; Le Caron, 213.

127. James Muldoon was a New York marine engineer. O'Brien and Ryan, 1, 95.

Official Report of the Work Done

over to Richardson and his receipts taken for that amount, the receipts specifically stating that the money was deposited for the purpose of "purchasing a whaling bark." The members of the committee were all written to and consulted about everything that was done, urged strongly to hurry up the various sums which had been collected and were not yet turned in, but considerable and unnecessary delay was caused by the negligence and want of energy displayed by officers in forwarding the money. As soon as the members of the committee received the money it was forwarded at once to the treasurer, who sent it as before stated. After a good deal of bargaining and examination of ships the Catalpa, which was then lying at Boston, was bought for $5,250, and the bill of sale made out in John T. Richardson's name, so that no suspicion might be aroused as to the object for which she was intended.

Inspected by a U.S. Naval Officer

"In order to make sure that everything was right, as soon as Richardson and his son-in-law, Captain Anthony, who had been chosen to command the vessel, had returned to New Bedford, a United States naval engineer, who was then on duty at the Boston Navy Yard—an Irish-American—who had been introduced to the Chairman of the committee by Mr. O'Reilly, was taken on board the Catalpa, and he gave her a thorough and complete examination, cutting out pieces of her timber to test it, and taking every other necessary precaution. He pronounced her fit to go anywhere, and sound in every respect. The only drawback, in his opinion, was that she was rather a slow sailer. On being asked how much she was worth, he said he could not speak so positively about prices as about construction and condition of a vessel, on account of the markets varying so much, but that she was worth at least $7,000, and might have cost $8,000, or even $10,000. On being informed of the actual price paid, he said we had got a great bargain.

"The Catalpa was taken to New Bedford as soon as the ice began to thaw, and the work of fitting her out was commenced at once. Though built originally as a whaler, she had been for some years previously engaged in the West India trade, and required several important changes before she could undertake a whaling voyage. A blubber deck had to be constructed; a furnace and trying apparatus put up, with a great deal of minor changes involving considerable expense. She had also to be coppered,[128] and whaling boats had to be built, care also being taken to bring along some extra ones for the use of the intended refugees. The latter boats, however, were bought second-hand, and repaired. Some sails, an anchor, a chronometer,

---

128. Coppering was required because of the length of voyages during which various marine growth accumulated that would otherwise destroy unprotected wood. Nathaniel Philbrick, *In the Heart of the Sea: The Tragedy of the Whaleship Essex* (New York: Penguin Putnam, 2000), 18–19.

Official Report of the Work Done

Catalpa "Jim" Reynolds, Treasurer of the Rescue Committee (Z. W. Pease, *The Catalpa Expedition*)

and many other necessaries were also provided, all of which were duly accounted for by the vouchers submitted to the Committee on * * * * at the last Convention, and pronounced correct. The bills for ship's stores, and all the accessories of a whaling voyage, such as oil and water casks, harpoons, bomb-lances, medicine chest, etc., were also submitted and pronounced correct. All these accounts are now open to the inspection of the Convention.

"Captain Hathaway superintended the fitting out of the Catalpa, without fee or reward, and the zeal he displayed was highly creditable to him. Having been over eighteen years a whaler, his experience was of invaluable assistance to Mr. Richardson, and many things which were usually put on board a whaler were left out on his advice that it was unnecessary. The organization was thus saved considerable expense, and, having taken some pains to consult reliable authority above all suspicion of interested motives or possibility of collusion, the undersigned have no hesitation in saying that, not alone was there no extortion in fitting out the vessel, but the Catalpa was fitted out cheaply. This statement can bear investigation; and, as reckless statements about extravagance and unnecessary expense have been freely circulated we challenge the most complete and searching investigation into the whole matter."

Official Report of the Work Done

Lesson of the Experience

Most of the balance of this report refers to matters that it is not well to publish now, and that portion will not be published unless the necessity should arise. One paragraph only which refers to the lessons taught by the experience of the rescue I will quote. It is as follows:

"The undersigned hope that when the ship returns with the rescued prisoners, the committee you will appoint to replace the present one, will draw up a complete statement of the whole matter, giving all the items and copies of the vouchers, to be laid before the whole organization by the governing body. When these facts and figures shall be seen, the organization can see for itself that its confidence has not been abused, and it is to be hoped that when next the organization undertakes an enterprise of this kind, there will be sufficient confidence in those in office at the time to entrust them with a sufficient amount of money to carry it out without having to impart information that can only be given with safety when all is over and the agents are beyond the enemy's reach. Having had practical experience of the danger attending an enterprise of this nature, when even its general outlines are known to thousands of men—among whom there may be a score of spies and hundreds of indiscreet and incautious men—we have no hesitation in saying, that if anything of the kind is attempted again, and the knowledge of it not confined to the governing body and the agents immediately connected with it, it must infallibly end in a miserable and disgraceful failure."

The United States Naval Engineer referred to was Lieutenant Tobin.[129] He and I dined at O'Reilly's house in Charlestown under the shadow of Bunker Hill on the Sunday after the purchase of the *Catalpa*. O'Reilly had introduced me, under my proper name, told him I had been in prison for Fenianism with him, that I represented a firm that was going to embark in the fruit trade, and, as I knew nothing about shipping, he would be obliged if he would come over and take a look at the vessel. Lieutenant Tobin entered into the examination with great zest, never for a moment suspecting our object. Some years later he called on me in New York, told me if he had known what we wanted the vessel for he could not have done what he did, but that he was very glad he did not know and that the expedition succeeded. He was a splendid fellow, and I hope he may yet be an Admiral.

129. A Rhode Island native, John A. Tobin (1849–1926) attended the United States Naval Academy at Annapolis, Maryland, and was commissioned an officer in 1870. "Lieut. John A. Tobin, Inventor," *NYT,* February 1, 1926, 23.

[V]

*[No heading in the original account. The chapter describes the
final preparations and departure of the Catalpa.]*

The fitting out of the *Catalpa* took considerable time, and the cost was very
much more than we had anticipated. I had to make several journeys to
New Bedford to hurry matters up and, as the cost of fitting out the vessel
loomed up, to visit several places to urge the voting of more money. In
every case when men heard that the probable outlay would be very much
more than the original estimate, it caused delay and sometimes aroused
suspicion. All this made our task more and more difficult and made a
heavier inroad on the time of more than one member of the Committee.
Even the men in New Bedford had underrated the cost of outfit, as will be
seen from the following letter from Hathaway, who continued to supervise
the work for us.

New Bedford, March 15, 1875.

To John Devoy, Esq.

Dear Sir:—You perhaps noticed my short stay in Boston in the presence of J. B.
O'R. I could have stayed a short time longer, but for fear we might be overheard as
he talked pretty loud.

I hope you had a good look at the Horse in Charleston and was satisfied with it.

I think it's a tip top bargain. I liked the looks of him first-rate and think will
bring more than we paid for him any day. We have already been offered $1,000
more than we paid for him, but I think he will more than pay for himself this
coming season on the track. We are going for him this week. The weather is now
very favorable, and think we can get him here by Thursday or Friday. I think he
will cost us nearly $17,000, but we will try to do our best and make everything
count. We have commenced this morning in earnest and will pay for the Horse
to-day. I hope you will be punctual in sending us the fodder, as grain is on the
rise here.

[The final preparations and departure of the Catalpa]

Please give my compliments to those other men, and hasten things as soon as possible.

Mr. R. sends his compliments. How did you like the looks of the man that we chose to take charge of the Horse? He is the right man for it.

Yours in haste,

H.C.H., Capt.

The Yankees Were Cautious

Speaking of the *Catalpa* as a horse was an illustration of the extreme caution of our Yankee friends in everything connected with the project. The reference to O'Reilly talking loud was another, although the talk was carried on in the *Pilot* office and there was nobody within earshot who was not entirely trustworthy. James Jeffrey Roche, the present editor of the *Pilot,* was O'Reilly's assistant editor, and the only other who might hear a chance word was Denis Cashman, who was himself an ex-prisoner who had been released with John Kenealy and the rest in Australia.

There were also difficulties about the selection of the man to take charge of the work and his subordinates, and a complication arising from a rescue project in Ireland, both of which will be dealt with fully in their proper place.

Finally the vessel was ready to sail and Reynolds was notified of the fact in the following letter:

New Bedford, April 22, 1875.

To James Reynolds, Esq.,

New Haven, Conn.

Dear Sir:—Mr. Richardson is very busy fitting the ship and wishes me to answer your letter. He says the vessel will go to sea next Tuesday morning, April 27th, without fail, as it will not do to detain her after she is ready, for several reasons, he wishes me to state that the amount that will be required for ship and outfits will be about $18,000.

This is a great deal more than we expected to sail for in the first place; but we have been as prudent as possible and bought everything at the lowest market price, and bought nothing but what is actually required for the voyage. I hope you and Mr. Devoy will be here in time to see her go, for I want you to see her as she is fitted for sea. You have got a good ship. Mr. Richardson is about buying another ship to be fitted shortly for the Atlantic Ocean.

I placed myself in a queer position when I put this job in the hands of Mr. Rich-

[The final preparations and departure of the Catalpa]

ardson, and although I am busy and anxious every day, there is quite a load taken from my shoulders by your visit to New Bedford, though I have the same interest now as ever.

Perhaps you had better telegraph to Mr. Devoy at once and be here by Sunday, or Monday sure, as there will be no delay in her sailing.

Please let us know by telegraph when you will be here.

Yours truly,
Henry C. Hathaway.

Cost of the Outfit

Even Hathaway's estimate of $18,000, made on the very eve of sailing, was below the mark.[130] Here are the items of the cost of the fitting out of the *Catalpa,* as they were afterwards presented and vouched for by receipted bills:

Ship	*$5,250*
Carpenter work	*1,500*
Coppering	*1,600*
Beef and pork	*1,130*
Flour	*700*
Steward's outfit	*300*
Small stores	*800*
Casks	*1,550*
Irons	*700*
Boats	*420*
Sails	*50*
Sail making	*145*
Cordage	*500*
Paint, etc.	*265*
Labor, wharfage, etc.	*700*
	$15,610
Advances and outfits	*3,400*
Total	*$19,010*

130. At the time, Devoy expressed alarm and surprise to Reynolds at the increased costs. O'Brien and Ryan, 1, 110.

[The final preparations and departure of the Catalpa]

These figures are given in detail now, ahead of the full account of the cost of the expedition, which will be given later, so that the reader may understand certain occurrences that will require mention before the close.

THE MAN TO GO ON BOARD

The announcement of the sailing brought us face to face with a difficulty that had to be met at once—the selection of the man, or men, to go aboard. There were plenty of men willing to go, but only one or two could with safety to the expedition be taken. If the Malays, Kanakas and Portuguese Negroes from the Azores and Cape de Verde Islands who formed the majority of the crew, and who were engaged for a whaling voyage only, had the slightest suspicion that anything else was on foot, the whole scheme would collapse at once. The taking aboard of any man who did not fill a legitimate function on the vessel, would at once arouse suspicion and sending a decent man as a sailor on a whaler was out of the question. It is the lowest grade of sailoring in the United States, so far as the crew are concerned. Every man, from the captain down, goes for his "lay," that is, for a proportionate share of the catch and the "lay" of the Malay is something that no white man would stand.[131]

We had gradually eliminated all the prospective candidates, originally numbering twelve or fifteen, until only four were left—Denis Duggan, Thomas Brennan,[132] John O'Connor[133] and Harry Mulleda,[134] and Hathaway, the captain, and Richardson had all along contended that one man would be quite enough, but that if two should go they should fill the positions of steward and carpenter. The steward should know all about cooking and restaurant work; a man without that knowledge attempting to fill

131. In addition to the captain and first mate, seven of the *Catalpa*'s crew departing New Bedford were probably white. By the late 1870s, over half of the members of a whaler's crew were generally black. Bark *Catalpa* Crew List, *New Bedford Port Society Records*; McKissack and McKissack, 128.

132. Thomas Brennan (1842–1915) was born in Dublin. He saw action in the 1867 rising at Glencullen and Stepaside but avoided arrest and escaped to New York. He was an active member of the Clan and a close associate of Goff. O'Brien and Ryan, 1, 105–6.

133. John O'Connor had been a messenger for Stephens and Kelly before the Uprising. He was a brother of James, a future member of Parliament for West Wicklow. After being deported to America, he returned to Ireland carrying messages and funds to the IRB. He remained there and became a senior IRB official. Devoy, 85; John Devoy, "Story of the Clan-na-Gael," [II], *GA*, December 6, 1924, 4.

134. Harry S. Mulleda assisted Ricard Burke and was imprisoned for purchasing arms. He was pardoned in 1871 and came to America aboard the *Cuba*. He died in New York in May 1876. O'Brien and Ryan, 1, 13; "Current Events," *Brooklyn Eagle*, May 15, 1876, 2.

[The final preparations and departure of the Catalpa]

the position would have a hard time. John O'Connor offered to take it—and he had learned all that was necessary during the hard times that followed his deportation in 1867 at the age of 17—on condition that Mulleda should go as a carpenter. Mulleda (an ex-prisoner) was engaged to be married and finally declined to go. That left only Duggan and Brennan, and Duggan was a coachmaker, who had turned to carpentering. He was one of James Stephen's bodyguard on the night that John Breslin released him from Richmond prison, was with Patrick Lennon[135] at Stepaside and Glancullen [*sic*], and was a cool, resolute man. The fact that he and I were at school together in School street model school certainly weighed with me, but no more than the fact that Thomas Brennan and I had been school-fellows at an earlier period in Marlborough street. I recommended Duggan because he was a carpenter and I had written votes of all the members of the Committee except one in favor of his selection. I still hoped that in some way Brennan could be taken on board. These personal details are given because for twenty-eight years there has been misrepresentation of the grossest kind about this matter.

THE FINAL SELECTION

When I received from Reynolds the letter from Hathaway given above, I at once wrote to Goff, apprising him of the situation and received the following reply:

Monday Eve.

Dear John,

Just received your note. Will get the Committee together soon as possible. Would like to go down myself. From what you tell me I presume Duggan to be a good man and fitted. I would prefer that not one man be taken from New York, if you can get along without.

Between John O'Connor and Tom Brennan, my choice is Brennan. Telegraph at once (when you get them). I will see Brennan at once.

This thing has come rather suddenly—has it not? I trust all the arrangements will be complete. This thing of selecting men should not have been left to the last

---

135. A Dublin man, Patrick Lennon fought in the 1867 Uprising, capturing two police barracks. He had received his military training in a New York cavalry regiment during the American Civil War. He was arrested, imprisoned, and released in the 1871 conditional pardon of Fenians. He came to America aboard the *Russia*. Devoy, 193–95; O'Brien and Ryan, 1, 28.

[The final preparations and departure of the Catalpa]

minute. Anything you require, telegraph, and I will respond. Have called upon Costello[136] for money.

> Fraternally,
> (Signed in cipher.)

There is no date on the letter, but the Monday mentioned was the one before the ship sailed. I started for New Bedford and found that Reynolds, who had arrived before me, his presence being required as Managing Owner, had at the urgent request of the agent, the captain and Hathaway, solved the difficulty by agreeing that only one of our men should be taken aboard, and Duggan was already installed as carpenter. Reynolds was confronted with a situation that required immediate action; he took the responsibility of acting, knowing that his colleagues had full confidence in him, and when I reached New Bedford and found what the situation was I endorsed his action. The vessel had been cleared and her papers, including a full list of her officers and crew, had been recorded in the Custom House.

The "Catalpa" Sails

On the day of my arrival in New Bedford I received a telegram from Goff stating that Brennan must be taken aboard and that he would bring him down on the following morning. They arrived, and both were very indignant at the state of affairs they found.[137] Reynolds and I had the written authorization of the rest of our colleagues to act for them, and we two had been appointed a sub-committee to manage the affair subject to the control of the whole Committee. We had the right to settle it and we exercised

---

136. Augustine E. Costello was a Clan member. He was on the ill-fated 1867 voyage of *Erin's Hope* (a ship from America carrying arms for the rebellion). Arrested with John Warren and General William Halpin when the ship reached Ireland, he was released in 1869. The detention of these men and others became a cause célèbre in the United States because they were American citizens. A congressional movement developed demanding that the president (initially Andrew Johnson and then Ulysses S. Grant) take steps to ensure the return of the citizens. Both presidents conveyed the sense of Congress to the British. Costello became a journalist in New York and published several books, including histories of the city's Fire and Police Departments. O'Brien and Ryan, 1, 148; D'Arcy, 369; Sullivan et al., eds., 67, 90; *U. S. House Executive Documents,* 1868, 40th Cong., 2nd sess., no. 167, and 1870, 41st Cong., 2nd sess., no. 170.

137. Some years later, Brennan's account of his involvement with the *Catalpa* rescue was published. In it he mentions Devoy once in passing and makes no reference to any of the difficulties described by Devoy. He credits Goff almost exclusively with the success of the mission. "Goff," *Tribune* (supra note 121).

[The final preparations and departure of the Catalpa]

the right. There was no quarrel, but the situation was strained as we all stood there on the dock and talked the matter over. A "row," or even a protest confined to the membership, would have spoiled all, and any alteration of the ship's papers, or putting on board of a man who did not fill a regular function on the vessel, would have been equally disastrous.[138]

Finally, on Hathaway's suggestion, the difficulty was compromised. All whalers, he said, were liable to have a man die during the cruise, or desert after reaching the Azores, and in this way a vacancy might occur. If we would send Brennan to Fayal or St. Michael's, the captain could either take him on board or not, according to his best judgment, and it would solve the problem. After a talk this was agreed to—and it was subsequently ratified at a meeting of the whole body and a letter of instructions for Brennan drafted by me, giving him explicit instructions, in the name of the governing body of the organization, to abide by the captain's decision in Fayal. After the settlement on this basis we then went out on the vessel into Buzzard's Bay and returned to New Bedford in a rowboat.[139] The *Catalpa* had started on her voyage.

Notes on the Catalpa

Some friends have written and some have called to make suggestions in regard to the story of the *Catalpa* Rescue, while some who are not friendly have made public comment on certain portions of the narrative. Suggestions from those in possession of information will be always thankfully received, and criticisms, whether friendly or otherwise, will be treated strictly on their merits.

Mike Hogan, of Omaha, who was in the thick of the fight in the John Mitchel election (and in the thick of every other fight in Tipperary when

138. Goff and Devoy had started feuding before the *Catalpa* expedition. Goff was infuriated that he wasn't chosen to make the address at Mitchel's New York memorial in 1875. (He then published an unauthorized notice in the New York *Herald* prohibiting the meeting.) Devoy suspended Goff's Club in 1876 for failure to obey the Clan constitution; Goff was expelled from the Clan. Devoy did credit Goff with raising a significant sum of money for the *Catalpa*. He and Devoy continued to feud for some years on a variety of subjects, including the *Catalpa*'s finances, but eventually became friends. O'Brien and Ryan, 1, 99–101; "Goff," GA (supra note 93); Devoy, "Clan," GA [IV] (supra note 123).

139. In a letter dated April 29, 1875, to James Reynolds, Devoy described accompanying the ship forty miles out to sea and having dinner on board (hard tack, salt beef, and cheese). He also mentioned that arrangements had been made for Brennan to go by steamer to the Azores. O'Brien and Ryan, 1, 105.

[The final preparations and departure of the Catalpa]

fighting men were needed), writes to point out an omission in the reference to that election. Mitchel, Mr. Hogan correctly says, was elected twice for Tipperary. The British Parliament annulled the first election and ordered a new one. Tipperary's answer was the triumphant re-election of Mitchel, and it was during the debate preceding the annulment of this second election that Mitchel died. Mr. Hogan says that the mental and physical strain imposed by these two elections really killed John Mitchel. I am glad to have these corrections made, although my references to the Tipperary and Cork elections were merely incidental and did not pretend to give a full report.

O'Donovan Rossa complains that he was treated badly because in giving a copy of John Mitchel's letter returning the check for $100, the fact that the letter was written to him was not recorded, and also claims that he, at Mitchel's request, presided at Mitchel's lecture at the Cooper Institute on his return from Ireland after the Cork election. Mr. Mitchel's letter, as I gave it in the story, was printed from a printed copy sent out in circular form at the time, without a word of change, omission, suppression or addition. The letter was written to O'Donovan Rossa, the check returned was O'Donovan Rossa's check, and I neither claimed, hinted nor implied that either check or letter was for me. Both were, of course, intended for the local New York Committee, having charge of the lecture.

As to presiding at the meeting, O'Donovan Rossa's memory is wholly at fault. Mr. Mitchel did request that *some one with a record in Irish affairs* should preside, and he did name O'Donovan Rossa, but just as clearly and distinctly he also named Thomas Francis Bourke and Thomas Clarke Luby. Anthony Fitzgerald,[140] now dead, explained to him that the selection of a chairman was wholly in the hands of the Committee, of which those who waited on him were only a sub-committee, but that his wishes would be laid before the full Committee. They were laid before it, and the Committee then selected Miles M. O'Brien as Chairman, and Mr. O'Brien presided at Mr. Mitchel's lecture, as a reference to the files of the daily papers will show. The introduction of Mr. Mitchel and his opening remarks are in the recollection of many old-timers who are still to the fore, and they corroborate my statement. The meeting over which O'Donovan Rossa presided was the Manchester Martyrs'[141] celebration in the same hall in November,

---

140. A New York Clan officer, Anthony Fitzgerald was from County Waterford. Devoy, 218.

141. William O'Meara Allen, Michael Larkin, and William O'Brien were executed in 1867 for their alleged involvement in a successful rescue at Manchester of two Fenians, Thomas Kelly and Timothy Deasy. A police officer was killed during the rescue. Connolly, 343.

[The final preparations and departure of the Catalpa]

1875, where we repudiated O'Connor Power[142] for his "college days" speech a short time previously. O'Donovan Rossa's name will occur several times in the course of the story because it forms part of it.

Another person who was never in a position to know anything of the *Catalpa* Rescue has publicly threatened to publish documents which will prove some unmentioned things about me. My answer to this person is, let him go ahead. I am perfectly able to take care of myself and to take whatever action may be necessary in the matter, should any action, or notice, be required. This person lives in an extremely thin glass house, and he may throw stones once too often. He has a libel suit on his hands just now which ought to be quite enough for him for the present. However, he is the best judge of his own affairs. I have all the documents in the *Catalpa* affair, but am not burdening the story with any that are not necessary to the proper telling of it.

J.D.

142. John O'Connor Power (1846–1919) was a Fenian organizer and fighter; eventually, he was expelled from the movement (1877) along with Joseph Biggar because of his willingness to take the oath of office when he became a member of Parliament for Mayo. The organization did not support parliamentary or constitutional agitation until the late 1870s, and opposed members of Parliament taking the compulsory oath of allegiance to the crown. Devoy also disliked Power. They first met when Power, representing the IRB, came to the United States in 1869. The purpose was to bring the IRB and the Clan closer together. Devoy described him as "the illegitimate son of a Peeler . . . a haughty person, very egotistical and arrogant in manner, and his terms for union were impossible." O'Brien and Ryan, 1, 74–76, 312; Devoy, "Clan," [II], *GA* (supra note 133).

[VI]

How John J. Breslin and Thomas Desmond
of San Francisco Were Selected to Do the Work —
An Appointment by James Stephens

The ship having sailed, the next thing was to select the man to effect the rescue. This was done at a meeting held shortly after the departure of the ship. I intended to go myself and I was assured of all the votes of the committee except one (and I am not even sure that even that would be against me), but conditions arose, owing to impatience and dissatisfaction on the part of men who had helped to raise the money, which made it absolutely necessary that I should remain in New York. In fact, my disappearance would have at once indicated that I had gone to Australia and the consequent loose talk would almost certainly ruin the chances of success. I gave up the idea very reluctantly, mainly at the request of Patrick Mahon, the treasurer, and James Reynolds.

John J. Breslin had just come from Boston to New York. His presence had not become widely known, so that his going away again would not cause any remark. He had liberated James Stephens from Richmond Prison and made a "clean job" of it. He was familiar with the British prison service, was a man of fine presence, good manners, high intelligence and very unusual decision of character. He was the ideal man for the work, but there was great difficulty in securing his selection. He was personally known to no member of the committee but myself and Goff, and only slightly to the latter, and he was not only not a member of the Clan, but belonged to a rival organization,[143] having branches only in Boston and New York. It was as a member of a conference committee to bring about a union which did not come off that he had met Goff with me. Breslin was a proud man, and if I told him he could only be selected on

143. United Irish Brotherhood. Amos, 216.

condition that he joined the Clan he would surely reject the offer. Yet when I proposed him for the chief command of the expedition that very condition was made, and it took some delicate negotiation to overcome his scruples. He finally was taken in quietly in Hoboken and all obstacles were removed. His selection was unanimous.

California had raised nearly half the money collected for the expedition and made no condition and no "kick." It made, however, a special and very earnest request that the selection of one man to take part in the work be left to John C. Talbot, California's representative on the committee, and the request was unanimously agreed to. John C. Talbot selected Thomas Desmond,[144] and he accompanied Breslin to Australia by steamer and gave a good account of himself when pluck and nerve were needed.

Breslin started with insufficient funds, as he had to go to Los Angeles to consult John Kenealy, who had been released from Australia, knew all about conditions there and was a man of high intelligence and sound judgment. We had to trust to luck to get in the necessary funds after Breslin's departure, and there were long delays and embarrassing disappointments before he and Desmond were finally able to sail for Sydney.

SENATOR CONOVER'S SERVICES

Breslin's instructions were clear and explicit as to the disposition of the prisoners and the vessel after the rescue had been effected. No matter what plans we might have discussed here, the rescue itself had to be left to the man in charge when he should get on the ground and was face to face with the situation. But we in America had to provide for the prisoners and dispose of the ship, so the same instructions were given to Captain Anthony and to Breslin. The *Catalpa* was to make for Fernandina, Florida,[145] land the men there and put out to sea again to cruise in the Atlantic for whale, so as to, if possible, clear the expenses of the expedition and pay back the advances made to the committee by a large number of clubs.[146]

---

144. Thomas Desmond (1838–1910) was born in Cobh, Cork and emigrated to America in 1854. He was an active Fenian and Clan member in California, where he became a wheelwright and carriage maker. *Sheriff's Star Bulletin,* Vol. 1, Issue 1, August 2000 [http://www.ci.sf.ca.us/sheriff/sheriffs.htm], October 2001.

145. Northeast of Jacksonville, on Amelia Island, Fernandina was an American port of entry. "Fernandina," *Britannica,* 4, 743–44.

146. Devoy originally envisioned the whaler going to and being sold at San Francisco after the rescue. O'Brien and Ryan, 1, 88–89.

Fernandina was selected for a very good reason. United States Senator S. B. Conover,[147] of Florida, was a member of the Clan, although he and both his parents were born in the United States. His grandfather was an Ulster Presbyterian rebel, who took part in the insurrection of 1798 and had to flee to America. Conover, who was an Irishman to the backbone, had been a surgeon in the Union Army during the Civil War, and in that capacity had made the acquaintance of Dr. Carroll, who later brought him into the Clan. There was not one Irish vote in the Florida Legislature which sent Conover to the United States Senate, so there could be no American politics in his connection with Irish affairs. The Collector of the Port of Fernandina was a follower of the Senator, and he arranged with him that the men should be taken on board the revenue cutter when the *Catalpa* reached port. We could then provide for them and arrange for their disposition quietly, instead of in the flurry and excitement of a reception in New York or any other big city. But "the best laid schemes of mice and men gang aft aglee,"[148] and this scheme was "knocked into a cocked hat"[149] by subsequent developments.

BRENNAN'S DISAPPOINTMENT

Brennan went to Fayal, as instructed, but failed to get on the ship. The Captain had got into trouble over some attempt to smuggle American tobacco,[150] had left Fayal before Brennan's arrival and gone to St. Michaels,[151]

147. Simon Barclay Conover (1840–1908) was a Republican who served in the United States Senate from 1873 to 1879. "Simon Barclay Conover," *Biographical Directory.*

148. "To a Mouse," Robert Burns (1759–1796). Howard Lowry et al., eds., *An Oxford Anthology of English Poetry* (New York: Oxford University Press, 1956), 574–75.

149. "Thoroughly beaten; altered beyond recognition; *hors de combat.* A cocked-hat, folded into a *chapeau bras,* is crushed out of all shape. In the game of nine-pins, three pins were set up in the form of a triangle, and when all the pins except these three were knocked down, the set was technically said to be 'knocked into a cocked hat.' Hence, utterly out of all shape or plumb. A somewhat similar phrase is 'Knocked into the middle of next week.'" E. Cobham Brewer, *Dictionary of Phrase and Fable,* 1898 [http://www.bartleby.com], October 2001.

150. Smuggling tobacco was a common practice among whalers. It assured the ability to barter in far-off places where standard currency might be useless. In the mid-1800s, it was estimated that the average American sperm whaler sailed with twenty-five hundred pounds of tobacco for the purpose of trading at ports of call. The Azorean authorities objected strongly to this and kept a close watch on the whalers. There is no reference to this incident in Pease's book or the *Catalpa* log, but it is mentioned in the Clan proceedings against Brennan. Mawer, 174–75; *Report of Eighth Annual Convention,* 22.

151. The *Catalpa* did not go to St. Michael's, an island of the Azores. It stopped at Flores on October 15 and went on to Fayal, anchoring on October 23. It left Fayal on November 6 heading southwest. *Catalpa Log.*

and from some things which had previously occurred had made up his mind not to take him on board. In this he was exercising the discretionary power given him, but Brennan, in his natural disappointment, jumped to the conclusion that the whole thing was a "put up job," for which I was responsible, and his resentment has grown with every succeeding year since then. All I had to do with it was to insist on the Captain having discretionary power, and after twenty-nine years I still stand by that decision.

With the subsequent events I shall have very little to say personally, but will allow John Breslin to speak for himself, giving only such portions of his story as are necessary to the general reader's proper understanding of it.

Notes on the Catalpa

Friends have informed me that some timid persons have arrived at the conclusion that I am "exposing the Clan-na-Gael" by telling what it did nearly thirty years ago. It will be a dreadful thing if the British government learns that the Clan really did this thing and how the money was raised and what difficulties had to be overcome. The same reasoning would apply to the Manchester Rescue, or the taking of Stepaside and Glancullen [*sic*] by Patrick Lennon and his men, or the capture of the Coast Guard station by John McClure[152] and O'Neill Crowley's[153] men.

The information is for the benefit of the present generation of Irish Nationalists and the British government derives no more benefit from the telling of the story than it does from any other chapter of Irish history. Our friends seem to forget that Le Caron's revelations were not all fake, and that they were published in every daily paper in England, besides being printed in book form by the London *Times* and circulated by tens of thousands. He could tell nothing about the *Catalpa,* but he knew all about the methods which our friends fear I am "giving away," he left nothing untold.[154] I know from evidence coming from every part of the country that the story is read with interest by the young men to whose lot the doing of bigger things will fall, I hope, in the near future, and I hope that other

152. John McClure, a veteran of the American Civil War, captured the Coastguard Station at Knockadoon with Crowley on March 5, 1867. Shortly after, he was captured and incarcerated. Pardoned in 1871, he was one of the "*Cuba* Five" who came to America. Devoy, 213–16; O'Brien and Ryan, 1, 12–13.

153. Peter O'Neill Crowley was a County Cork farmer who fought in the 1867 Uprising. He was with McClure at Knockadoon and was mortally wounded at Kilclooney Wood. Devoy, 213–16.

154. Le Caron's treatment of the *Catalpa* in his book is very brief with some inaccuracies, e.g., "whaler was chartered . . . manned by trusted men of the organization." Le Caron, 72.

events in recent Irish history will be chronicled before long by those in possession of the necessary information.

In reply to criticism of another kind regarding my connection with the Rescue and my reason for taking an interest in the soldier Fenian prisoners, I give here a reason which will be sufficient for honest Nationalists. I had charge of the Fenian organization in the British army during a very trying period and most of the men were convicted on evidence of their connection with me, as will be seen by reference to James Jeffrey Roche's "Life of John Boyle O'Reilly."[155] I was appointed to that position after the arrest of William F. Roantree, my predecessor in the work, and while there was a warrant for my own arrest and my name was in the *Hue and Cry*,[156] in the following document brought to me by Edward Duffy[157] from James Stephens:

"Thursday, October 26, 1865.

"My Dear Friend:—

"There is a lull just now on the part of the enemy, and we should make the utmost of it. To this end I hereby appoint you Chief Organizer of the British troops here in Ireland. While in this service your allowance will be £3 a week, but this sum must cover your support, traveling expenses and refreshment to any soldier you may have to meet. I also authorize you to appoint a staff of eight men to act under you. Two of these should be civilians and the other six soldiers. All should be staunch, steady men. Use your very best judgment in their appointment, but make them rapidly as you can. The allowance to each of the two civilians (your aids) may be from 15$^S.$ to £1 10$^S.$ a week, according to the circumstances and requirements of the men. The soldiers (unless they be men of superior tact and prudence) could not be given much money. Five to ten shillings a week will be amply sufficient for most of them, but, should you meet with a really clever and reliable man, don't hesitate about allowing him £1 a week. Should you find it wise to add to the number of your military aids, let me know. Bearer will give you £6. Send me weekly returns of expenses.

"Yours faithfully,

"J. Stephens."

---

155. James Jeffrey Roche, *Life of John Boyle O'Reilly, together with His Complete Poems and Speeches,* Mrs. John Boyle O'Reilly, ed. (New York: Cassell Publishing, 1891).

156. The *Hue-and-Cry* was a publication of the Head Police Office (Dublin), Royal Irish Constabulary. It contained details of crimes and wanted persons. Devoy, 131.

157. Edward Duffy (1840–1868) was an organizer, a deputy of Stephens. He died in Millbank prison. According to Devoy, it was Duffy who instructed him to plead guilty at his 1866 trial with the expectation he would be rescued. (No rescue occurred.) O'Brien and Ryan, 1, 10, 166.

"P.S.—Send off the man you write about."

"Be very prudent now. You owe me this, to justify the appointment of so young a man to so responsible a post."

This document properly belongs to a history of Fenianism in the British army, which I will write later. I have the original, which was preserved for me by a member of my family, and the handwriting of James Stephens can be verified by Colonel Thomas J. Kelly,[158] to whom I made daily reports of my work.

---

158. A Union veteran of the American Civil War, Thomas J. Kelly was sent by the Fenian movement as an envoy to Ireland. Impressed with the potential for an uprising, he remained and succeeded Stephens as head of the Irish Republican Brotherhood. He was arrested and imprisoned. It was Kelly who would be successfully rescued in the 1867 Manchester Martyrs incident. Devoy, 57, 70, 244.

[VII]

AUSPICIOUS BEGINNING OF THE EXPEDITION

by Captain Anthony Succoring a Ship in Distress—Caught Whale in the North Atlantic—John Breslin's Official Report of the Enterprise—Anxiously Waiting for Ship's Arrival

After the sailing of the *Catalpa,* other difficulties and causes of delay arose. I will dwell on them as lightly as possible, so as to let John Breslin tell his own story of the Rescue.

The agent sent us more bills for the vessel just as we were sending Breslin off, and Mr. Mahon, of Rochester, the treasurer, who was a sharp and clear-headed business man, refused to pay them until he should have an opportunity to examine them and hear explanations. After that examination and explanation he was perfectly satisfied, and paid the bills. A note which Richardson gave me instead of a receipt for the first installment of the price of the vessel was retained in his personal possession by a member of an auditing committee and that made a bad hitch for a time. We had to keep Breslin waiting idly in San Francisco for want of sufficient funds to enable him and Desmond to start, and an audit at a convention had to be faced, with the possibility of an exposure of the scheme. When Brennan failed to get on board at Fayal, instead of returning to New York, as, by vote of the committee, he was instructed to do, a number of his friends contributed money to enable him to go to Australia and join the expedition there. He did so, arriving the day before the rescue.[159] It was necessary, they afterwards claimed, to have one honest man on board, presumably to prevent the captain running away with the ship and to keep me from stealing ship, cargo, prisoners and all. To prevent the "crooked work" which they claimed to suspect, they adopted crooked methods and sowed the seeds of dissension and disorder. However, these same men who

---

159. Brennan arrived in Bunbury on April 1. See Breslin's report, Chapter 8.

Auspicious Beginning of the Expedition

were acting in this absurd and factious way, preserved the secrecy of the project as strictly as those who were acting in perfect co-operation with the committee.

In the course of the preparations a man prominent in the National movement at the other side of Atlantic visited this country on a business mission.[160] He was informed in a general way of the project, having, from his position, a right to the knowledge. Before returning he took up a public attitude wholly at variance with the principles of the Nationalist movement and soon afterwards severed his connection with it. His difference with the Clan-na-Gael here made him adopt a peculiar and very uncalled for course. Owing to the receipt of letters from the military prisoners by relatives in Ireland, a movement for their rescue had been started there, but, although he knew all about it, he never gave a hint of it when I told him what we were doing here. On his return to the other side, he used the knowledge acquired here to hurry up matters and carefully refrained from giving the men at home the slightest information as to what we were doing on this side. The result of this was the collection of about £1,000, and the sending of two good men to Australia to carry out the same mission. As they made connection, accidentally at first and then through the soldier prisoners, with our men, their part will be dealt with in its proper place.

First News of the Catalpa

The first news we got of the *Catalpa* was in the following item from the New Bedford *Standard,* which was enclosed in a letter from Captain Hathaway:

"Brig Florence of Annapolis, N.S., with salt, arrived at St. Stephen, N.B., yesterday, 63 days from Liverpool. May 10th a violent gale carried away her foremast, maintopmast, and all the sails but the main staysail. The provisions ran short, and the vessel drifted helplessly about for 20 days, the crew suffering intensely from hunger and thirst. May 30th, bark Catalpa, Anthony, of this port, rendered assistance, and jurymasts were rigged, enabling the vessel to reach the mouth of the St. Croix. During the gale a French sailor named Le Blanc was fatally injured by falling from aloft."

160. Ó Lúing suggests this may have been "Long John" O'Connor. O'Connor came over in 1874 seeking support for a new rival organization to the IRB: the U.B. of Ireland. Devoy and his Clan colleagues offered no support and O'Connor returned home empty handed. The organization, based in Cork, soon collapsed, and he rejoined the IRB. Ó Lúing, 107; Devoy, "Clan," [I], *GA* (supra note 90).

Auspicious Beginning of the Expedition

Following is Captain Hathaway's letter:

New Bedford, June 15th, 1875.

To John Devoy, Esq., New York.

Dear Friend: I see by to-night's Standard that the Catalpa was seen May 30th, and rendered assistance to an English brig. I think we will have letters from Captain A. [Anthony] in a few days. I received your dispatch yesterday and am glad to know that everything is settled right. I shall now wait anxiously for Mr. R. to tell me that everything is satisfactory, then my mind will be at ease, I cannot write any more now as I am very busy, and you know my mind as well as I can write.

Yours in haste,

H. C. Hathaway

Then two days later came the following:

New Bedford, June 17th, 1875.

To John Devoy, Esq., New York.

Dear Friend: Mr. R [Richardson] received a short letter from Capt. A., dated May 8th, nine days from home. Boiling a sperm whale. Seven days from home he saw whales and killed four of them, but owing to the rough weather they only succeeded in saving but one of them. He did not write how much oil the whale would probably yield, as he wrote but a few lines in haste to send by a passing ship. In all probability we will get letters from him in a few days as he must have sent letters by the vessel he supplied provisions to on the 30th of May. This is a first rate commencement and I am glad to hear of it so early in the voyage, as it will keep the officers and crew in good spirits. Capt. A. writes that he is very much pleased with the ship and crew. Well, he might be, for we were very particular in shipping good men and having things as near right as possible on shipboard. I think this voyage will be a success for all concerned. I have great faith in Capt. A., he being a young man who is looking ahead.

Mr. R. received a letter from Reynolds last night dated June 14th, stating he would send the balance of the money in a day or two. I am glad that this part of the job is drawing to a close; it will take a big load from my mind.

I will now close, hoping to hear from you soon.

Yours truly,

Henry C. Hathaway.

As to the amount of the catch, Mr. Richardson wrote later to Reynolds:

Auspicious Beginning of the Expedition

New Bedford, August 11th, 1875.

Friend Reynolds: I have just received a letter from Capt. Anthony, dated June the 29th. He had taken 110 lbs,[161] of sperm oil (one hundred and ten pounds). He likes his ship first rate, and his crew. He thinks he will get a big catch this season. I should have sent you a letter before this time, but I had no news to send you before this time. If I should receive any more I will let you know.

Your true friend,

J. T. Richardson

And so matters went, letters coming from Richardson, Hathaway, O'Reilly, and reports from Breslin, writing under the name of Collins, as to his progress up to the last moment, when the cable announced the success of the expedition. All these would be very interesting reading in a book, but would make this sketch unnecessarily long. I shall now let John J. Breslin tell his own story:

Breslin's Official Report

New York, August 20, 1876.[162]

To the ——

The following report is respectfully submitted: ——

Started from New York at 10 o'clock A.M. by the Hudson River Railroad, to take Lake Shore and Michigan Southern route to San Francisco, on July 19, 1875, with instructions to proceed to Western Australia and attempt the rescue of the Irish political prisoners, James Wilson,[163] M. J. Hogan,[164] Michael Harring-

---

161. This is probably a transcription error because whale oil quantities were usually expressed in barrels (bbls.) or gallons.

162. This report was originally submitted to the Rescue Committee in 1876, and then in 1877, to the Clan's annual convention, in Cleveland, where it was incorporated into the convention's report.

163. James Wilson was born James McNally in 1836 in Newry. He became a Fenian in 1864 while a member of the Fifth Dragoon Guards. Before that he served seven years with the Bombay Artillery in the 1850s. Devoy considered him to have a great mind. A good recruiter for the cause, he deserted the army in 1865, was court-martialed, and was sentenced to life. He was transported to Australia aboard the *Hougoumont*. Like Harrington, he was a quarry constable at Fremantle. O'Brien and Ryan, 1, 172, 179; Amos, 290; Ó Lúing, 29.

164. Martin Joseph Hogan was born in 1833 in County Limerick. He became a Fenian in 1864 while a member of the Fifth Dragoon Guards. He had been a coach painter before enlisting. In his seven years in the army he was considered a superior swordsman. A good recruiter for the cause, he deserted in 1865 to avoid arrest, was court-martialed, and was sentenced to life. He was transported to Australia aboard the *Hougoumont*. During the voyage, the Fenians organized evening concerts in which Hogan frequently sang. His repertoire ranged from Stephen Foster's "My Old

Auspicious Beginning of the Expedition

ton,[165] Thomas Darragh,[166] Robert Cranston[167] and Thomas H. Hassett,[168] or as many of those as I could get; to use my own judgment as to the means and manner of the rescue, and to expect the arrival and co-operation of the Catalpa in January, 1876. Arrived at San Francisco, July 26, 1875; left San Francisco for Sacramento on the 29th by steamer up the Sacramento river, and arrived at Sacramento on the morning of the 30th; called on J. C. Talbot and handed him a letter of introduction from John Devoy.

Mr. Talbot telegraphed my arrival to John Kennealy in Los Angeles, and Kennealy sent Thomas Desmond on to Sacramento. Before leaving New York, Mr. Devoy had informed me the Western men had preferred a request to the Committee that they might be allowed to send a man to assist. I told Mr. Devoy that unless I approved of the man they had selected I would decline to accept his services, and

---

Kentucky Home" to Rudyard Kipling's "The Galley Slave." When he first arrived at Fremantle, he threatened to kill a warder and was subject to separate confinement for three months. His subsequent behavior was satisfactory and he became a painter at the prison. Letters home from Hogan caused the IRB to organize its own mission to Fremantle. Hogan also wrote a letter that came to Devoy's attention. O'Brien , I, 83, 179; Amos, 127, 222, 290; John S. Casey, *Journal of a Voyage from Portland to Fremantle on Board the Convict Ship "Hougoumont,"* Martin Kevin Cusack, ed. (Bryn Mawr, PA: Dorrance, 1988), October 12, 1867; C. W. Sullivan, ed., *Fenian Diary* (Dublin: Wolfhound Press, 2001), 66, 70, 73.

165. Michael Harrington (1825–1886) was born in Goleen, County Cork. He was an apprentice boat builder who enlisted in the army, serving for twenty years. He saw action in the brutal India campaigns of 1849 and 1856, in which he was wounded and decorated for bravery. He was arrested in 1866 for desertion from the Fifty-third Foot, was court-martialed with John Boyle O'Reilly, and was sentenced to life. He was transported to Australia aboard the *Hougoumont*. His initial experience at Fremantle was poor. For some type of misconduct he was sentenced to bread and water and labeled as requiring special attention. In time, however, his conduct improved and he rose to a position of trust as a quarry constable. O'Brien and Ryan, 1, 178–79; Amos, 290; "Funeral of a Nationalist," [New York] *Irish American* (hereafter *IA*), February 27, 1886; Ó Lúing, 28; George Russo, *Race for the Catalpa* (Perth, W.A.: Lynward Enterprises, 1986), 23; James Hurley, "In Search of a Forgotten Fenian," [Cork] *Irish Independent,* December 16, 1964.

166. Thomas Darragh, a Protestant, was born in 1834 in Broomhall, County Wicklow. His family were Protestants. He served in South Africa with the Second (Queen's Own) Regiment. Later, he was decorated for bravery in the China campaign. Returning home, he became the Fenian center of his regiment. After nineteen years of service, he held the rank of color sergeant and was also on the commission list. He was arrested in 1865 for failing to report mutinous conduct and being a Fenian, for which he was convicted and sentenced to death. His sentence was commuted to life, and he was transported to Australia aboard the *Hougoumont*. At Fremantle, he was the Protestant chaplain's groom, acted as school monitor, and trained the Church of England choir. Darragh presented no problems to the authorities while incarcerated. O'Brien and Ryan, 1, 172, 179; Amos, 232, 289; Ó Lúing, 26.

167. Robert Cranston was born in 1842 in Stewartstown, County Tyrone. He enlisted in the Sixty-first British Infantry in 1863 and later joined the Fenians. He was arrested in 1866, sentenced to life, and transported to Australia aboard the *Hougoumont*. On the voyage over, his behavior was so exemplary, he was commended by the *Hougoumont*'s surgeon. Several times, he participated in the on-board concerts, offering comic songs. At Fremantle, he worked in the Prison Stores as a letter carrier. O'Brien and Ryan, 1, 179; Amos, 128, 232, 289; Ó Lúing, 28–29; Cashman, 68, 78.

168. Thomas Henry Hassett (1841–1893) was born in Doneraile, County Cork. He became a carpenter and joined the Phoenix Society. He saw action in a different venue than the other military

Auspicious Beginning of the Expedition

he agreed that I should be at liberty to do so. I told Mr. Talbot, at our first interview, that unless I found the man they had selected a person whom I could trust and work with I would decline having anything to do with him. Mr. Talbot agreed that it would be optional with me whether their man went or not, but added, "We have selected our best man and I think you will like him."

Desmond arrived in Sacramento a few days afterwards. I did like him. And I now believe that if Desmond alone had been sent, the rescue would have been as successfully accomplished, and at far less cost to the organization; for, while my expenses, from the position I had to assume, were necessarily rather heavy, Desmond was self-supporting, and his sojourn in Western Australia did not cost the organization anything.

Remained in Sacramento four weeks waiting for remittances, and received one hundred dollars each from J. C. Talbot.

Left Sacramento, August 26th, for Los Angeles via San Francisco, stayed two days in San Francisco, and sailed for Los Angeles by the steamer Ancon, August 28th; arrived in Los Angeles September 1st, saw John Kennealy and obtained all the information he could give about Western Australia; remained in Los Angeles six days and arrived in San Francisco on the morning of the 10th September. Received letters and notice of remittance the same day, and, after considerable difficulty, with the valuable assistance of Judge John M. Cooney,[169] of San Francisco, obtained from the telegraph office the amount of cash remitted. September 11th engaged passage for myself and Desmond to Melbourne and exchanged greenbacks for gold. Spent Sunday with Stackpoole[170] and a few friends, and on Monday morning, September 13th, sailed for Sydney at 11:20 A.M.

Fenians: he joined the Irish Papal Brigade, a unit that fought (unsuccessfully) for Pope Pius IX against Victor Emanuel. He was wounded at Perugia. Upon his return to Ireland, he enlisted in the Twenty-fourth Foot in 1861 and joined the Fenians in 1864. He deserted in 1866, was arrested, and was transported to Australia aboard the *Hougoumont*. Of the six prisoners, he appears to have been fairly impulsive. When he learned he was to be arrested, for example, he simply walked off from his guardpost and marched, in full uniform, to a pub where Devoy was meeting! (He had been the center for his regiment.) At trial, he pled guilty to treason. While at Fremantle, he had two violations: one for drinking and one for insolence. Then he escaped in 1870 and remained at large for ten months. When caught, he was subject to six months' solitary confinement and three years' hard labor. Afterwards, he was assigned to the Fremantle Prison Shop. O'Brien and Ryan, 1, 179–80; Amos, 202, 232, 289; Ó Lúing, 27; Pease, *Catalpa,* 50; "A Famous Fenian Dead," *IA,* December 18, 1893, 1.

169. Born in Ireland in 1839, Michael (not John) Cooney came to the United States as a child and grew up in the Midwest, becoming a teacher. He went to California, where he became a politically active lawyer and Fenian. He served one term as a justice of the peace of San Francisco. Oscar T. Shuck, ed., *History of the Bench and Bar of California* (Los Angeles: Commercial Printing House, 1901), 811–12.

170. M. W. Stackpoole's correspondence is found in *Devoy's Post Bag,* but no biographical note is offered. His first letter is dated 1874 from Paris. It addresses the then current effort to combine the Clan and the IRB. Subsequent letters on business letterhead have both a Paris and San Francisco heading, and other correspondents mention his activities in San Francisco. O'Brien and Ryan, 1, 70, 86, 134.

Auspicious Beginning of the Expedition

Arrived in Sydney

Arrived in Sydney, Friday, 15th October, 1875, inquired for and found E. J. Kelly,[171] who introduced us to two friends in Sydney named King and A.[172] Finding that there was no steamer leaving Melbourne for King George's Sound before the 4th of November, under the names of Johnston[173] and Collins, Desmond and I remained in Sydney until the 19th, when I sent Desmond on to Melbourne and stayed in Sydney to receive some money promised to me by King and A. Received two hundred pounds from A. the following week, and gave back thirty pounds to be used for the expenses of B.,[174] who had been telegraphed for, to come on to Sydney and raise funds from the branches in New Zealand. Left Sydney for Melbourne on the 26th, arriving in Melbourne on the 30th. In Melbourne visited C. and some other friends; sailed for Albany, King George's Sound, November 4, 1875, arrived at Albany on the 13th November, took passage by the Georgette[175] to Freemantle,[176] and arrived in Freemantle on the 16th November, 1875.

Before leaving San Francisco Judge Cooney prepared and gave me a legal document, in reading which the natural inference would be that I, James Collins, possessed large interest in lands and mines in Nevada and other States of the Union. I believe my West Australian reputation as a millionaire is due chiefly to the fact that

171. John Edward Kelly (Edward Kelly, Edward John Kelly) (1841–1884) was another prisoner transported on the *Hougoumont*. He was born in Kinsale, Ireland, emigrated with his parents to Canada, and then moved to Boston, where he became a printer and joined the Fenians. In 1863, he returned to his native land. For his involvement in the 1867 Kilclooney Woods engagement, his sentence was initially death but was subsequently commuted to life. He was conditionally pardoned in 1869 and remained for several years in Australia. Amos, 290. For more details, see section "Irish in Australia at Work" in John King's narrative, chapter 12 of this book; Devoy, 213–15; Roche, 235–36.

172. "A" was James McInerney, who had emigrated to Australia many years earlier from County Clare. His brother owned and operated a stone quarry near Sydney. Amos, 218–19; Ó Lúing, 92.

173. Most accounts spell the alias Johnson, but Breslin, in "A Descriptive Poem of the Rescue of the Fenian Prisoners from Freemantle, Australia," spells it like this.

174. Michael Cody (alias James Dunn, Michael Byrne) was a Dublin boilermaker and committed Fenian taking part in Stephens's rescue. Devoy commented that Cody had "a weakness for punching peelers." He was arrested in 1866, convicted, and transported to Australia aboard the *Hougoumont*. Following his 1869 pardon, he remained in Australia for the rest of his life. Through a network in New Zealand and New South Wales, he and John Edward Kelly provided monetary assistance, through John King, to the *Catalpa* rescue. Amos, 84–85, 196, 219, 289; O'Brien and Ryan, 1, 184.

175. The *Georgette* was a 211–ton iron screw-steamer. She was built at Dumbarton on the Clyde, Scotland, in 1872 by McKellar McMillan and Company. She was an iron-hulled, two-masted steam schooner, screw driven, registered at 211 tons, 151'9" long. She arrived in Fremantle in September 1873, and engaged in the Western Australian coastal trade, principally between Albany and Fremantle, until she sank with the loss of twelve lives near Margaret River later in 1876. Graeme Henderson and Kandy-Jane Henderson, *Unfinished Voyages*. Vol. 2, *Western Australian Shipwrecks, 1851–1880* (Nedlands, W.A.: University of Western Australia Press, 1988), 207–12; Jack Wemp, "The *Catalpa* Saga, 1844–76" [1998, copy in the editors' possession].

176. Breslin consistently misspells the town of Fremantle throughout his report.

84

Auspicious Beginning of the Expedition

The jail at Fremantle, where the prisoners were confined (Z. W. Pease, *The Catalpa Expedition*)

this document was left, "with intent to deceive," loosely in my room so that it might be read, my style and actual cost of living being in reality below that of an ordinary commercial traveler.

On the day after I arrived at Freemantle I rode to Perth, but finding Freemantle the best base of operations determined to make it my headquarters. Engaged a room in the Emerald Isle Hotel, Patrick Maloney [sic],[177] proprietor, and Desmond went to Perth and found immediate employment in a carriage factory.

Connected with the Prisoners

Having learned during the following week that one of the Fenian ex-prisoners, named William Foley,[178] was at large in Freemantle, I made use of him to convey to

177. The police suspected that Patrick Moloney, originally from County Clare, was probably the Fenian Head Center for Western Australia. He was also one of the trustees for the prisoners' fund about which Wilson so bitterly complained. Amos, 260; "Two Limerick Fenians," GA, April 22, 1922, 6; Ó Lúing, 93.
178. William Foley (1838–1876) was born in Waterford. He was a military Fenian who was sentenced to five years and transported aboard the *Hougoumont*. Following his release, he remained in Fremantle and was able to provide Breslin with introductions to the prisoners. He then left in January 1876 and made his way to New York and witnessed the arrival of the *Catalpa*. He died several months later. Amos, 290; "The Rescue," *Irish World* [hereafter *IW*], June 24, 1876, 1.

85

Auspicious Beginning of the Expedition

James Wilson notice of my arrival and arrange our method of communication. The exploring expedition under Giles[179] accomplished the overland journey from Adelaide to Perth[180] the same week that I arrived in the colony, and, about the middle of December, I visited the prison, or, as they call it in the colony, "The Establishment," and, in company with two other gentlemen, was shown through the interior by the superintendent, Mr. Donan [sic],[181] visiting all the corridors, both chapels, punishment cells, hospital, cook-house, workshops and storeroom, and found it to be very secure and well guarded. By the 1st of January, 1876, I had several interviews with Wilson and determined the plan for escape.[182]

All the prisoners I wanted were working outside the prison and communication with them was comparatively easy.[183] Not expecting the Catalpa to arrive at Bunbury[184] before the last week in January, and as some parties in Freemantle began to express surprise that I remained there so long without any ostensible business, I determined to take a trip inland, and accordingly visited Perth, Guildford, York, Northam, Newcastle, and the smaller villages on the route.

Awaiting the Ship's Arrival

January, February and March passed by and no sign of the vessel I waited for. The prisoners I wanted had been shifted around, communications with them had become difficult, and they were not so easy to be found when wanted.[185]

---

179. Between 1872 and 1876 Ernest Giles led five expeditions in South Australia, the Northern Territory, and Western Australia, and crossed more undiscovered country than any other Australian explorer. Friends of the State Library of South Australia Publications [http://www.slsa.sa.gov.au/friends/ernest_giles.htm], October 2001.

180. A distance of about thirteen hundred miles.

181. Joseph Doonan was the assistant superintendent of Fremantle Prison. Amos, 251–52.

182. Wilson would later recall, "The [only] disputed point was as to how we were to get from Fremantle to the coast. I was in favor of going on horseback, for I thought if we were pursued we would have a better chance of escape. The gentleman (Mr. Collins), however, said that it would be difficult to obtain horses enough for us all without exciting suspicion, and that it would also be difficult to use them for the same reason since we must make our escape in the daytime." "The Escaped Fenians," [New York] *Evening Post,* August 21, 1876, 1.

183. One Fremantle resident recalled as a youth meeting kindly Thomas Darragh, who seemed to move freely around town. The boy delivered soft drinks to him weekly. On one occasion, he came across Darragh with a young lady picnicking with a white cloth on the ground and a bottle of wine. Keith O. Murray, "Fenians' Escape," [Western Australia] *Western Mail,* January 19, 1950.

184. At the time, Bunbury was a flourishing port and favorite resort of American whalers. Alexandra Hasluck, *Unwilling Emigrants: A Study of the Convict Period in Western Australia* (Melbourne: Oxford University Press, 1959), 74.

185. Based on correspondence he had received from Breslin and Desmond, Judge Cooney wrote Devoy from San Francisco expressing considerable alarm that the *Catalpa* had not arrived at Fremantle as of March 26 (the plan had called for it arriving in January). He quoted the clearly exasperated agents: "Every day now is a day lost, and we will not adopt any other course until we hear

Auspicious Beginning of the Expedition

About the end of March an American whaler named the Canton put into Bunbury, and I telegraphed to her captain to know if he had any news of the Catalpa, of New Bedford. He replied that he knew nothing of her. I was now beginning to get anxious about the vessel and determined to go to Bunbury and wait there for some time. I expressed myself anxious to see that portion of the colony lying between Perth and Vasse, and, on the 5th of March, engaged a seat on the mail car from Perth to Bunbury.

On the 5th of March King arrived by the Georgette, bringing me three hundred and eighty-four pounds from New Zealand. I gave him back twenty pounds so that he might be at liberty to return to Sydney, but he was so anxious to remain until the escape was effected that he stayed in Freemantle and ultimately became one of the rescuing party.

Monday, March 6th, left Freemantle for Bunbury, distance 120 miles, and remained in Bunbury until the following Saturday evening, when I retuned to Freemantle by a small coasting vessel called the Mary. I remained in Freemantle with an occasional visit to Perth.

King, under the name of Jones, passed for a gold-miner, who had come to the colony on the reports of gold having been discovered in the northwest. Desmond remained all this time at Perth, working at his trade with an employer named Sloan,[186] and was pretty well known as "the Yankee"; he came to Freemantle occasionally and saw me there.

---

from you or until we are satisfied that he will not come; hence we hope you will write to our New York Correspondents with the greatest dispatch and let them say whether they will keep their part of the contract and whether Anthony (the vessel) will come or not!!" O'Brien and Ryan, 1, 171–72.

186. This would have been William Sloan (1829–1899), an ex-convict who established a thriving coach building and wheelwright business. He had been convicted in Glasgow in 1852 for robbery, was transported, and was conditionally pardoned in 1859. Erickson, *Bicentennial Dictionary of Western Australians pre–1829–1888* (Nedlands, W.A.: University of Western Australia Press, 1988), 2840; Rica Erickson and Gillian O'Mara, *Convicts in Western Australia, 1850–1887* (Nedlands, W.A.: University of Western Australia Press, 1994), 503.

[VIII]

John J. Breslin's Graphic Account
*of the Escape of the Six Prisoners, the Dash for the Boat, the Long and Weary Pull for the Ship, the Arrival on Board in the Nick of Time, and the Sharp Parley With the "*Georgette*"—The Victory Won*

Breslin's Report—(Continued.)

March 29th, at 6:30 P.M., found by the bulletin board that the Catalpa had put into Bunbury the day before, March 28th. As soon as the office opened, at ten o'clock, I telegraphed Captain Anthony:

"Any news from New Bedford? When can you come to Freemantle?"

I received in reply in the afternoon:

"No news from New Bedford; will not come to Freemantle."

I engaged a seat by the mail car for Bunbury, and left Freemantle the following morning, arriving in Bunbury at four o'clock P.M., on Friday, 31st. I met Captain Anthony ashore and explained to him what I proposed doing with the ship; he expressed himself perfectly willing to do what I required of him; but his crew were in a very discontented state and attempting to desert the ship—four of them took a boat forcibly and made off for the bush; three of them were brought back and put in irons on board and the fourth was confined in Bunbury lock-up.[187]

The part of the coast I had selected for embarking from was distant from Freemantle about twenty miles south, at a place named Rockingham. It lies at the head of the sound, and a narrow passage at the end of Garden Island leads out to the sea. I intended the Catalpa should stand well out to sea, ten or twelve miles outside Garden Island, and a whale-boat put into Rockingham and pull out to the ship,

---

187. On March 30, four crewmen stole a boat and went ashore. Three had joined the ship at the Azores: Joseph McCarty, George Durgin, and Harry Duggin; the fourth, Cyrus Keill, was an original crew member. The authorities were alerted and caught the men that same afternoon. McCarty was put in jail because he insulted an arresting officer. The other three were returned to the ship, where they were kept in irons until April 8. *Catalpa Log,* March 30 through April 8, 1876.

when we would get on board, a distance of fourteen or sixteen miles, which could be easily done, under ordinary circumstances, in four or five hours.

I was anxious that the captain should see the coast outside of Rockingham and know exactly where his ship should be, so I arranged with him to come up with me to Freemantle by the Georgette, which was due in Bunbury with the colonial mails on Saturday, April 1st. By this arrangement the captain would have time to see the coast, know the spot where I intended to embark the men and be back in time to put to sea, and leave me free to make the rescue on the morning of Thursday, April 6th.

Saturday evening, while waiting for the Georgette to leave for Freemantle, Thomas Brennan, who left New York to join the Catalpa at Fayal, turned up unexpectedly as a passenger from Melbourne on board the Georgette. He recognized the Catalpa and came ashore to find out what he was to do; I had already more men than I could conveniently take to provide for, and again, he could not go on board at Bunbury without exciting suspicion, so I determined to let him come on to Freemantle and then do the best I could for him.

Going Carefully Over the Ground

Sunday morning, April 2d, from the bridge of the Georgette Captain Anthony had a good view of the coast outside Rockingham, and noted the positions of Rottnest, Garden Island and other principal landmarks. Arrived in Freemantle and found her Brittanic Majesty's gunboat Convict,[188] carrying two guns and thirty men, schooner-rigged and fast sailing, had arrived and anchored on the previous day. As the wind was for the most part light and variable, and the Catalpa a dull sailer unless with a stiff breeze, the chance of escape from pursuit was too slim to be risked. So the presence of the gunboat upset my plan for Thursday morning. On the afternoon of Monday I learned that the gunboat came to Freemantle on an annual visit, would remain eight or nine days and then proceed to Adelaide or Sydney; also that another gunboat was expected to call at Freemantle and take Governor Robinson[189] to visit the Northwest.

I asked Captain Anthony to overhaul his vessel and paint her, and be in no hurry to get his wood and water on board, as we must wait until the gunboat sailed. I also explained to him the details of my plan and drove him out to Rockingham

---

188. The correct name of the ship was the HMS *Conflict*, carrying two guns and thirty men. Amos, 221.

189. William Cleaver Francis Robinson (Sir William after 1877) was governor of Western Australia three times: 1875–1877, 1880–1883, and 1890–1895. *Australian Dictionary of Biography*, 6 (Melbourne: Melbourne University Press, 1976), 50–51.

John Breslin's Graphic Account

that he might see and know the spot I intended to embark from. The road from Freemantle to Rockingham, for the first ten miles, is good for Western Australia; from the Ten-Mile Well to Rockingham Hotel, about six miles, heavy and cut up with sand patches; from the hotel to the beach, about four miles, a mere track through sand and bush. We made the distance, without stopping, in two hours and twenty minutes.

Code of Signals Arranged

Thursday, April 6th, Captain Anthony left Freemantle for Bunbury, and I arranged to telegraph to him as follows: When the gunboat had sailed, the telegram: "Your friend (N or S, meaning north or south) has gone home. When do you sail?" This meant: "The gunboat has sailed north or south; all right; start from Bunbury." In case the gunboat to take the governor to the northwest should arrive I would telegraph: "Jones is going overland to Champion Bay. When do you clear out of Bunbury?" And when the coast was again clear—"Jones has gone to Champion Bay; did not receive a letter from you." Meaning: "All right again."

Tuesday, April 11th, the gunboat Convict sailed from Fremantle, and I learned that she was bound for Sydney. At ten o'clock A.M., I telegraphed to Captain Anthony: "Your friend S has gone home; when do you sail?" I expected an answer that he would start that afternoon, and we would start April 13th.

Wednesday, April 12th, 11:3o A.M., received the following telegram: "I sail today. Good-bye. Answer if received. G. Anthony."

This sailing, according to our arrangements, would leave the ship ready for my leaving with the men on Friday morning, and Friday being Good Friday, a government holiday, I could not do so. I immediately telegraphed: "Your telegram received. Friday being Good Friday I shall remain in Freemantle and start for York on Saturday morning. I wish you may strike oil. Answer if received."

At half past seven P.M., I received the following telegram: "Yours received. Did not leave to-day; wind a-head and raining. Sail in the morning. Good-bye."

This fixed the start for Saturday morning, and I made all arrangements to be ready to leave.

Hitches and Disappointments

I had an interview with Wilson shortly after the arrival of the Catalpa and arranged a signal I was to make to him, which meant: "Get ready; we start tomorrow morning." This signal I could not give on Friday, but I had a letter conveyed to him on that morning and an answer that he had received it. This letter contained

John Breslin's Graphic Account

all necessary instructions, and concluded with the words: "We have money, arms and clothes: let no man's heart fail him, for this chance may never occur again." Desmond came from Freemantle to Perth with a good pair of horses and a four-wheeled wagon on Friday evening, and I had a similar conveyance and the best pair of horses I could get in Freemantle engaged for Friday and Saturday. I took the horses out for a drive on Friday afternoon to be sure that they went well together and were in good condition, and on my return to my hotel found the following telegram waiting for me:

"Freemantle, 14, 4, '76, 3:18 p.m. From Bunbury.
"J. Collins, Esq.—It has blown heavy. Ship dragged both anchors. Can you advance more money if needed? Will telegraph again in morning.—G. Anthony."[190]

By a fortunate chance, Cranston had been sent from the prison into the town with a message that evening; had the telegram read to him and my order of the morning countermanded. I thought the ship, having dragged both anchors, must have gone on the bar and a delay of some weeks would follow before she would be ready for sea again. Sent Desmond back to Perth and prepared to wait the turn of events.

Saturday, April 15th, half-past 10 A.M., received the following telegram: "I shall certainly sail to-day. Suppose you will leave for York Monday morning. Good-bye. —G. Anthony."

I immediately replied: "Your telegram received. All right. Glad you got off without damage. Au revoir.—J. Collins."

Hard to Get Good Horses

I then engaged the same horses for Sunday and Monday and sent King to Perth on a horse I bought some months before to give Desmond notice to get his team and come to Freemantle on Sunday evening. Saturday afternoon I walked to the jetty, and when I was sure Wilson saw me I gave him the signal which means: "We start to-morrow morning." The following morning being Sunday, I saw he was somewhat puzzled; so, keeping him in sight, I walked leisurely across where the

190. Accounts vary as to whether or not this was a near disaster or a coded message. According to an unidentified participant in the rescue, "This was a disguised despatch to let him know that he could not go to sea on that day." "The Fenians," [New York] *Herald,* August 20, 1876, 4. The log entry describing Friday afternoon indicated pleasant weather except for some light rain squalls. (Two days earlier, the anchors did drag, according to the log.) Also, on Friday morning, Anthony learned that jailed crewman McCarty had been released. Anthony may prudently have decided to wait and see if McCarty would appear (apparently he never did). *Catalpa Log,* April 12, 14, 15, 1876.

John Breslin's Graphic Account

prisoners were working and sufficiently near to say: "Monday morning," without being observed by the warder or any of the other prisoners.

Easter Sunday Desmond came to Freemantle, about 2 P.M., with a very poor looking pair of horses, the former pair having been engaged to go to York when he returned them on Sunday. He offered the hostler two pounds to get him a good pair, but they were all engaged. I then went to get the horses I had engaged and found that Albert, the owner, had given the best horse of the pair to Mr. Stone,[191] the superintendent of water police, to go to Perth with; his brother-in-law, the sheriff, having been thrown from his horse in Perth and lying in a critical condition. Albert also informed me that I could not have the horses I had engaged on Monday morning, that his clerk had done wrong in hiring them to me, as he himself had promised them to Thompson a week before to go to Perth regatta on Easter Monday.

Ready for the Start at Last

Monday, April 17th, at half-past five A.M., I had the hostler called and the valises put in the trap, waked up King and Desmond; Brennan was already awake and dressed, and left for Rockingham at 6 A.M. At seven o'clock A.M. I went to Albert's stables and found the pair of horses I wanted and a nice, light four-wheeled trap already harnessed and waiting. I told the hostler to let them stand about twenty minutes, and then went and told Desmond to get his horses harnessed up and be ready to leave at half-past seven A.M.

I had arranged with Desmond for him to leave Freemantle by a side street which, after a few turns, took him out on to the Rockingham road, while I drove up High Street as if going to Perth, turning sharp round by the prison and on to the same road. King, being well mounted, was to remain after we started for a reasonable time, and then to follow and let us know if the alarm was given.

At half-past seven A.M. I drove slowly up the principal street, and, turning to the right, walked my horses by the warders' quarters and pensioners' barracks. The men were beginning to assemble for parade. I had arranged with our men that I would have the traps in position on the road at a quarter to eight, and would remain so, the nearest being within five minutes' run of the prison, until nine o'clock A.M.

Being ahead of my time I drove slowly along the Rockingham road, and Desmond, coming up shortly after, drove by me. Coming to a shaded part of the road we halted, and, having divided the hats and coats three to each trap, I commenced to drive back to Freemantle, Desmond following; time, five minutes to eight.

191. John F. Stone. Amos, 236.

John Breslin's Graphic Account

The Men Get Out

A few moments after I saw three men in prison dress wheel round and march down the Rockingham road. Driving up to them I found the men were Wilson, Cranston and Harrington. I directed them to pass on and get into the trap with Desmond and drive away.

Desmond wheeled his horses around, and they were only seated and ready to start when the other three came in sight, and, on driving up to them, I found one man carrying a spade and another a large kerosene can. As soon as I came near enough to recognize them he who carried the spade flung it with vim into the bush, and the holder of the kerosene can bestowed a strong kick upon it in good football fashion. I found the men were Darragh, Hogan and Hassett. I now had all the men I wanted and felt glad.

My horses got restive and refused to wheel around. Darragh caught one by the head, but he jibed and kicked so I was afraid he would break the harness. I told Darragh to let him go, and, whipping both of them up smartly, they started fairly together, and when I got them on a wider part of the road they wheeled around nicely. I now drove back and took up my men. Desmond was already out of sight, and King shortly after rode up and told me all was quiet when he left.

With regard to the method or plan of communication between the prisoners themselves it may be well to state that their good conduct and length of imprisonment had entitled them to the rank of constable, which enabled them to communicate with each other with greater ease and freedom than the other prisoners. Wilson and Harrington worked in the same party at the construction of harbor works in Freemantle. Hogan was a painter by trade, and on the morning of the escape was employed painting the house of Mr. Fauntleroy,[192] outside the prison walls. Cranston was employed in the stores and as messenger occasionally. Darragh was clerk and attendant to the Church of England chaplain and enjoyed considerable facilities for communication with the other prisoners, and on the morning of the escape took Hassett with him to plant potatoes in the garden of Mr. Broomhole, the clerk of works for the convict department.

Slipped Away Unsuspected

After breakfast on the morning of the 17th of April all the political prisoners were engaged outside the prison wall. Cranston passed out as if going on a message, and, having overtaken the warder, who was marching the working party in which Wilson and Harrington worked, showed him a key and told him he had been

---

192. William Robert Fauntleroy was the acting comptroller-general at Fremantle Prison. Erickson, 1022.

John Breslin's Graphic Account

sent to take Wilson and Harrington to move some furniture in the governor's house, which was the nearest point to where they expected to meet me. The warder told Wilson and Harrington to go with Cranston, and they marched off. Darragh took Hassett, as if going to work, in the same direction, and was joined by Hogan, who made an excuse for temporary absence to the warder who had charge of him; both parties met at the Rockingham road.

[EDITORS' NOTE: The following inserted passages are not part of Breslin's report. They are from a newspaper article, "Daring Escape of Six Fenian Prisoners," *The Herald* (Fremantle), April 22, 1876. They provide the reader with an Australian perspective of events.]

["On the morning of the day in question, the men, who have escaped, were engaged at various work. Wilson and Harrington were employed at the works near the sea jetty—two others, Cranston and Hassett were at work at the prison—another Hogan, was engaged painting at the Comptroller's house—and the other, Darragh, was the prison clergyman's messenger or orderly. About eight o'clock that morning—Cranston one of the two men working outside the prison, visited the party at work near the sea jetty and informed the warder—(Booler) that Wilson and Harrington were wanted to assist in removing some furniture at Government House, Fremantle. The warder not suspecting anything wrong, allowed the men to go. Between 9 and 10 o'clock, Hogan, the man who was painting at the Comptroller's residence, was missed from his work and could not be found. As he was a Fenian prisoner, suspicion of concert with the other Fenians was aroused, and inquiry was at once made for the other Fenian prisoners, where it was found that the six men above named were missing. The police were at once communicated with and mounted patrols sent in search of the runaways." *The Herald*]

I now drove on, letting King fall behind, and in half an hour was close behind Desmond. We held on without accident or incident until we reached the Rockingham Hotel, when Somers, the proprietor, who knew me, called out to know what time was the Georgette expected at the timber jetty. I told him the Georgette was at the jetty in Freemantle when I left, but I did not know when she would be at Rockingham. At half-past 10 A.M. we made the beach and got aboard the whale boat. The men had been instructed to stow themselves in the smallest possible space, so as not to interfere with the men at the oars, and in a few minutes all was ready and the word was given, "Shove off, men; shove off."

Now fairly afloat the word was: "Out oars and pull for your lives! Pull as if you were pulling after a whale!" The boat's crew was somewhat disconcerted and scared

94

John Breslin's Graphic Account

at the sudden appearance of so many strangers armed with rifles and revolvers, and pulled badly at first, but the voice of the steersman rallied them, and cries: "Come down Mopsa; come down, you big Louis. Pull, Toby, pull. Give them stroke, Mr. Silvee. What do you say, men? Come down all together. Pull away, my men, pull away," soon warmed them to their work and they fell into stroke and pulled well.

When about two miles off shore we saw the mounted police ride up to the spot where we had embarked, and then slowly drive the horses and wagons we had used up the beach towards the Rockingham jetty.

["In the mean time information had reached the police that two four wheeled carriages with two horses each, one two-wheeled trap with one horse and a man on horseback had been seen going at a tremendous pace along the road towards Rockingham. The mounted police were at once dispatched and reached Rockingham, a distance of 14 miles, within an hour and 10 minutes after leaving Fremantle. They found the horses tied up, and in the carriages three prison hats, revolver cartridges, a breech loading rifle cartridge, a bottle of wine, and a woolen gun cover. From this it is quite certain that the occupants of the traps were fully prepared to resist capture had it been attempted on the road journey. About 1 o'clock a person named Bell, residing at Rockingham, arrived at Fremantle bringing the news that about 9 o'clock that morning a whale boat with a crew of six colored men, and another man of Yankee look, came alongside the landing place of the Rockingham Jarrah Timber Company. Some two hours after Bell saw a man on horseback, followed by eight or ten men in traps galloping from the direction of Fremantle. When they arrived at the landing place they got out of the traps and went at once on board the boat and pulled out to sea. Before they started, he (Bell) asked them what was to be done with the traps and one of them said 'let them go to h——' and gave him a sovereign. Bell rode the saddle horse into Fremantle and gave information." *The Herald*]

Breslin Takes Leave of the Governor

I now remembered a letter which I had addressed to the governor, and fastening it to some wood sufficient to float it well I posted it to him by the ocean mail, as we were well inside Garden Island and the wind and tide setting full on shore, I have no doubt it reached its destination. The letter read as follows:

"Rockingham, April 17, 1876.

"To His Excellency the British Governor
of Western Australia—
"This is to certify that I have this day released from the clemency of Her Most

John Breslin's Graphic Account

Gracious Majesty Queen Victoria, Queen of Great Britain, etc., etc., six Irishmen, condemned to imprisonment for life by the enlightened and magnanimous government of Great Britain, for having been guilty of the atrocious and unpardonable crimes, known to the unenlightened portion of mankind as "love of country" and "hatred of tyranny." For this act of "Irish assurance" my birth and blood being my full and sufficient warrant. Allow me add that—

> In taking my leave now I've only to say,
> A few cells I've emptied (a sell in its way);
> I've the honor and pleasure to bid you good day;
> From all future acquaintance excuse me, I pray

In the service of my country,
John J. Breslin.[193]

At half-past twelve we were clear of the reefs seaward of Garden Island, and hoisting the boat's sails, stood away to the southeast in search of the ship; held on this course until four o'clock P.M., when, there being no sign of the ship, we took in sail and rowed to the westward. About half-past 5 P.M., Toby raised the ship fifteen miles ahead of us, and the men bent to their oars in order to get as near to her as possible before dark; at half-past six we had gained on the ship and could see her topsails quite plain from the crests of the waves. Made sail on the boat. At this time the weather had become gloomy, with rain squalls, and we were all pretty thoroughly soaked.

An Anxious Night in the Water

The boat made good headway under sail and we were rapidly overhauling the ship, carrying all sail and the whole boat's crew—sixteen men in all—perched on the weather gunwhale, with the water rushing in from time to one lee side, when, about seven o'clock a squall struck us, carrying away the mast, which broke short off at the thwart, and, by the time we had the mast and sail stowed away, the ship had disappeared in the increasing darkness.[194]

["As the American whaler 'Catalpa' had cleared out from Bunbury on the Saturday previous, and as no other vessel was known to be off the coast, it was at once con-

---

193. While this letter is described in many accounts, only one suggests it was ever received by the authorities: William J. Laubenstein, *The Emerald Whaler* (London: Andre Deutsch, 1961), 199.

194. "In following her up our mast broke about seven in the evening, and we were nearly being capsized and drowned in consequence." Darragh quoted in "The Catalpa Six," *IW*, August 26, 1876, 5.

John Breslin's Graphic Account

cluded that the boat in which the prisoners had escaped belonged to that vessel, and arrangements were at once made to go in pursuit. The Superintendent of Water Police at once dispatched the Police Boat in pursuit, in charge of the Coxswain, Mills. She left Fremantle at 1:30 and off Sulphur Bay—Garden Island—spoke a fishing boat who reported having seen a whale boat pulling out of the South Passage between Perron Point and the South end of Garden Island. After clearing the passage the boat set sail and steered South. The Police boat coasted along close in shore as far as Murray Head which she made at ½ past 7 o'clock. She then steered out to sea under easy sail keeping a good look out. She remained at sea all night, but saw nothing, and returned to the Murray Head early next morning." *The Herald*]

We pulled in the direction of the ship until about ten o'clock with the hope of being able to see her lights, but without success. We then hoisted the jib on an oar and steered the course we supposed the vessel had gone. There was an ugly sea running, and the weather threatened to become more severe. However, towards morning it moderated considerably. At a quarter to 7 A.M. we raised the ship and steered for her. She was coming towards us and we could see her lower sails, when, on looking behind, I saw the smoke of a steamer, and soon after was able to make out the Georgette steaming out of Freemantle with all sail set.

["It having been brought under the notice of the Government that owing to the wind being westerly the ship assisting in the escape of the prisoners could not work off shore and might possibly be within territorial waters and so subject to jurisdiction it was determined to place the steamer 'Georgette' in commission and send her in pursuit. The agent, Mr. John McCleery, having been communicated with, his consent obtained and indemnity given, active preparations were made to equip her for the pursuit and possible encounter with the ship 'Catalpa.' Mr. John Stone, Superintendent of Water Police, was placed in command with instructions to go alongside the ship and endeavour to ascertain if the prisoners were on board, and if they were, to demand them, warning the captain of the consequences of his act if he refused to give them up. No force was to be used and the 'Georgette' was to return by noon of the next day, Tuesday, if possible. It took until nearly 9 o'clock to get the 'Georgette' ready and then somethings—among others, a 12 pounder, artillery piece, was left behind. About 9 o'clock she left the jetty having on board in addition to her usual crew, 18 pensioners, of the Enrolled Pensioner Force, under the command of Major Finnerty,[195] and 8 policemen all armed." *The Herald*]

195. Major Charles Finnerty (1815–1881) had arrived in Western Australia in 1859. Erickson, 1049.

John Breslin's Graphic Account

It was her regular day for sailing for Albany with and for the colonial mails, and for a short time we were in doubt whether she was in pursuit or going on her regular trip. A little further observation convinced me that she was too far out of her regular course to be going to Albany, and a slight alteration in her steering decided the question, showing us that she was making for the Catalpa, which she must have seen before we did.

A Narrow Escape

We now plied oar and sail to reach the ship, but it soon became apparent that the Georgette was gaining too fast on us and would fetch the ship much sooner than we could. She was also coming close enough to make us out under sail, so we determined to take down the sail and lie to, taking the chance of her passing by without seeing us. The Georgette passed without having seen our boat, steering direct for the Catalpa, now distant about five miles. As soon as she had passed far enough ahead, we pulled after in her wake, judging it to be the safest position we could occupy if she was in search of us, and also bringing us nearer to the ship. Situated thus we saw the Georgette run alongside the Catalpa, and after remaining alongside about ten minutes, steam slowly away, the ship holding on her course and the Georgette steaming in the same direction, but gradually sheering off and going more in shore.[196]

["The 'Georgette' rounded Rottnest in the night and made about 30 miles S.W. of the Island by daybreak. The ship's course was then laid S.E. and about 8 o'clock a barque under light canvass was sighted standing south. Observing the 'Georgette' she made all sail and stood away, but the wind being light the 'Georgette' gained upon her and she then shortened sail. The 'Georgette' was got ready for defence, the pensioners, policemen and crew (the latter having been sworn in), being under arms. About 10 o'clock the 'Georgette' was alongside, and the vessel proved to be the 'Catalpa,' of New Bedford, flying the Stars and Stripes of America. In reply to questions put by the Superintendent of Water police, the mate stated that the Captain was at Fremantle, that no boat had been seen and that he was awaiting the return of the Captain. In reply to the question:

'Can I board your ship and search?'

---

196. "At 8 Am the Steam Ship Georgette hailed me and her captian [*sic*] asked me if I had seen a boat with a lot of men in it—I told him no—another man asked me if the Captian [*sic*] was on board—I told him no—Asked if I had any strangers on board—I told him no—then asked if he might come on board—I told him no—the steamer then left me and I stood on my course—On the wind heading S s.w. and about 15 miles off." *Catalpa Log,* April 18, 1876.

The mate coolly replied:—

'Don't know, got no instructions, but guess you'd better not.'" *The Herald*]

It was now about half-past eight A.M., and we made all the sail we could and put out every oar and paddle to overtake the ship. The ship held on her course on the wind, heading south-southeast, and both the ship and the Georgette kept increasing their distances from our boat. About half-past eleven A.M., watching the ship and the steamer alternately, the ship being about twelve and the steamer about eight miles distant, I noticed the steamer heading too close in shore to be on her course for Bunbury, where we thought she was bound after parting with the Catalpa.

"The Phantom Ship"

Observing her movements more closely, we shortly afterwards saw the steamer turn right around, and heading for Freemantle, come under steam and sail along the coast, evidently in search of our boat. We were now almost in the steamer's track, and if she stood out to sea a little could scarcely hope to escape unobserved. However, we still struggled on in the course the Catalpa was sailing, although she was fast receding from our view, and some of our men began to call her the phantom ship,[197] as the more we strove to approach her the farther off she appeared to sail.

The Georgette now began to get dangerously close to our boat, and we took down our mast and sail, but continued to work our oars and paddles. The Georgette still continued to come closer, and we had but slight hopes of escaping unseen. We lay as low as possible in the boat and ceased rowing for a short time.

About half-past 12 P.M. the Georgette passed across our wake so close that we could distinguish men on her deck and a look-out man at her masthead. For a time I expected to see her turn right down on us, but she passed on, and as soon as we sunk her hull we made sail again and stood after the Catalpa. We now commenced to gradually gain upon the ship, which continued to loom up larger, and about 2 P.M. we saw that the Catalpa had altered her course and was coming toward our boat.

I placed Wilson in the bow of the boat holding aloft a blue flag, and, about half-past 2 P.M. felt certain that we were observed from the ship, as she was now headed directly for our boat.

---

197. While sea tales of phantom or specter ships predate Christianity, the men may have had the more recent *Flying Dutchman* in mind (the legend of a wandering vessel found most often near the Cape of Good Hope). Horace Beck, *Folklore and the Sea* [American Maritime Library, 6] (Middletown, CT: Wesleyan University Press, 1973), 389, 390, 406; Peter Kemp, ed., *The Oxford Companion to Ships and the Sea* (New York: Oxford University Press, 1976), 319.

John Breslin's Graphic Account

["The ship was about nine miles off shore to the west of cape Bouvard. As it was reported to the officer in charge that there was only coal enough for part of a day's consumption it was deemed advisable to return to Fremantle and the steamer's course was shaped in that direction. On the way to Fremantle, about half an hour after leaving the ship a boat was sighted some 6 miles south of the Murray Heads which proved to be the police boat. After speaking her, instructions were given to the Coxswain in charge to cruise along the coast and keep a good look out, as there could be no doubt the ship's boat with the escaped prisoners was concealed somewhere in the vicinity of the Murray Heads. The 'Georgette' then bore up for Fremantle and came along side the jetty about 4 o'clock." *The Herald*]

Safe on the "Catalpa"

About the same time we saw another boat under sail making for the ship, and about equally distant on the land side as we were to seaward. A few minutes more and we recognized the boat as the water police cutter, and it now became a race which boat should reach the ship first.

At 3 P.M. we ran up to the ship on the weather side, the police boat being close up on the lee side, and scrambled on board in double quick time.[198] As soon as my feet struck the deck over the quarter rail, Mr. Smith, the first mate, called out to me:

"What shall I do now, Mr. Collins? what shall I do?"

I replied: "Hoist the flag and stand out to sea."

And never was a manœuvre executed in a more prompt and seamanlike manner. The "Stars and Stripes" were flying at the peak, our boat was hoisted and in its place at the davits, the ship wore and was standing on her course inside of two minutes.

The police boat was dropping alongside. As we went past I stepped to the rail and kissed my hand to the gentlemen who had lost the race; their boat dropped astern, and their officer shouted, "Goodby, Captain, goodby."

["The police boat stood to the southward about two miles to leeward of the 'Catalpa' until past noon when the ship tacked and stood to the north. The police boat tacked also and soon after saw a whale boat ahead and to leeward. Chase was at once given, the police boat gaining fast, when the 'Catalpa' bore down under all

---

198. Darragh: "We certainly thought the cause lost, but the superior seaman ship of the mate of the *Catalpa* stood to us splendidly. He run his vessel in between the police boat and us, lowered his grapples, and took the boat, crew, and all on board at one hoist." "The Catalpa Six," *IW* (supra note 194).

100

John Breslin's Graphic Account

The town of Fremantle, Australia (Z. W. Pease, *The Catalpa Expedition*)

sail, picked up the whale boat and stood away. At the time the whale boat was picked up by the ship, she was not more than 400 yards ahead. After picking up the whale boat the police boat passed to leeward of the ship within 20 yards and saw distinctly the escaped Fenians looking over the bulwarks, some of them in prison dress. A person named 'Collins,' who had been living in Fremantle for some months past, and who is suspected of being the organiser of the escape, was also recognised. The police boat did not hail the ship nor did the ship hail the boat. The ship stood away south and the police boat returned to Fremantle, which place she reached about 10 o'clock that night. The men on board the ship appeared to be armed and it was quite evident from the behaviour of the escaped prisoners while the police boat was within range, that they were only restrained from firing upon the boat by the influence of the captain." *The Herald*]

Twenty-eight hours in an open boat, with a liberal allowance of rain and seawater, cramped for want of room, and cheered with the glorious uncertainty as to whether we should gain freedom or the chain-gang, a suit of dry clothes, a glass of New England rum and a mug of hot coffee were just the things to put "where they would do the most good," and were put accordingly. After supper we walked about the deck and enjoyed what we supposed to be a last look at the shores of Western Australia, the ship working to windward with a light breeze in the direction of Cape Naturaliste.

John Breslin's Graphic Account

The "Georgette" Loomed Up Again

All hands, except the watch on deck, retired for the night about 9 o'clock P.M. and slept soundly. At 5 A.M. I came on deck and found the ship's course had been altered and we were working to windward on a light breeze, steering north-north-west, which would bring us past Freemantle again outside Rottnest Island.

["Particulars having been transmitted to head quarters by telegraph, it soon became rumoured that the Governor would visit Fremantle personally to give instructions and that a second attempt to capture the runaways would be made by the Authorities. Arrangements were at once made with the agent for the 'Georgette' for a second cruise—for four or five days if necessary. Alarm, excitement, bustle and activity were exhibited on all hands. Never were the people of Fremantle so upset or excited. Business was almost entirely suspended and the imposing Masonic ceremony of laying the foundation stone of the new Freemasons Hall, which was to take place at 4 o'clock, was almost forgotten, and attracted but little if any attention. In the course of the afternoon His Excellency, accompanied by the Colonial Secretary, drove down, and after consultation with the Superintendent of Water Police, the Comptroller General and other officials, and the agent for the 'Georgette' it was decided to dispatch the 'Georgette' again to the 'Catalpa,' with a view to intercept the boat, or to demand the surrender of the prisoners from the captain, if they were on board. The pensioners and police were embarked, a 12 pounder field piece was shipped and fixed in the gangway; provisions were put on board, and a fatigue party of pensioners were engaged in coaling—30 tons being put on board in a short time. By 11 o'clock arrangements were completed and the 'Georgette' steamed away at the jetty. Not a few, both on board and on shore, but gave way to gloomy forebodings as to the result of this second trip to the ship. Certainly, the arrangements made by the authorities warranted those who were not acquainted with international law or aware of His Excellency's instructions, in concluding that the Governor had determined upon resorting to force, if necessary, to capture the fugitives. By early morning the 'Georgette' was outside of Rottnest and at daylight sighted a ship bearing S. S. E., under full sail. The 'Georgette' hereupon hoisted her pennant and the ensign, and all hands were put under arms." *The Herald*]

About half-past 5 o'clock the man on the lookout reported a sail on the lee bow. I thought when I first saw her she was a small coasting vessel, but Mr. Smith quickly pronounced her to be the Georgette. As the daylight advanced we saw that he was right—it was the steamer Georgette standing across our course, and evidently in search of us.

102

John Breslin's Graphic Account

About 6 A.M. we passed the Georgette, she lying about half of a mile to windward of us, with a man-of-war ship and vice-admiral's flag flying. We set the "Stars and Stripes" as we passed, and held on our course. The Georgette turned and followed us, still keeping to windward. The breeze freshened about 7 o'clock and the Catalpa began to drop the Georgette astern. They then fired up and made all sail on the Georgette, and the breeze dying away they began to overhaul us very fast. At a quarter to 8 o'clock the Georgette was so near that I could see she had guns, an artillery force, and the water police on board; a whaleboat belonging to the water police hung at her davits, to be used in boarding, and they seemed quite eager and determined to capture us.

The men of our party were all assembled in the cabin with their rifles and revolvers ready. Of the watch not a man visible from the Georgette but the lookout and the man at the wheel. I now stepped down into the cabin and explained to the men the position in which we stood. I told them that if the officials on board the Georgette were determined to fight for their re-capture they would, most probably, succeed, as they had the advantage of us in every way—more men, better armed, cannon, and a steamer with which they could sail round and round us. I also explained to them that while those of our party who had not been in prison could only suffer imprisonment, the men who had been imprisoned could be hanged in case any life was lost by their resistance. I then said it was simply a matter of dying now or waiting to die in prison, and gave them the option of fighting or surrendering, if the officials in the Georgette fired into or boarded us. Their answer was "We'll do whatever you say." I then said, "I'll hold out to the last," and went on deck again.

A Shot Across the "Catalpa's" Bows

The Georgette was now very close on the weather side, with a company of artillery on board, a field piece pointed at our ship, and the gunners at their quarters. At 8 o'clock A.M. the Georgette steamed ahead and fired a round shot across our bows. Captain Anthony then put a question to me, to which I replied, "Hold on, and don't take any notice of the shot yet."[199]

After a lapse of about three minutes, the artillerymen having gone through all the regulation motions of sponging out, reloading and pointing their field piece,

---

199. Most accounts, including the *Catalpa's* log, report only one shot being fired from the *Georgette*. However, the *Times*, August 11, 1876, 3, citing a [Boston] *Pilot* article, describes an earlier shot under the *Catalpa's* stern. James Wilson also stated this in interviews with New York papers including the [New York] *World*, August 20, 1876, 1. Captain Anthony is quoted describing two shots in the *Standard*, August 21, 1876, 1. While several Australian papers reported the one bow shot, one described two shots: "Escape of Fenian Prisoners," [Western Australia] *Inquirer and Commercial News*, April 26, 1876; *Catalpa Log*, April 19, 1876.

John Breslin's Graphic Account

and the steamer and the Catalpa sailing side by side within easy speaking distance, I said, "Now ask him what does he want?"

Captain Anthony stepped on the weather rail and raised his speaking trumpet; as he did so the Georgette hailed:

"Bark ahoy!" and the answer went back,

"What do you want?"

"Heave to," came back from the Georgette.

"He says, heave to, ask him, what for?"

"What for?" shouted our captain, through his trumpet. No reply, and the question is repeated still louder. "What am I to heave to for?" After quite a pause the Georgette hailed—

"Have you any convict prisoners on board?"

Answer: "No prisoners here; no prisoners that I know of."

The Georgette then hailed—"I telegraphed to your government; don't you know that you are amenable to British law in this Colony? You have six convict prisoners on board. I see some of them on deck now."[200]

I then said to the Captain, "This fellow is lying and trying to bluff us; he can't send a message to Adelaide before Saturday next."[201] The Georgette then hailed:

"I give you fifteen minutes to consider and you must take the consequences; I have the means to do it, and if you don't heave to I'll blow the masts out of you."

"Tell him—That's the American flag; you are on the high seas: if he fires on the ship he fires on the American flag." The Captain then shouted, pointing to his flag:

British Threat Aroused Yankee Ire

"That's the American flag; I am on the high seas; my flag protects me; if you fire on this ship you fire on the American flag."[202]

---

200. The officer misspoke. Western Australia's only telegraph service at the time of the *Catalpa* incident was local and limited to its coast. There was no transcontinental or international access. Not until the end of 1877 was there even a link with the rest of Australia. While an international cable link existed at Port Darwin, Western Australia was still working on a connection in 1876. (At the end of the next decade Western Australia did establish its own international cable.) K. T. Livingston, *The Wired Nation Continent: The Communication Revolution and Federating Australia* (Melbourne: Oxford University Press Australia, 1996), 84, 98, 124.

201. Breslin had arranged that McCarthy and Walsh, two IRB agents left behind, would cut the local telegraph lines from Perth to King George's Sound so that the warship HMS *Conflict* could not be contacted. According to Amos, the schoolteacher Frank O'Callaghan accompanied McCarthy late Sunday night to do this. (O'Callaghan has received little recognition for his help in the *Catalpa* rescue. In a letter to Devoy, Wilson had said to send replies in care of O'Callaghan.) The authorities were able to repair the wires by noon the next day. O'Brien and Ryan, 1, 220; Amos, 233, 236. (See John King's report starting in chapter 12 of this volume.)

202. An Australian newspaper reported, "It would appear that there was a desire to obtain correct legal information on international law, for about the time of Captain Anthony's visit to

John Breslin's Graphic Account

The threat of firing on the flag highly incensed the first mate, Mr. Smith. He damned the scoundrel in good strong nautical phrase, and he exclaimed, "Damn him, let him sink us; we'll go down with the ship; I'll never start sheet or tack for him." Mr. Smith now asked, "What will you do if he attempts to board us?" I replied, "Sink his boat when it comes alongside. You have a couple of good heavy grindstones; let us have them handy to heave over the side." The Captain now reminded Smith of some heavy logs of timber which were in the hold and bade him order the crew to pass them on deck; these logs were quickly passed on deck and laid on the main hatch ready for use.

The lookout reported a sail on the lee bow, and we saw a small sail between us and Rottnest Island. This called the Captain's particular attention to the position of our ship, and, judging that we were coming too close in to the land and liable to run into British waters, he wore ship and stood on the other tack, bearing down close on the Georgette, which backed out of our way. This movement appeared to disconcert the parties on board the Georgette. Our fifteen minutes' grace and several other minutes had expired, and, as the Georgette steamed slowly across our stern, I looked for a raking shot among the masts. She did not fire; and, as she ranked alongside again, I knew that the game of bluff was played out. The party on board the Georgette, with a battery of glasses and their spokesman, whom I believed to be Colonel Harvest,[203] called out:

"Won't you surrender to our government?" No reply. And again he called out

"I see three of those men on board now."

Our Captain replied—

"You are mistaken, sir; the men you see are my ship's crew."

Our men were all in the cabin from the time the Georgette first bore down on us, with strict orders not to come on deck until I called them. After about ten minutes more sailing side by side, the Georgette hailed:

"Can I come on board?"

To this Captain Anthony replied:

"No, sir; I am bound for sea and can't stop."

The Georgette still kept us company, as if loath to part, until half-past nine A.M., when she slowly swung off, and without having the courtesy to bid us bon voyage, steamed back to Freemantle.

Fremantle, Johnson [Desmond] called upon Mr. Howell, the solicitor in Perth, and asked him several questions as to the limit of neutral waters, from which we would infer that the captain knew what he was about when he told Mr. Stone that his flag protected him where he then was, against misdemeanour or felony either." "Escape," *Inquirer and Commercial News* (supra note 199).

203. Breslin is mistaken. Colonel Edward Douglas Harvest was not aboard the *Georgette*, nor did any account suggest he was at Fremantle for the crisis. Harvest was the military commandant of Western Australia at the time, based at Perth. "Harvest," Erickson, 1390.

John Breslin's Graphic Account

The remaining incidents of the voyage are written in the log of the good ship Catalpa.[204]

["As the 'Georgette' did not gain upon the ship and the wind was freshening, a gun was fired under the vessel's stern—and she then run up the American flag. She took no further notice of the signal and the 'Georgette,' under full steam and all sail gave full chase. As the ship did not attempt to shorten sail, or take any notice of the signal, when the 'Georgette' had steamed to within a quarter of a mile of her, a gun was fired across her bow and the captain of the ship then got into the quarter boat. The 'Georgette' stood on until within hailing distance, when the Superintendent of Water Police, Mr. J. F. Stone, addressing the Captain said:

'I demand six escaped prisoners now on board this ship—in the name of the Governor of Western Australia. I know you and your vessel. I know the men I want are on board, for the police saw them go on board yesterday; if you don't give them up you must take the consequences.'

The Captain answered:—

'I have no prisoners on board.'

Mr. Stone replied:—

'You have and I see three of them.'

To this the Captain rejoined:—

'I have no prisoners here, all are seamen belonging to the ship.'

---

204. From the *Catalpa* log for April 19: "This day commences with Light, breeses from the w and clear pleasant weather—Ship heading at S.SW—At 2 pm wore Ship heading N.N.W—At quarter past 2 raised the boat bearing N by E—Kept off for her—At 3 pm She came along side with 10 passengers—Coast guard boat in Sight. She hoisted her flag—we set course And wore ship—The Coast guard boat run along by us and they bid the Captian good by—Middle part. Light baffaling baffaling [*sic*] winds working into the westward—Latter part fresh breeses from the WNW—Still working to the windward—At 5:30 Saw a Sail to the windward—Ship on the starboard tack heading N—the Sail [undecipherable word] off for us and proved to be the Georgette—She had her flag set and we set ours. At 8 Am the Georgette fired a gun across our bow—the captian stood on the weather rail and raised his Speaking trumpet. the Georgette then hailed bark Ahoy—the captian answered what do you want. Georgette then hailed heave to—the Captian asked what for and again asked what am I to heave to for. After Sometime the Georgette hailed have you any convict prisoners on board—Captian answered no prisoners and again no prisoners that I no of—Georgette then hailed I telegraph to you government do know that you are amenable to British Law in this colony you have six convict prisoners on board—I see some of them on deck—Now Captian answered you are mistake Sir the men you see are my ship crew—Georgette hailed again. Give 15 minutes to consider and you must take the consequences—I have the means to do it. And if you dont heave to I will blow the mast out of you—the Captain said I am on the high Seas that the American flag—my flag protects me—if you fire on this ship you fire on the American flag—Ship continued her course At 8:30 wore Ship heading SW. S—Georgette hailed again wont you surrender—held on our course—Georgette hailed again can I come on board—Captian answered No Sir I am bound to Sea and cant Stop—At 9:30 Am She left and we kept on our own course heading SW—So ends this day."

106

John Breslin's Graphic Account

The wind compelling the 'Georgette' to get away from the ship, Mr. Stone said to the Captain:—

'I will give you 15 minutes to consider what you will do.'

At the end of that time the 'Georgette' again went alongside and Mr. Stone re-demanded the prisoners in the same words as before. The Captain again replying:—

'I have none on board.'

'If you don't give them up' said Mr. Stone, pointing to the gun, 'I will fire into you and sink you or disable you.'

At this time the pensioners' [*sic*] and police were in order with arms ready, and a man at the gun with lighted match. Nothing alarmed at Mr. Stone's threat or the demonstration made, the Captain coolly replied:—

'I don't care what you do. I'm on the high seas and that flag'—pointing to the American flag he was flying—'protects me.'

Mr. Stone replied:—

'You have escaped convicts on board your ship, a misdemeanour against the laws of this colony, and your flag won't protect you in that.'

The Captain returned:—

'Yes it will or in felony either.'

Mr. Stone then asked:—

'Will you let me board your ship and see for myself?'

And was answered:—

'You shan't board my vessel.'

'Then your Government will be communicated with' said Mr. Stone 'and you must take the consequences.'[205]

---

205. A review by the editors of 1876 U.S. congressional records and diplomatic correspondence between Great Britain and the United States failed to find any reference to the *Catalpa*. There were no congressional bills or resolutions about the *Catalpa*. On June 9, a single, brief reference to the *Catalpa* escape is found in the records of the House of Commons. The most important diplomatic matter addressed in that period was the negotiation of a new extradition treaty. The sticking points related to the political nature of offenses, granting asylum to political prisoners, and whether one would be tried for the same crime for which he was extradited. These negotiations started years before the *Catalpa* affair. Interestingly, an August 7 [London] *Times* editorial about the *Catalpa* makes no reference to the treaty. Both before and after that editorial, the *Times* ran lengthy ones about the treaty. In his history of Western Australia, J. S. Battye wrote that Britain's secretary of state decided the escape was not a matter for diplomatic negotiation. National Archives and Records Administration, "Despatches from U.S. Ministers to Great Britain, 1790–1906" (Microfilm Publication M30, rolls 125–26); "Diplomatic Instructions of the Department of State, 1801–1906" (Microfilm Publication M77, roll 83); "Notes from the British Legation in the United States to the Department of State, 1791–1906" (Microfilm Publication M50, roll 100); "Notes to Foreign Lega-tions in the United States from the Department of State, 1834–1906" (Microfilm Publication M99, roll 46); O'Brien and Ryan, 1, 88; *CIS US Serial Set Index, Part II, 35–45th Congresses, 1857–1879*, Subindexes A–K, L–Z, (Washington, DC: Congressional Information Service, 1977); *Hansard's Parliamentary Debates* (Microform) Third Series, Vol. 229 (London: Cornelius Buck, 1876), 1040–52; Battye, 333.

John Breslin's Graphic Account

'All right' said the Captain, and the interchange of civilities ceased. Mr. Stone had gone as far as he dared go, even a little beyond his instructions, but it was useless, and he had nothing else to do but return to Fremantle which he reached about one o'clock." *The Herald*]

[IX]

BRESLIN'S DIFFICULTIES WITH THE MEN
on the Homeward Voyage—Complained of Food and Treatment and Were Discontented—Demanded to Be Put Ashore and Forced a Change in the Plans—Arrived in New York

BRESLIN'S REPORT—(CONTINUED).

July 27th, 1876, Latitude 20° 12′ north, longitude 46° west, at 1 o'clock P.M. sighted a ship steering west, and, when we came near enough to signal, found that she hoisted American colors, the first American ship we met since leaving Western Australia. The captain proposed going on board to find out whether he could purchase any sugar or molasses, ours having ran out, to get what news he could, and other purposes.

After the boat had lowered and put off, James Wilson came to me and said that he "wanted to be put ashore if that ship was going to an American port." I told Wilson that the captain said to me it was most probable that the ship was bound to Barbadoes for sugar, and I could not tell whether the captain could get on board her or not, as Mr. Smith, the first mate, had told the captain he could not overtake her in his boat, and declined to go.

Wilson then said, "You refuse to put me on board. Life is life; my health is getting worse every day; I want to be put on shore."

I replied, "I did not refuse to send you on shore. I have only explained the situation to you; but you can note down, if you like, that I have refused. Life is life to me as much as to you, and I believe we are all anxious to get on shore."

He replied, "We ought all to be on shore long ago, and might have been but for you," or words to that effect.

Wilson's tone and manner were decidedly insolent and threatening, and, in my opinion, calculated to provoke strife and dissension.

109

Breslin's Difficulties with the Men

The ship proved to be the Kentuckian, of Boston, from Liverpool bound to New Orleans, with scarce provisions enough for her own crew, and in such a hurry to proceed on her voyage that Captain Anthony returned after a few moments on board, with a few newspapers only.

Complaint of Breslin's Treatment

Later in the afternoon Dennis Duggan, Thomas Brennan and Thomas Desmond requested to speak to me privately. Captain Anthony having withdrawn from the cabin, I requested these gentlemen to be seated, and Brennan commenced the conversation by remarking, "Well, who's to open the ball? I suppose I will."

He then commenced to state that, as members of the organization, they found fault with my conduct on board the ship; that I directed the movements of the ship without consulting them, and that was not right. Also that the men we brought from Freemantle were suffering from bad health, and from being unable to make use of the food on board, and ought to be put ashore at Fernandina, or some other port, without delay; that they believed they were not free men until they were placed on American soil, and they, Duggan and Brennan, believed that it would give greater satisfaction to the organization to go into port than to remain out four weeks longer and chance the taking of ten or fifteen thousand dollars worth of oil; ending with a request that I would ask Captain Anthony to go into port.

I asked if that was all? and, having received an answer in the affirmative, replied to the first part, or charge against myself, by asking the gentleman who spoke to point out a single instance where I had taken direction of the ship, or conducted myself otherwise than as a passenger from the time the ship left Western Australia. (On that morning I took direction of the ship, and required nothing from them but obedience to orders). He had to admit that he could point out no instance, and stammered out something about, "He thought."

Men Had All Improved

I then said, with regard to the food, I considered I had been accustomed to as good food as any of the men on board, that they all had the same food on board as I had; and we would all have been very glad to get on board at Freemantle with a prospect of much harder fare. Every man of the ex-prisoners had improved in appearance since coming on board, and the two men who complained of ill-health had suffered in the same manner for years, the voyage appearing to benefit them more than otherwise.

Breslin's Difficulties with the Men

Brennan agreed that they had all improved in appearance; Duggan asserted that they had not. I said that I felt perfectly satisfied with the captain's conduct, that he was acting for the best interests of the owners, and I knew of no better chance of making the same amount of money for the organization in the same time.

To this Brennan and Duggan replied, that there was money enough in the organization, and it would give greater satisfaction to have the men home for the Convention.[206]

With regard to the fear of the ex-prisoners for their freedom, I said that question had been decided at Freemantle, when they did not dare to take us almost in their own waters they would never attempt to molest us on the shores of America; I believe the flag protected them as much now, and they were as free as on American soil. Duggan said he believed so, too, but the ex-prisoners could not be made to believe it. I said I did not see sufficient grounds for interfering with the captain and declined to do so.

Duggan then said, that if Lennon or Cody were in my place they would take the ship from the captain. I asked him if he thought they would be sustained in such action by the organization? "Well, he didn't know."

After considerable angry discussion, in the course of which Brennan asserted that he had been sent out to watch the interests of the organization, and that he had watched the interest of the organization for six years; and in the course of which I found that the ill-health of the ex-prisoners had about as much to do with the matter as the anxiety of Brennan and Duggan to be home for the Convention in August.

Demand to be put Ashore

Desmond proposed that they write out a protest against the ship being stopped on the whaling ground, and I agreed that if they took the responsibility of guaranteeing the captain that, by going into port, he would be giving the greatest satisfaction to his owners, I would act upon it. The enclosed protest or note was handed to me in the evening:

"On Board Bark Catalpa,

July 27th, 1876.

"John Breslin:
"We the undersigned do hereby request that this ship be brought into port without delay for the following reasons:

206. The Clan-na-Gael convention of August 1876.

Breslin's Difficulties with the Men

"1st. Owing to the innutricious [*sic*] quality of the food, the ex-prisoners believe it injurious to their health.

"2d. Owing to the ill-health of some of the ex-prisoners it is deemed dangerous to prolong the voyage.

"3. The ex-prisoners consider themselves not actually free men until placed on American soil.

"4th. By complying with the above we believe it will be satisfactory to all parties interested in this undertaking.

"Thos. Desmond, Thomas Brennan, Denis Duggan, John King, Martin J. Hogan, James Wilson, Robert Cranston, Thomas H. Hassett, M. Harrington, T. Darragh."

I then assembled the men who had signed the note and asked them if they understood the nature of the request they had made. I read the note, paragraph by paragraph, and refused to endorse the opinions contained in the first and second paragraphs, giving my reasons for so doing. I then explained to them that compliance with their request would compel the captain to throw away an almost certain chance of making ten or fifteen thousand dollars, and asked if they preferred a month ashore to making ten or fifteen thousand dollars for the organization. Their reply was, that they understood the nature of their request and preferred to have the ship go into port.

I told the men that from the time we started from Western Australia not an hour —not a minute that the ship could make—had been lost on the passage homewards; if we had had bad weather on the passage we might have been detained much longer than a month despite our utmost efforts to make a port; and that we were six or seven days sail from the whaling ground, where there was any likelihood of delay. Duggan agreed that, up to the present time, there had been no delay, but all adhered to the demand that the ship go into port.

Laid Protest Before the Captain

I then laid their protest before the captain, and explained to him the state of feeling I found existing among these men. I told him I had found out that a man whose signature was attached to the protest claimed to have more authority from, more influence with, and a greater interest in the concerns of the owners than I had.

The captain then told me he had heard that before, and understood, through the carpenter (Duggan), that Brennan had more authority to act for the owners than I had. I further stated my belief that this impression had been made on the

Breslin's Difficulties with the Men

minds of the ex-prisoners, and that they had been led to believe that they were treated on board in a manner far different from what their friends expected and provided for them.

After a short consultation with the captain the following reply was returned to the signers of the protest:

"On Board Catalpa,

July 27th, 1876.

"Gentlemen:

"In reply to your note received this evening, I beg to state:

"The food on board the Catalpa is good, sound, ordinary ship's food; the water is good, and in sufficient quantity.

"The ex-prisoners are in as good a state of health to-day as when they came on board.

"The ex-prisoners are anxious to get on shore, believing they are not free men until placed upon American soil.

"The ex-prisoners take the responsibility of all loss to the owners incurred by my compliance with their request to into port.

"The signers take equal responsibility with the ex-prisoners.

"We endorse this statement as correct, and request the captain to go into port.

"Denis Duggan, Thos. Desmond, Thos. Brennan, John King, Martin J. Hogan, Thomas H. Hassett, James Wilson, M. Harrington, Robert Cranston, Thomas Darragh."

I then read this reply to all the men that signed the protest. Brennan said that he did not want all the responsibility left on the ex-prisoners, that he took an equal share of the responsibility with them. I then added the words "the signers take equal responsibility with the ex-prisoners," and they all signed.

I then told the captain that, under the circumstances, and considering the discontent and ill-feeling that prevailed amongst the men, I felt justified in taking the ship into port, and requested him to steer for New York. We were then steering north by west, intending to pass through the western whaling grounds, in the track of homeward bound American vessels, with the chance of meeting an American vessel willing to take our party on shore and leave the Catalpa free to cruise the season out; or to get all the fresh provisions we needed off some of the whalers cruising there, and remain out a month cruising, which we could have done without any danger or inconvenience.

"It was too late to go into Fernandina, and, for other reasons, I had already determined not to go there.

Captain George S. Anthony, Commander of the *Catalpa*
(Z. W. Pease, *The Catalpa Expedition*)

Coming into Port

July 28th, 1876. After breakfast this morning I informed the men that the ship was going into port, and requested them to take notice that they had forced the captain to this decision contrary, in my opinion, to the best interests of the owners, and before any delay had occurred, or any chance to put them ashore been neglected.

I regret having to report that I must attribute the chief cause of the discontent and ill-feeling exhibited by the men to the influence of Duggan and Brennan. These men, I understood, when leaving New York for Western Australia, could be relied upon to assist me in any way. I have received no assistance whatever from either of them; on the contrary, both of them, I have been informed, have presented my simplest acts and expressions in the worst light, and expressed their determination to get me into trouble when we got home—and this at a time that each of them professed to be perfectly satisfied with what had been done, and on friendly terms with me.

We had not been at sea a fortnight when I was informed, by one of the prison-

Breslin's Difficulties with the Men

ers, that Brennan meant to do me all the mischief he could, and I shortly after learned that Duggan and he combined for that purpose. Brennan gave the ex-prisoners to understand that he was a person of great importance in the organization, and that I was a sort of interloper who had lately joined. Duggan was asked about it, and confirmed the impression of Brennan's high position in the organization. Duggan also informed the mate of the ship that Brennan had more authority in this matter than I had. Duggan told the men that the provisions provided for their use had been given to the crew and to other ships; that everything had been provided by their friends—canned meats and fruit, and even condensed milk for their use. Brennan was understood to be taking notes of all these matters, and threatening to have the captain and myself punished for all these shortcomings.

Discontent of the Rescued Men

Thus matters went on until the occurrence just related; under a smooth exterior discontent gnawing deeper, until the men, I believe, considered themselves injured by being taken on board the Catalpa. Harrington declared they were better treated on board the convict ship, for they got a glass of wine every day,[207] and Cranston wished himself back in Freemantle because the slapjacks were not fired to his liking one morning. Hogan suffered fearfully because the cook refused to supply him with boiled onions. Hassett found out that he must have been a freeman in Western Australia, for he was deprived of his liberty on board the Catalpa, and Wilson was knave enough to pretend that he could not use the food, that he found himself becoming weaker and would die if not put ashore. Darragh was the only one of the six who showed common sense and common decency, and was willing to remain out longer so as to catch oil. Duggan told Desmond that he would not stay out two days if by so doing he would catch ten thousand dollars worth.

As to the ill-health of the prisoners, their own signatures attest the fact that they enjoyed as good health as they did in Freemantle, and I have no hesitation in saying they all appeared very much improved in condition.[208] The men who complained of ill-health were Wilson and Harrington—Wilson complained of a pain in the chest in the region of the heart, which attacked him at times, and which he believed was disease of the heart. A stimulant called "pain killer" always relieved him; a glass of rum or brandy had the same curative effect, and he told me he did not have these pains so often on board the ship as when he was in prison.

207. Unlike their British or French counterparts, American whalers were generally "dry." Mawer, 169.

208. Virtually all the newspaper accounts of the arrival commented upon the good appearance of the prisoners.

Breslin's Difficulties with the Men

Harrington complained of dysentery. After coming on board the mate gave him a bottle of patent medicine, and the use of it, according to his own account, made him better than he had been for years. Both Harrington and Wilson had been working daily at the construction of harbor works in Freemantle up to the morning of their release as healthy, able-bodied prisoners, under the inspection of duly qualified and efficient medical officers. I saw nothing indicating the increase of ill-health in the appearance of these men; I have had an hospital experience of four years and claim to have some knowledge of the symptoms of ill-health.

Of the general conduct of the men I have no reason to complain; on the contrary, it has been rather better than I expected to find it.

[EDITORS' NOTE: The following portion of Breslin's report was not printed in the *Gaelic American*. It is a part of the printed convention report of the 1877 Clan-na-Gael. Reprinted with the kind permission of The American Catholic History Research Center of the Catholic University of America.]

["Of their conduct while in prison, waiting for the *Catalpa*, it may be well to state that, at my first interview with Wilson he told me some money would be of service to them. I asked him how much he wanted, he said a pound a man would be quite sufficient, and, upon his assuring me that he could take it in without any danger of being searched, I gave him the money. A few days after that I learned, through a prisoner who had been discharged, that Hassett had been found lying drunk in his cell with a bottle of liquor and some twelve or fourteen shillings in his possession, for this he had been punished, deprived of his privileges as constable, and confined to the interior of the prison: and I looked on his case as hopeless. At my next interview with Wilson he never mentioned this to me, and would not have done so only I asked him what effect Hassett's conduct would have in causing a stricter watch over them, he then said he did not mean to tell me about Hassett for fear it would discourage me. I had particularly cautioned and requested Wilson to destroy all letters received from me, and on no account to let any man know anything of the intended escape but the men whose names I gave him. I find that Wilson kept one of my letters for three weeks and then enclosed it in a letter to J. Walsh[209] of San Francisco; also that a ticket-of-leave Irish political prisoner named Delany[210]

---

209. John Bennett Walsh had been transported on the *Hougoumont*. He received a full pardon in 1869 and went to San Francisco. The remaining military prisoners at Fremantle would write Walsh, who in turn forwarded their letters on to the Clan. Amos, 290; Ó Lúing, 65.

210. Thomas Delaney was a military Fenian (Fifth Dragoons) transported on the *Hougoumont*. Due to exemplary conduct while incarcerated, he received a ticket-of-leave in 1871. Thereafter his ticket was revoked on numerous occasions for a variety of offenses apparently related to alcohol abuse. When Devoy wrote of six military Fenians at Fremantle, he was unaware that Delaney had been returned to the prison and was serving a short sentence at the time of the rescue. Amos, 205.

Breslin's Difficulties with the Men

—a man of drunken and disreputable character—was, by Wilson, made fully cognizant of the whole matter, and was with difficulty prevented from attempting to join the party on the morning of the escape. Cranston informed another prisoner, who had not even the merit of being a political prisoner, named Brennan, of the intended escape, and placed in his possession a letter addressed to Cranston's mother, containing written evidence of the matter.

About two weeks before the escape, two friends from the home organization[211] arrived in Freemantle, acting on the belief (derived from letters written by the prisoners) that passage money and clothes were all they required to escape. One of these men, through —— and ——[212] had an interview with Wilson, and, on an intimation that money would be acceptable, gave Wilson five pounds. Of this money Darragh, Hassett and Cranston allege they never received any portion or account, but I have been informed that a considerable portion of it was spent on brandy for the party in which Wilson and Harrington worked; and that, a few nights before the escape, Wilson was so drunk as to attract the notice of the other prisoners but was fortunate enough to escape the observation of the warders.

The prisoners also received six pounds of the money in the hands of C.O'——,[213] at the time Foley left Freemantle, making a total of seventeen pounds during my stay in Freemantle.

Of my connection with Denis Duggan in this matter I have merely to state, that my first interview with him in this business of the escape of the political prisoners took place in Spencer's hotel in Bunbury, when Captain Anthony introduced him to me as the carpenter of his ship; this was in the presence of strangers, and as a matter of form to account for my recognizing and talking with him. I was already acquainted with Duggan, was aware that he was on board the ship, and that he could recognize me in case the captain had any doubts of my identity. Duggan appeared to me to be discontented and excited about something, but had no appearance of being under the influence of liquor. I went on board the *Catalpa* with Captain Anthony, and he explained to me how he felt himself situated. He told me that he felt very anxious and doubtful about putting into, or remaining at Bunbury, principally on account of the conduct of the carpenter. The carpenter, he told me, went ashore at Fayal, went on a drunken spree with the crew, and became so drunk that, when returning to the ship, he fell out of the boat three times, and had to be

211. Walsh and McCarthy from the IRB.

212. Father J. Carrerras was a Catholic priest whose pastoral duties included the prison, and Frank O'Callaghan was a teacher at the local government school. Amos, 223.

213. This was Cornelius O'Mahoney of Macroom, Cork. He had been a secretary to Stephens and a writer for the *Irish People*. He was sentenced to five years for treason and transported aboard the *Hougoumont*. Following his release, he remained in Australia, where he became a teacher, and later principal, of a Catholic school, first in Perth and then in Melbourne. McGrath, "The Fenians in Australia," 51; Amos, 270.

hauled on board by making him fast to a rope. He could not tell what the carpenter might have told the crew as to the ship's object in going into Bunbury, or how much his own liberty and the safety of the ship were at the mercy of a crowd of discontented sailors. Four of the crew had attempted to desert the ship, three were on board in irons, and one in the lock-up in Bunbury; the carpenter, he said, had insulted him, and made use of language towards him for which, only for the peculiar circumstances in which he was placed, he would put the carpenter in irons. He was afraid to give the crew liberty on shore, and the men, in consequence, were growling and discontented; he said he felt very much discouraged in the affair from the manner in which the carpenter acted, he having been placed on board as a most trustworthy man, and he did not know but he would have to work with men like the carpenter in Western Australia. Some of the officials at Bunbury had told him that if Captain Gifford[214]—the captain who had taken O'Reilly out of the colony—was ever caught in the colony he would be hanged. Altogether he felt himself in a very awkward and uncomfortable position, and was most desirous to get to sea. The carpenter, he said, commenced drinking when he got ashore at Bunbury, and he requested me not to let him have any money to spend on shore and to get him to go on board, as the crew, the second and third mates were growling at the carpenter being allowed to remain ashore; and that it looked suspicious in the eyes of any person who understood the discipline of a ship to see the captain and carpenter on terms of equality ashore, and living at the same hotel. The first mate, Mr. Smith, was present and confirmed the captain's statement. I had a long conversation with the captain and mate and showed them that the ship was perfectly safe unless found with the prisoners on board; that the only danger to be apprehended from any information received by the authorities would be the arrest of the parties endeavoring to effect the escape at Freemantle. Explained my plan of action to the captain and showed him that, before I committed any act that would compromise his safety or that of the ship, the ship would be at sea beyond British jurisdiction; and that he was free to proceed on his voyage homeward if I did not make an appearance at a certain point of the sea-shore on a given day and hour. I also stated my belief that, no matter how drunk Duggan might have been, I thought him incapable of betraying the confidence reposed in him. I promised that I would have Duggan come on board and stay there. I advised the captain to give his crew liberty on shore; that, from my knowledge of the country, if any of the crew attempted to desert, a few days in the bush would make them willing to come on board again.

214. David R. Gifford was captain of the bark *Gazelle* that rescued John Boyle O'Reilly in 1869 at Bunbury. Evans, 134.

Breslin's Difficulties with the Men

Before I left the ship the captain and first mate promised to take the ship any place I required her, and to assist me in every way to the best of their ability; before coming on shore the captain ordered Mr. Smith to give the starboard watch liberty on shore the following morning, and the consequence was that, before the day was ended, every man of the watch was on the jetty waiting to go on board the ship.

I had a private conversation with Duggan the next morning, he complained bitterly of the harsh treatment he received on board the ship. I told him what I thought of men who got drunk when engaged in any business requiring secrecy, and asked him to go on board in order to prevent any further grumbling or discontent, he promised to do so; he then asked me for some money; I asked him what he wanted the money for; he said he wanted to buy some cigars and give them to the sailor who was in the lock-up,[215] that he was a good fellow and an Irishman. I asked him if ten shillings would be enough; he said yes, and I gave him the money. I explained to him how matters stood in Freemantle, and what I proposed doing; he asked me if he was going to Freemantle; I told him no, I had more men than I wanted, and any more would do more harm than good. He appeared to be very much annoyed at this, said it was too bad, that he calculated all along on being present at the prison when the men were escaping, and was very excited about it. I told him it was no use talking to me in that manner, I had determined on my plan, and did not mean to take him to Freemantle merely to bring him back again, as he could do no good there. I told him I required him to act his part on board the ship, and that he could be of much more service to the cause there than on shore. Duggan seemed so much put out at the idea of his not taking a more active part in the immediate rescue of the prisoners that I subsequently asked the captain to allow Duggan to come off in the boat which was to take them to the ship; the captain said he was no good to pull an oar, and he did not want to bring any one but a good oarsman.

After coming on board for the homeward trip the captain told me that from the time I came to Bunbury he had no fault to find with Duggan.

From expressions made use of by Duggan on the voyage I believe he harbors the opinion that I have treated him unfairly and not in accordance with my instructions. It would be a simple matter of justice to me to have the committee disabuse his mind of these errors.

My connection with Thomas Brennan in this business amounts to this—He was introduced to me at New York as the man who was to join the Catalpa at Fayal, and I

---

215. The crewman was McCarty, who had jumped ship at Bunbury and was jailed for insulting a police officer. *Catalpa Log,* March 30 and 31, 1876.

expected to find him on board at Bunbury. On Saturday evening, April 1st, while waiting in Spencer's hotel for the sailing of the *Georgette* to Freemantle, Brennan came into the sitting room where I was, and without waiting to see whether I would recognize him or not, called out in a loud voice—

"Don't you know me; don't you recollect seeing me in New York?"

It was no part of my plan at that time to appear to know every stranger who came into the Colony, and in such abrupt fashion. I have no doubt I gave him a rather chilling reception. I said I knew him, and asked him to step out on the sidewalk, where I could talk to him apparently as a traveller; he did so, and commenced the conversation with—

"You know I was a delegate to the last Convention?"

I told him I was aware of that important fact, and asked him to tell me what had occurred since he missed the ship at Fayal. He gave me a hurried account of the exertions he had made to get to Western Australia, and stated that if he could be of any service he was willing to do anything in his power, if not he could work at his trade for some time and get back the best way he could. His presence under the circumstances was more of an embarrassment than an assistance to me. The character I had received of him was that he was a good, sober reliable man, and his own account showed that he had made extraordinary exertions to be in time. The captain was averse to taking him on board at Bunbury for fear of exciting remark amongst the crew, so I determined to do the best I could for him at Freemantle, without interfering with my plan. He came on to Freemantle, and I told him to stop at Harwood's, a hotel opposite Maloney's, where I was staying. He did so, and we arranged signals by which he knew when I wanted to communicate with him. King and I had several interviews with him on the outskirts of the town, and he was very severe on Duggan's conduct; he told us that he had found out the sailors who had deserted the *Catalpa* at Fayal, and learned from them that Duggan had been on a drunken spree with them, that Duggan had boasted he would meet a friend at Fayal who would have lots of money and that he would have plenty of money when he got to Bunbury. Brennan remarked that John Devoy knew the sort of man Duggan was and had no right to send him. He was also of opinion that our object was known to too many persons even in the Colony. There was a good deal of truth and common sense in his remarks, but he was rather too despondent of success. So matters ran on until the morning of the 17th of April, about 2 o'clock A.M. All hands had retired for the night. I remained awake and on watch, and about 5 o'clock A.M. met Brennan in the passage way leading from my room; he was quite excited—every thing was wrong—he had been waiting an hour—he would be late—he wanted to see the men. I told him he was quite time enough, that he could walk the distance in the time, and asked him to make no noise, but remain in my room while I called up

Breslin's Difficulties with the Men

—— and get the hostler to harness up his trap. I left the room for that purpose and he followed me along the passage, tramping with a heavy pair of boots; I again asked him to remain where he was, but he refused and attempted to bully me, insisting that he wanted to see the men, meaning Desmond and King. There were two men staying at Moloney's hotel that I had particular reasons for avoiding to awaken on that morning: one was a commercial traveler named Rosser, the other a clerk named Searle; in fact I had spent a considerable portion of the previous night in inducing these men to drink sufficient to make them sleep sound in the morning. King slept in the room next to Searle and Desmond in the room opposite Rosser. I was very much provoked by Brennan's manner, and if he had persisted much more the whole affair might have had a different ending.

While waiting at the beach with the boat, the captain told me Brennan proposed to cut the throat of a man who came up to see what they were doing,[216] for fear he would go away and give the alarm, but he changed his sanguinary intentions into giving the same man a pound to bring back the horse and trap he had used to Perth.

To Brennan's presence on board I attribute the refusal of the ex-prisoners to remain at sea for the purpose of catching oil, as he had impressed them with the belief that his presence and theirs at the Convention was a matter of the utmost importance to them. His conduct on board the *Catalpa* at New York amounted to mutinous disobedience of orders, and in this he was abetted by Duggan and the ex-prisoners.

I believe he considers himself aggrieved, and I would feel obliged if the committee would investigate any complaint he has to make and see justice done in the matter.

I enclose my cash account statement, and hold myself ready to give any further particulars or explanations that the committee may require.

I remain, gentlemen,

Yours fraternally,

John J. Breslin.

John J. Breslin swore to the matter herein contained that came under his own personal observation. April 17, 1877. John J. Rossiter, President Napper Tandy Club.

Bro. Breslin then replied verbally to the charges made against him by Brennan. {See Appendix B.}

Bro. Desmond then took the floor and corroberated {*sic*} the statement of Bro.

---

216. John Bell (a Bunbury timber-getter). Amos, 233.

Breslin's Difficulties with the Men

Breslin, and condemned in the strongest terms the conduct of Brennan on board the ship. He explained that he only signed the demand to take the vessel into port to prevent bloodshed, as he had good reason to believe a refusal would result in a mutiny.

Bro. Desmond was cross-examined on this point, but solemly (*sic*) reiterated his statement, that he had reason to believe that bloodshed would follow a refusal to take the vessel into port.

A motion offered by Bro. Devoy, that a Special Committee should be appointed to investigate the whole A.P.R. enterprise from beginning to end, and that funds should be placed at their disposal to examine witnesses, was laid on the table.

A motion was then made that the verdict of the trial committee in the case of Bro. Brennan be re-affirmed. A substitute was offered that Brennan be expelled, which was declared carried by the Chair, by a vote of 32 to 29.

Bro. John Egan, of New Jersey, appealed from the decision of the Chair, and called for the ayes and nays on the appeal. The decision of the Chair was sustained, there being 39 ayes, 34 nays, and 8 not voting {Devoy and Breslin were among those that abstained}. . . ."]

Part of Report Omitted

The portion of Breslin's report which is omitted is not necessary to the telling of the story and does not make pleasant reading. It will not be made public unless there should arise a public necessity for doing so. I hold it and other documentary evidence subject to that reservation. [The missing portion has been inserted above in brackets.]

The report was presented first to the committee, together with the balance of the money in hand, a few days after the arrival of the *Catalpa* in New York, and then to a convention[217] in the following year. By that convention it was approved and ordered printed. Thomas Desmond at that convention fully endorsed Breslin's report, and stated that he only signed the demand to be put ashore in order to prevent very serious trouble, owing to the feeling among the men. King made a similar statement.

The portion of Breslin's report which told of the actual escape was published in the *Herald,* giving that paper a three-column "scoop" two days after the *Catalpa* arrived in New York. For this Breslin was paid $75, and that was the only money he made out of the affair.

217. The Clan-na-Gael convention of 1877.

[X]

Unexpected Arrival of the Vessel

in New York Creates Many Difficulties — Factional Attempt to "Capture" The Men from the Committee Foiled by Patrick Lennon's Quiet Threat to Use Force — Work of Providing for the Soldiers

[Devoy's Account Resumes]

The cruise of the *Catalpa* was over, the rescued men had arrived in New York, the vessel was anchored in the bay, and thousands of Irish people, proud of the victory over England, crowded the Battery Park to get a view of the vessel, or were rowed out in boats to board her and shake hands with her officers and crew. The men were overwhelmed with congratulations and hundreds of old friends crowded O'Donovan Rossa's Hotel and gave vent to their enthusiasm with characteristic warmth.

The rescue had been accomplished, and it only remained to provide for the men and wind up the business end of the expedition. In this a new set of troubles confronted us.

The *Catalpa*'s arrival in New York was utterly unexpected and no provision whatever had been made here for the reception of the men.[218] As

218. Because the cable between Australia and Java had been broken soon after the escape, news of the escape did not reach either America or Britain until June. The [London] *Times* first reported the escape on June 6, 1876, citing the receipt of letters from Australia as the source. The New York dailies began to report on the escape June 7, with the *Herald* doing an extensive article based on an unidentified source. The papers mentioned that the *Catalpa* had not violated any international law. The captain simply took on board a boat load of people he had come across! The possibility that prison staff had been bribed was also mentioned in several articles. (They also reported that the cutting of the cable was a prearranged signal to the rescue organizers. Devoy thought that the break might have been a signal. O'Brien and Ryan, 1, 167. There is, however, no evidence at all that the cable was cut by Fenians.) Thereafter a number of reports were published on both sides of the Atlantic. At the end of the month, William Foley arrived in New York and was able to provide first-hand details of the escape plans, though he had left Australia three months before they were carried out. His recollections were published in the June 24 edition of *Irish World*. "The Escaped Fenians," *NYT*, August 11, 1876, 2; "The Escaped Fenians," [New York] *World*, August 20, 5;

Unexpected Arrival of the Vessel

before stated, the arrangement was that she should put into Fernandina, Fla., where United States Senator Conover's friend, the Collector of the Port, was ready to attend to them and notify us of their arrival.[219] That would give us time to put matters in proper shape and avoid the dangers and inconveniences inseparable from the sudden throwing of the men into the excitement of a reception in a big city. Such a thing as the demand of the men to be put ashore anywhere but at the place arranged beforehand had not been dreamed of. They were soldiers, accustomed to discipline, none of them having less than seven or eight years' service in the British army, and in the Fenian organization in that army all of them had always obeyed orders implicitly. Civilian Fenian prisoners previously released had cheerfully carried out all arrangements made for them by committees, and these soldiers, rescued at a great sacrifice of time and money and personal risk to the rescuers, were expected to do at least as well. The reader who has followed Breslin's report can readily see how the unexpected happened, but it took some time to have that knowledge reach those in charge of affairs at that time.

The convention, which cut such a figure in the discussion on board the *Catalpa,* had already been held, but many of the New York men who attended it had not yet got home. A reception committee, composed of men residing in various cities, had been appointed, mainly with a view to raising a fund for the men on their arrival; but only a few of the New Yorkers on it were in the city. I was laid up with a bad cold, due to a drenching in a rainstorm, in the house of Dr. William Carroll, in Philadelphia—the man who had interested his old army friend, Senator Conover, in the work and who had suggested the landing in Fernandina. The first notice I received of the ship's arrival in New York was a telegram from Denis O'Donovan, eldest son of O'Donovan Rossa, informing me that she was in port; that there was some trouble about providing for them, and asking me to come on at once. I at once wired back to have the men brought to his father's hotel on Chatham Square,[220] and started for New York by the next train.

I found the men there in the clothes that had been hastily provided for them in Australia, and which, after three months on a whaling bark, were

---

"The Rescued Fenians," *Republican Standard,* August 21, 2; "The Escaped Fenian Convicts," [London] *Times,* September 6; "The Rescued Fenians," *Republican Standard,* August 24, 3.

219. Dr. Carroll wrote Devoy several times in June inquiring about preparations for and the arrival date of the *Catalpa* at Fernandina. He was also a friend of Senator Conover. O'Brien and Ryan, 1, 185–87.

220. Chatham Square is located at the intersection of Park Row and Worth Street in lower Manhattan. At the time, the neighborhood was known as Five Points, a notorious slum ruled by Irish gangs. Jackson, 414–15.

not exactly fit for the drawing-room. I had been intimately associated with all of them in Ireland, except Darragh, and was known to them as the man in charge of the organization in the army. But I had known them as soldiers, full of enthusiasm and spirit, and I was not prepared for the change which ten yaers [*sic*] of the iron discipline of England's prison system had wrought in some of them. Their welcome was hearty and effusive, but I had not been five minutes in the room till I heard a volley of the most absurd complaints against Breslin. They had been "ill-treated," "half starved," their just complaints were ignored, etc., etc. I found most of them full of the notion that the vessel sent to receive them ought to have been little short of a floating palace. It did not take me long to disabuse them of these notions, although it did take some plain talk; but I never succeeded in removing the feeling of positive hatred, not to speak of ingratitude, which they entertained for Breslin.

Faction Shows Its Hand

I found that before the men left the vessel a bold attempt had been made to take them away from the committee and put them in charge of a little knot of "kickers"[221] in New York. That would not have lasted long, but had it succeeded even for a day it would have made a newspaper scandal. It did not succeed, even for a minute, because one very resolute, but very quiet-mannered man, with a well-earned reputation for straight shooting, happened to be in New York and took charge of the landing. This man was Patrick Lennon, who had commanded the Dublin men at Stepaside and Glancullen in 1867, and who had seen plenty of service, both in the British army and in the American Civil War. Lennon was a member of the Reception Committee and went down with two carriages to the Battery. Duggan had been with him in the Dublin hills, and the rescued men had all heard of him. As the men were about to go with Lennon and his friends two other carriages appeared on the scene in charge of a man who was not a member of the Reception Committee and who is rather well known in commercial life in New York. There is no particular need of mentioning his name, but I may express the opinion after twenty-eight years that there would have been no trouble worth speaking of in connection with the expedition but for his special talent for making mischief and his doubtless sincere conviction that he was the only really honest man in the

---

221. "One who protests, objects, or rebels; one who breaks away from his party. Chiefly U.S." *O.E.D.*

Unexpected Arrival of the Vessel

movement. This man was introduced to the rescued men by Brennan, and he proceeded at once to try to get them to go with him. Lennon reminded him that he was not a member of the committee and had no business there. He blustered a bit, but Lennon stepped over to him and very quietly said:

"So-and-so, if you don't get out of here in two minutes I'll put a hole in you."

"So-and-So" knew the man's reputation, so that ended the attempt to "capture" the rescued men, and Lennon took them to O'Donovan Rossa's hotel, where they were when I arrived from Philadelphia. They were very much troubled about their shabby clothes and were impatient to make themselves presentable. Mr. Mahon, the Treasurer, lived in Rochester and it would take a few days to get the necessary money, but they wanted clothes at once and were impatient. At their urgent request I took them to a tailor who clothed a large contingent of the *Herald*'s staff and who was a good tailor, although his store was on South street, and he made a specialty of sailors' outfits. Dan Kirwan, William McGarrahan,[222] Dominick May and other famous reporters of that day patronized him, and they dressed as well as their fellows. I brought the six rescued men, Duggan and Brennan there, and got them such an outfit as could be procured in a hurry for eight men in a small shop, because the clothes had to be got on credit and I knew the tailor. This transaction was described during many subsequent years as taking the men to "a sailors' slop shop" and supplying them with "shoddy clothing," but it met a temporary emergency in the only way that was then practicable.

Slander Mars the Good Effect

Within a few hours of my arrival in New York I was told by one of the rescued men, who had never any communication with the eastern colonies of Australia, that King had followed a vile occupation in Australia, and among New York men I soon found that a story had gained circulation that he had "cheated the men out of their money at cards" on the vessel. I called the men together at once and told them that this blackguardism must be stopped at once, and demanded the name of the liar who had told

---

222. William McGarrahan was a *Herald* journalist closely associated with the Irish American community. "W. M'Garrahan's Funeral," *NYT*, March 10, 1889, 3.

Unexpected Arrival of the Vessel

them these stories. I did not get it immediately, but I got it later and, so far as the men were concerned, the vile talk was finally stopped, but it was carried on outside by those who originated it until it finally culminated in the publication of a foul and ruffianly lie in the press.

Within two or three days after his arrival Breslin turned over to the organization over four hundred pounds in Australian sovereigns, yet within a month stories were privately circulated through the country that he had made away with a lot of money. He did not receive and never asked a dollar of the money collected for the prisoners, yet a story was published in a New York paper and telegraphed all over the country that he had demanded a share of it and that a shooting affray had occurred because one of the rescued men had protested against the demand.

I make brief mention of these matters to show the difficulties we had to contend with, even after the men had landed—difficulties created entirely by our own people and in no sense due to any action of the enemy. We got over them all, and when we were through with them all the National movement in America was an efficient fighting force, animated with a high spirit and having a more perfect discipline than had ever existed in the American Fenian organization. The rank and file were filled with a new enthusiasm, the good effect on our people everywhere was very marked and the steady progress made in subsequent years was mainly due to the impression made by the success of the rescue.

CONGRATULATIONS ALL ROUND

Congratulations poured in on us from all sides. John Boyle O'Reilly's editorial in the Boston *Pilot* sounded the keynote, but I will not quote it here. The general effect may be judged by a few individual expressions selected from a large number. James J. O'Kelly, now Member of Parliament for one of the divisions of Roscommon, was traveling as correspondent for the *Herald* with Dom Pedro, Emperor of Brazil, and when the news of the success of the rescue was cabled was in Montreal. He wired as follows:

"Dated, Montreal, June 7, 1876.

"To John Devoy,
Herald Office, New York:
"Accept my congratulations. Many mistakes have been wiped out.

"O'Kelly"

Unexpected Arrival of the Vessel

M. P. Curran was then night editor of the Boston *Globe* and Boston correspondent of the New York *Herald*. He was not connected with the Clan and looked at the matter from another point of view. He wrote as follows:

"Boston Daily Globe,

"August 20, 1876

"John Devoy, Esq.

"My Dear Sir—I beg leave to congratulate you on the successful issue of one of the boldest and best-planned and executed schemes in history. I do this both as an Irishman and a journalist—as an Irishman because I take a natural pride in seeing the noble Lion of Britain humiliated, and because I want to see every man who risked his life for a noble principle which has the same object for all, however they may differ as to the advisability of the means, as free as the air of heaven; and as a journalist because it is natural for the guild to be clannish.

"I had been aware since the published reports of the escape that you were an active agent in the affair, but not till now did I know the amount of personal labor which you devoted to the glorious work. I can imagine how much objection a sanguine man with a clear head and ready wit would be compelled to overcome in trying to persuade men of inferior intellect, and of more conservative views, into an appreciation of the grandeur of the scheme and the rewards of its successful accomplishment. But you have succeeded and doubtless you will find many of the lukewarm ones of times gone by eager to share now in the renown. Your Boston friends, at least O'Reilly and Cashman, who are my warm friends, too, are not sparing of their praise of your generous and persistent efforts to rescue the poor fellows, and I trust they did their share of the work also.

"I never have had the pleasure of meeting you but once, but even if I had never done so, the feeling would not deter me from paying my humble share of honest tribute to such high-minded devotedness to a cause and the victims of its consequences. I trust when you next come to Boston that I shall have the pleasure of meeting you.

"Believe me,
"Very respectfully yours,
M. P. Curran,
"Night Editor Globe."

I would not have given the above letter if it had not been for remarks made by some of Mr. Curran's present associates to the effect that I had "some indirect connection" with the rescue. Next week I shall deal with the raising of the fund for providing for the men and give the financial

Unexpected Arrival of the Vessel

report of the expedition. Later I will give John King's accounts of his meeting with the two men sent on the same mission, one from Ireland, the other from England, both of whom arrived in New York, via San Francisco, a day or two after the landing of the rescued men.

[XI]

Work of Raising Funds
*for the Rescued Men and the Winding Up of the
Expedition — The Slander-Monger at Work —
Financial Statement of the Enterprise*

The money to provide for the rescued men had to be raised outside of the regular funds of the Clan-na-Gael, which could not be touched for such a purpose. The method used was to get up receptions for them in the various cities, either in the form of public meetings in halls or of picnics, charging an admission fee. The men were divided up into squads and sent to attend these gatherings. In all cases their presence attracted a large crowd and the demonstrations realized a considerable sum of money. The total amount was about $15,000 but the traveling expenses of the men were deducted from this and the balance divided among them.

When it came to the final distribution of the money the rescued men (or most of them) protested against any portion of it being given to their rescuers. None of these had asked any of it, but the committee in control of the fund had discussed the question of dividing it equally between the rescuers and the rescued, as that was the original intention when the appeal was issued. But both in the circular making the appeal and in the *Irish World,* which acknowledged the subscriptions and proceeds of demonstrations, the headline, "Rescued Prisoners' Fund," was used, more for newspaper reasons regarding the length of the line than for any other reason. This, the prisoners used as their pretext for protesting against giving anything to the men who had risked life and liberty to give them their freedom.[223]

---

223. In a letter dated November 29, 1876, Dr. Carroll expressed frustration with the rescued prisoners: "I wish you [Devoy] were well rid of them all, and they given to understand that having been given their liberty, a handsome sum to begin life with anew, and the best wishes of their countrymen, their future will depend entirely upon themselves." O'Brien and Ryan, 1, 217–18.

But the scandal to avert which this action was taken was not averted. There were some men determined to throw dirt and they used the opportunity supplied by one of the rescued men making a fool of himself while drunk and getting arrested to secure publication for a lie made out of whole cloth that his arrest followed a shooting scrape in which Breslin and I figured as the chief villains. A meeting, the published story said, had been held to distribute the money, I refused to give a proper account of it, Breslin demanded a share of it, and the result was a row in which pistols were drawn and the arrest followed. The persons who gave this ruffianly lie to the papers knew that no such meeting had been held and that none of the incidents described had occurred, but the publication gratified their sense of injured self-importance.[224]

The Final Settlement

Things dragged on for months until I was finally empowered to go to New Bedford and effect a final settlement. In order to keep my appointment and prevent a further hitch I was obliged to be away on that day that John O'Mahony's body was put aboard the steamer for transmission to Ireland

224. Martin Hogan was the ex-prisoner and the article appeared in the [New York] *World*: "Mr. M. J. Hogan's Story of His Vain Attempts to Get Any. Martin J. Hogan, who had been bound in $300 for an alleged assault on John J. Breslin, was yesterday discharged by Justice Duffy at the Tombs Police Court, on his own recognizance. The story of Mr. Hogan is as follows: He and five others were the band of English convicts rescued from confinement in Australia by the Catalpa. A subscription for the benefit of these gentlemen was started by the Irish World newspaper. Messrs. O'Donovan Rossa and John Davoy [*sic*] being made the custodians of the funds subscribed. This fund amounts to over $15,000 cash, and has been in the possession of the custodians some time. Mr. Hogan has frequently urged Messrs. O'Donovan and Davoy to distribute it, but without avail, till finally a settlement was promised for Christmas night last. It was agreed that the party meet at O'Donovan Rossa's hotel in Chatham square, and that the distribution take place then and there. The gentlemen were there as agreed, and also Mr. John J. Breslin, by whom the escape was managed. Mr. Breslin put in a claim for a share of the fund, and the ex-convicts refused to allow it, answering that Breslin had been amply rewarded by his lectures, and on the escape. Breslin was persistent, and the meeting broke up without any result. Last Tuesday Mr. Hogan met Davoy and Breslin at O'Donovan's hotel. Hogan had been drinking and as the interview progressed he became exasperated and pulled from his pockets two pistols, and, placing them on the table, challenged either Davoy or Breslin to fight a duel, and was arrested at Breslin's instance." "The Fenian Benefit Fund," [New York] *World,* January 4, 1877, 7.

In response to this article, Cranston was asked to sign a statement prepared by Carroll. He did so and it was dated January 6, 1877: "From Robert Cranston to the Public—Having seen with pain and indignation the local article in the N.Y. World unjustly reflecting upon the conduct of Messrs. John Devoy, O'Donovan Rossa, and John J. Breslin, in reference to the distribution of the Fund contributed by our countrymen for the benefit of the rescued Irish Political Prisoners, I, Robert

for interment—an event which no Nationalist living near New York wanted to miss.

After much delicate negotiation I succeeded in effecting a settlement on this basis. Mr. Richardson had hired the crew for a genuine whaling voyage; the vessel had gone out of her way to take the rescued men aboard and the latter had forced the abandonment of the cruise in the North Atlantic, which would have certainly yielded several thousand dollars and enabled the agent to pay the crew in the usual way; that is, by giving them a certain proportion of the profits of the voyage. We agreed to make an average of the catch taken by a certain number of other sailing vessels sailing from New Bedford and of the prices received for the oil and to assume that the *Catalpa* had made that average. Each man's "lay," from the captain's down, was calculated at that average, and the men were paid off. When that agreement was made the ship was appraised by the same method and turned over to Mr. Richardson to make the settlement. I learned afterwards that the price realized by the sale of the ship did not come up to our calculations and that therefore Mr. Richardson, Captain Anthony and Captain Hathaway came out much worse than the financial report which is appended would make it appear.

Cranston, one of the six rescued soldiers, hasten to state, that except when enjoying the hospitality of our friends elsewhere, out of New York, Mr. Devoy has paid from the Fund all our expenses of every kind since our arrival, and in addition gave me $300, when leaving New York for Phila. That the rescued men have been entirely satisfied with the stewardship of the Fund in the hands of Messrs. Devoy, Rossa and the other gentlemen of the Reception Committee. That neither the Prisoners nor their Rescuers ever made any demand for the distribution of the money, leaving that entirely to the discretion of the Committee through whose exertions it was raised. That although it was announced that the Fund was to be distributed on Christmas no meeting was held for that purpose as the contributors, who appointed the Reception Committee, postponed the day of distribution until 14 Jan., 77 in hopes of increasing the amount. Finally, that having known Messrs. John Devoy and O'Donovan Rossa personally for over thirteen years, I wish publicly to add my testimony to their honour, honesty and unselfish patriotism and this I do, not that they require such endorsement, but to save myself and rescued comrades from the suspicion of base ingratitude to honourable and patriotic Irishmen, and especially to Mr. Devoy, without whose self-sacrificing labours, and those of his agents, I would to-day be serving out my life sentence of imprisonment in Fremantle jail, for the crime of loving and trying to serve Ireland." O'Brien and Ryan, 1, 227–28.

Carroll wrote Devoy that had Cranston not signed the statement, he (Carroll) would have moved to have the funds returned to the contributors as was being suggested by some Clan officials. O'Brien and Ryan, 1, 227–28.

Work of Raising Funds

FINANCES OF THE CATALPA

Statement of the A.P.R. Fund, from February 6, 1875, to September 5, 1877.

RECEIPTS.
Per Treasurer's report, July 15, 1875, as follows:

From District ———	$8,473.69	
From District ———	1,759.17	
From District ———	880.00	
From District ———	1,556.50	
From District ———	404.00	
From District ———	7,065.63	
From District ———	50.00	
		$20,188.99
Error in above		10.00

Per Treasurer's report, August 8, 1876, as follows:

From District ———	$516.00	
From District ———	370.25	
From District ———	200.00	
From District ———	199.60	
From District ———	500.00	
Interest	42.48	
		1,828.33
J. T. Richardson, agent for oil $3,0000 [sic], less interest		2955.83
(Report $4,794.68 and interest $43.17 equal to $4838.15, less on hand $5,399 equal to $4,784.16)		
To cash, gold received in California by J. J. Breslin		1,200.00
To cash, gold received in Sydney by J. J. Breslin		850.00
To cash, gold received from Sydney by J. J. Breslin, £384		1,920.00
To Profit of voyage, by J. T. Richardson		2,391.10
To cash allowed for Catalpa		6,000.00
To interest, per Treasurer		180.06
		$37,524.31

DISBURSEMENTS

By cost and outfit of Catalpa and advances to crew	$18,914.82
By expended through J. W. Goff	372.53
By expended through J. Devoy	289.57

Work of Raising Funds

By expenses of J. J. Breslin, as follows:		
Paid him by Goff	118.48	
Paid him by Treasurer	400.00	
Paid him by Treasurer	600.00	
Paid him by Treasurer	407.35	
Paid him by Sheares Club	1,000.00	
Expenses of Breslin besides above advances	824.95	
		3,350.78
By expenses of T. Desmond		1,000.00
By expenses of J. Reynolds		35.00
By transfer to general fund		14.65
By expense of treasurer to New Bedford		30.46
By expense, Garaghy family		69.10
By D. Duggan, account of family		35.00
By telegrams, etc., Devoy		8.50
By Thomas Brennan, per Goff		125.00
By expense of Reynolds to New Bedford		56.66
By expense of Devoy to New Bedford		29.80
By D. Duggan, per A		40.00
By Smith, per A		5.00
By John King		500.00
By J. J. Breslin		1,000.00
By J. T. Richardson, outlay		3,044.40
By J. T. Richardson, advanced to Committee, and interest		3,142.50
By H. C. Hathaway		1,000.00
By Captain Anthony		1,000.00
By S. P. Smith		200.00
By balance on hand		3,260.54
		$37,524.31
Net cost of the enterprise to the Committee		26,070.47
Less $208.25 and $4.20		212.45
		$25,858.02

Statement of the Sales of Oil and Expenses of Voyage, per J. T. Richardson's Report

RECEIPTS

1876

Jan. 1	Sale of oil to George Delano, at 30 days:		
	359 gallons dark sperm oil at $1.55		556.45
	824 gallons sperm oil at $1.60		1,318.40

Work of Raising Funds

Mar. 14	Sale to George Delano at 60 days:		
	5,158 gallons sperm oil at $1.50		7,737.00
	57 fat lamp oil at 90c		51.75
1877			
Feb. 2	Sale of 39 barrels at $1.24 per gallon, per account sales. See S.		
	Potter's report, page 1, total $11,092.56, less $9,663.60.		1,428.96
	Balance of interest, See ditto		299.65
	$11,392.21		

DISBURSEMENTS

1875			
Dec. 10	To China Mutual Insurance Co., insurance on oil landed		51.00
" "	To Hart and Akin, one barrel coal, omitted in outfit		1.15
" 31	To Bark Addison and owners bill, freight on oil		57.40
1876			
Jan. 3	To Captain Anthony, draft, gold	$700.00	
	Loss on ditto	91.00	
			791.00
	To Taber's Wharf, wharfage on oil		1.52
" 6	To Captain Anthony, draft, gold	$333.78	
	Loss on ditto	42.00	
			375.92 [sic]
	To Custom house entry oil		0.50
	To Bark General Scott for 1,207 gallons cask		72.42
Feb. 10	To power of attorney to Ellay, Boston		1.20
Mar. 4	To amount McKim's bill filling oil		2.10
	To Bark Osw. How's bill, freight and expenses		209.29
	To Deane & Co., bill, freight on oil from Boston and cartage		68.40
	To telegram to Boston, account of oil		1.92
Apl. 19	To Oriental Mutual Insurance Company, insurance on oil		188.75
	To draft, Captain Anthony, gold $300		339.00
1877			
Feb. 2	To expenses on return and in New York, with watching and		
	wharfage to date		465.39
	To Captain Anthony, share of voyage		2,165.63
	To S. P. Smith, first mate, share of voyage		1,388.66
	To balance, officers and crew		2,329.79
	To commission		490.07
	To balance, as profit		2,391.10
			$11,392.21

Work of Raising Funds

J. T. Richardson, Agent, In account with Committee
Dr.

To profit on voyage		$2,391.10
To barque Catalpa		6,000.00
		$8,391.10

Cr.

By one-eighth vessel, original outlay		$2,702.12
Interest	285.51	
Taxes	50.77	
		3,044.40
By cash	3,000.00	
Interest	142.50	
		3,142.50
By H. C. Hathaway		1,000.00
By Captain Anthony		1,000.00
By S. P. Smith		200.00
By cash paid J. Reynolds		4.20
		$8,391.10

Average of Seven Ships Which sailed in April, 1875, and Made A Basis of Average in Settlement

NAME	AGENT	TONNAGE	BARRELS
Abbott Lawrence	Lewis	160	320
Charles W. Morgan	Wing	314	375
Peru	McCullough	259	600
Pioneer	Allen & Co.	228	700
President Second	Tucker	123	700
Sarah B. Hale	Allen	183	400
Janet	Lewis	154	750
		1,421	3,845
Average		203	549

Say 550 bbls., 31 1/2 gals. each, equal to 17,325 gals., at $1.50 per gal. $25,987.50

AMOUNT PAID CAPTAIN ANTHONY:

Share of voyage as per average	$2,165.63
Gratuity for rescue	1,000.00
Total	$3,165.63

AMOUNT PAID MATE, S. P. SMITH

Share of voyage as per average	$1,443.75
Gratuity for rescue	200.00
Total	$1,643.75

Work of Raising Funds

STATEMENT OF THE AMOUNT PAID THE CREW

		LAY	PAID
George S. Anthony	one-twelfth	$879.99	$879.99
Samuel S. Smith	one-eighteenth	586.66	586.66
Antoine Farnham	one-thirteenth	308.94	528.94
George H. Bolles	one-forty-eighth	191.34	191.34
Thomas F. Knifie	one-eighty-fifth	108.05	288.05
Henry Parrott	one-one hundred and twentieth	87.99	342.99
Antoine Ferris	one-one hundred and fortieth	75.43	330.43
Mopsy Ross	one-one hundred and seventieth	54.02	216.02
Walter E. Sanford	one-one hundred and ninetieth	55.58	180.34
Cyrus S. Hall	one-one hundred and eightieth	51.02	213.02
Henry D. Paine	one-one hundred and ninetieth	55.57	142.97
John Cockin	one-one hundred and eightieth	51.02	213.02
Mike Malay	one-one hundred and eightieth	51.02	186.02
Lombard Malay	one-one hundred and eightieth	51.02	186.02
Ginggy Malay	one-one hundred and eightieth	51.02	186.02
Thomas Kanaka	one-one hundred and twentieth	76.54	256.54
Denis Duggan	one-fiftieth	211.19	211.19
Antoine Silvester		256.77	302.50
Frank Perry		6.80	142.50
Manuel Antoine		6.80	142.50
Louis Toaquin		6.80	171.00
Antoine Manuel		6.80	142.50
George Duigan		7.38	135.00
Joseph H. Dutton		7.38	135.00
		3,245.13	6,310.56
	Overpaid	3,065.43	
Total amount paid crew			$6,310.56
	Less George S. Anthony	879.99	
	Less Samuel P. Smith	586.66	
			1,466.65
			4,843.91
	Less advances		2,617.71
			$2,226.20

[EDITORS' NOTE TO FINANCIAL REPORT: The method of calculating the lay was quite simple. On the credit side of the ledger were the earnings (the lay) of the crew member. Usually this was only one entry, though

Work of Raising Funds

occasionally there might also be a monthly guarantee or a prize for spotting a whale. (With the latter, one is reminded of Captain Ahab's gold coin enticement to the crew to spot Moby Dick.) With "seasoners," crew members who were hired for short periods, the lay would likely be a small fixed amount rather than a percentage calculation.

On the debit side of the ledger was where many entries were made. Interest on any loans or advances would be entered here along with slop chest purchases—both guaranteed since crew members rarely had any cash during the voyage and relied on credit for these necessary articles. Any other miscellaneous or extraordinary expenses would be listed. For example, if the crew member deserted and was captured, the cost associated with that would be applied to his account.

The first column of figures on the above table is the calculated lay. The second column is the amount paid and in every instance except for Anthony and Smith, the amount paid exceeds the lay. Bear in mind that "amount paid" is any cash paid to the crew member and expenses incurred on his behalf. In the case of the *Catalpa,* there were costs associated with hiring replacement crew members, for instance. Those costs would have been charged to the accounts of the crew members who deserted. If crew member X received an advance of $50, made purchases of $75 from the slop chest, deserted, and the captain had to pay $75 for a replacement, Mr. X has cost the ship's owners a total of $200. This would be the "paid" amount. Even if a crew member deserted, the standard contracts of the day called for his being entitled to a prorated lay. These schedules also have some minor addition errors.]

[XII]

THE EXPEDITION WOUND UP

After Many Difficulties — John King's Narrative of His
Part in the Work — The Fenians in Australia Had a Rescue
Project of Their Own — Meeting with Breslin —
How He Ran the Quarantine

In last week's issue pressure of space made it necessary to leave out part of the *Catalpa* story, and the work of cutting it in a hurry was botched. One of the interesting things left out was a letter from James Reynolds, who had been obliged to go to New Bedford to endeavor to make a final settlement of the voyage, but was unable to do so, owing to difficulties created by some of our friends here who wanted to treat the whole matter as a huxter's[225] bargain, or the sale of a cow or a pig at a fair, instead of treating our Yankee friends as men who had rendered us a great service at considerable risk to themselves and their business.

Captain Anthony's action had made it impossible for him to enter an English port again. I had arranged with him that the *Catalpa* was to wait off shore outside the three-mile limit and the men were to be taken out in boats procured in Australia, so as to keep the Captain and ship from being made amenable to international law. When Captain Anthony got to Bunbury, however, he at once saw that no boats procurable there would be fit for the work, and that ordinary oarsmen unaccustomed to work in the open sea would be utterly unable to cope with the conditions. He therefore determined to take the men off in the vessel's whaleboats, pulled by his own men, and to take charge of the work himself, regardless of consequences as to his seafaring career. The result showed that but for this

---

225. "A person ready to make his profit of anything in a mean or petty way; one who basely barters his services, etc., for gain; a mercenary; an overreacher of others." *O.E.D.*

139

The Expedition Wound Up

decision of Captain Anthony the attempt at rescue would have been a total failure. The committee fully recognized the extent of the obligation that this bold and generous action of the captain had put us under, but we were hampered at every step, not only by the public circulation of slanders against ourselves, but of damaging statements in regard to the agent and the captain.[226]

The same men who spread these stories of improper handling of money were also busy sowing distrust of our Yankee friends without whose help we could have done nothing. They were described as a lot of sharks anxious to make money on the poor Irish, and Reynolds and I as either simpletons imposed on by shrewd Yankees or dishonest men in league with them. We wanted to deal generously with all the men who had enabled us to carry out the rescue, to make a good impression that would be of service in future enterprises. Our critics insisted on making a huxter's bargain with them and treating them as if we suspected them of a desire to cheat us. Their campaign of slander had some effect on our people and made the work of winding up the affair peculiarly difficult. Many journeys had to be made to New Bedford and our Yankee friends did not fail to see that a hostile influence was at work against them. The following letter from Reynolds will give a better idea of the situation than anything that could be written now.[227]

226. Among other items, Goff and his allies issued a circular in June 1878, charging that the Clan had been "robbed of nearly $20,000"; Richardson allegedly allowed a gross cost overrun; Anthony sold tobacco abroad at great profit; thousands of dollars in provisions were missing. O'Brien and Ryan, 1, 224.

227. The final negotiations were unfortunately full of ill feelings among the various parties, as Reynolds makes clear in this letter. Hathaway wrote Devoy less than a month after the *Catalpa*'s arrival, expressing, in a forthright manner, concern that no word had been heard from New York and wanting to know about a final settlement and disposition of the bark. Carroll wrote Devoy soon after that "those N.B. people set a high value on their services." Looking at Richardson's settlement figures, he suggested getting a good lawyer. Even Breslin was impatient about settling. In an 1877 report, the Clan committee seeking to make settlement with all *Catalpa* parties found that a valid contract existed between Richardson and the Clan, that the contract had been breached by the ship being brought directly into New York, and that therefore Richardson had a valid claim against the Clan. It further reported that negotiations with the captain and mate were difficult and the proposed settlement was "reluctantly accepted." Patrick Mahon, the ever vigilant Clan treasurer, felt the prisoners ought to contribute several thousand dollars from their rescue fund to the settlement with Richardson (the prisoners did not agree). Carroll feared that Anthony "feels we are frauds." Devoy, responding to one of Reynolds's suggestions, wrote that he couldn't go to New Bedford right then (August 1877) and that even if he could, he wouldn't! He also expresses harsh words about Richardson. No suggestions of hard feelings are found in Pease's book. He wrote that "a liberal settlement with the crew" was made. O'Brien and Ryan, 1, 204, 211, 214, 225, 232, 268, 272; Pease, *Catalpa*, 183.

140

The Expedition Wound Up

Reynolds Describes the Difficulties

Providence, at Capt. Revin's, cor.
Point and Richmond Streets

October 16, 1876.

My Dear John:—I am here after returning from New Bedford, and I hasten to inform you of my experience.

I found Richardson rather moody in spirit on account of our apparent neglect in not coming to time. After a few moments' conversation we became more familiar and went to business.

He sent for his bookkeeper in order that everything might be made as plain as possible, and I find after a thorough investigation that Mahon's figures are nowhere.

In the first place, it cost Richardson over $3,000 over their lay to settle with the men before the mast.[228] Smith, the mate, is not settled with and will not take a settlement unless it is a very profitable one to him.

Some of our New York patriots told him that his share of the work was worth $13,000, and he is falling back on that.

The next case is that Richardson does not propose to lose anything. He wants every cent he laid out and his percentage, to say the least; that is, he does not, and I think he should not be expected to suffer in any way by the acts of our dictators on board the ship by cutting off the profits of the voyage by at least one-half.

All extras must be paid by us, no matter from what source. In short, we are indebted to him $1,057, with Anthony's figures, at his actual lay on the oil taken. Smith the same and all supposed paid. Those are actual figures, and of course, this will not settle with Smith or Anthony.

This is enough to show you the condition of affairs, from a business standpoint, except that this would leave the ownership of the vessel just as it was before, 1/8 Richardson's, 7/8 the Committee, and he estimates her now as she stands at $6,000 with what provisions is [sic] left after the voyage. So, now you can see at a glance that it was not possible for me to do anything by way of settlement.

At about this time Capt. Hathaway dropped in on us and after another general chat I suggested that Richardson would meet me at some future time in New York for a final settlement. This he flatly refused to do. I tried to urge on him and Hathaway the necessity of so doing. He thought Hathaway, if any, was the man to meet my friends. Hathaway then suggested that Richardson himself and Anthony should

---

228. Originally this was where the crewmen's quarters were located: in the forecastle or forward of the mast. It also became a term to describe seamen. "Before the Mast," Kemp, 73.

The Expedition Wound Up

go. I accepted that offer and promised if they did it would not cost them a penny, but to no purpose. Richardson was immovable and continued so until I left. Hathaway, however, thinks he will be able to get him, and if so he will write to me so that I can hear from him by Wednesday. If they conclude to meet us they will bring all books and papers with them, also their bookkeeper; if not, we must do the best we can to satisfy them. If a meeting is effected, I told Hathaway that I thought I could arrange it for one week from next Saturday.

So, you see, as near as I can tell you in writing how we stand. Would like very much to have an interview with yourself, the doctor and Mahon, if possible, before we meet those men in New York, and would like, if possible, to have the meeting one week from next Sunday, in the same place; if this cannot be, we will have to go to New Bedford to settle, and Richardson says that is the place to do it—in his office.

I wish you would send this to the doctor and I will write to Mahon when I get home; if they decide on meeting us I will write to the doctor at once asking him to fix time and place.

Yours as ever,
Reynolds.

P.S.—I have written a letter more in detail to Mahon and asked him to send it to the doctor, so you need not send this.
R.

The settlement was finally made as described last week, and the small balance which remained of the fund was distributed pro rata among the branches which contributed it.

AN EXPEDITION FROM IRELAND

I shall only make brief mention of the expedition from Ireland sent to carry out the same object, and will leave to John King the telling of his meeting with the men sent out to Australia. The two men in question were Denis F. McCarthy, of Cork, now a resident of Chicago, and John Walsh, of Middleborough, England.[229]

---

229. Probably unknown to Devoy, a letter, signed by the seven Fremantle prisoners (including Keilly), dated August 3, 1875, was sent to Michael F. Murphy of Cork. Murphy, an active Fenian, knew some of the prisoners, but, more important, had a family connection to Charles Guilfoyle Doran (1835–1909), then the leader of the IRB's Supreme Council. Along with the letters sent home by Hogan, this additional appeal by the prisoners no doubt spurred the IRB into action,

The Expedition Wound Up

In consequence of letters sent by Martin Hogan to his family in Limerick, a movement had been started at home to effect a rescue, and a sum of £1,000 had been collected for the purpose, none of those connected with the raising of the money, except one, having any knowledge of the fact that we in America were engaged in the same work. That one, for personal reasons, kept his associates in ignorance of the fact, and the result was a practical demonstration of the absolute necessity for a closer union than had prevailed up to then between Nationalists at both sides of the Atlantic. The larger portion of the money was contributed by our people in the North of England, but a portion was subscribed by well-known public men. Two contributions that I heard of (my knowledge of this home movement being obtained later in America) may be specially mentioned. Joseph Ronayne,[230] later a member of Parliament, contributed £100 and Joseph Biggar[231] *lent* £50 to those in charge of the work. Biggar had probably more money than Ronayne, and the personal characteristics of the two men were well illustrated by the manner and amount of their contributions, for both were decidedly hostile to England, and in favor of rescuing the prisoners. Biggar's money, I am informed, was returned to him.[232]

---

and the two agents, McCarthy and Walsh, were dispatched in January 1876 (arriving in Fremantle in March). The prisoners' letter was thirteen pages and included strong, bitter passages, i.e., "They [the Clan] have even turned a deaf ear to our calls for assistance." Thus, even though the *Catalpa* had already sailed from New Bedford, and Breslin and Desmond were about to leave California, the prisoners were apparently still unaware of those actions and believed they had been forgotten. Walter McGrath, "The Great Catalpa Rescue of 1876, Long-hidden Records from the Valuable C. G. Doran Papers," [Part 2], [Cork] *Evening Echo,* February 17, 1977. See also Amos, 222.

230. Joseph Ronayne was a Young Irelander and an engineer who made his fortune building railroads in California. He returned to Ireland, built railroads there, and was elected member of Parliament for Cork City. O'Brien and Ryan, 1, 166.

231. Joseph Gillis Biggar (1828–1890) was a prominent nationalist politician and member for Cavan. He was a Fenian until 1877 when he was expelled, along with O'Connor Power, because of the movement's opposition to parliamentary agitation and the compulsory oath of allegiance to the crown that all members of Parliament were required to take. Connolly, 46; O'Brien and Ryan, 1, 312.

232. Devoy probably included King's report here because the IRB was dissatisfied with Breslin's report on the *Catalpa*—specifically, that more credit was not given to its two agents, Walsh and McCarthy. Breslin mentions the agents once, not by name, in his report, and omits their contribution (cutting the telegraph wire between Perth and King George's Sound) and the risk they took in remaining at Fremantle after the escape. (He may have felt it was inappropriate for him to report on the IRB activities.) In a letter dated December 12, 1876, to an unidentified person, Walsh provides his report and expresses obvious dissatisfaction with matters:

"You asked me to write some details of our late trip, and it surprises me why you should need them, when you have one at your elbow able to give you all you require of me. However, I will give the principal points.

"When we arrived we opened a safe channel of communications which the others had failed up to then in accomplishing. This was the one used after for all purposes. Without this channel Capt. A's [Anthony's] last message could not be communicated to the inside parties before 10

The Expedition Wound Up

JOHN KING'S NARRATIVE

The late John King, who formed the rear guard of the rescuing party, remaining in Fremantle to watch the police after Breslin and Desmond had started off with the men, and then galloping after them, some years ago contributed to the Passaic *Sunday Chronicle* a personal narrative of his part in the Rescue. He first sketched the events which led up to the expedition, which were fully recorded in the earlier chapters of this story, and there-

---

o'clock on Easter Monday, and even then it would rest on chance as to whether Cranston or the other man would be sent to the post office for the letters; their only mode of communication being to watch Cran. during this journey. The men were locked up at 6 o'clock in the evening, and it being after that hour on Saturday when the message came, there was no chance of seeing one of them before Monday morning at 7 a.m., and C. could not be seen before 10 a.m., and then only [by] chance, and the time of starting was 8 a.m.

"We offered ourselves, our money and materials to be placed in any position they thought proper in order to prevent the possibility of failure. The post assigned to us was the cutting of the wires to prevent communication with the warship Conflict at the sound. To remain on land in order to to [*sic*] able to succour them, in the event of any accident befalling the Catalpa that would prevent her being at the time and place appointed, in which case our friends would be obliged to take to the bush, where they would surely perish without some friendly hands to succour them. This we undertook, and after supplying them with arms of which they were deficient, and giving a small share of money to the prisoners, and managing the wires, were on the ground at the start. If a row took place we would be in it. We parted with them and if they carried out their part of the programme, as we did, they would have nothing to fear. But they did not, and if the authorities on board the Georgette had not committed another greater [blunder?] than theirs, they would have failed miserably and disastrously.

"The last words of advice we imparted to them was to allow no one to pass them coming to Fremantle, but compel them to turn back. There was two Islands close to the place of embarkation where they could be left; but exulting in a short-lived triumph which proved disastrous to the cause before to-day, they allowed the man Bell to return to town; one of them actually giving him a sovereign to take a glass and give the account. This man found one of their horses saddled ready, and rode into town just when a party of mounted and native police had returned after a fruitless search in the bush. The next step was to be a search of the shipping and the suspected houses, but Bell arrived at this juncture, and then wires were brought into requisition, but were found to be deficient and when they had repaired them and wired the Sound they found that the Conflict had cleared out for Adelaide an hour and a half previously. If this had not occurred and the Conflict was the pursuing vessel instead of the other, they would have a different story to tell, and the fault would be their own. But even the others would have them cheap but for they being also duffers. When they fell in with the ship on Tuesday morning they the fugitives, had not reached the ship, but were about 3 miles distant at the time. If they were seen at this time they were done, but they were not and here the shore blundered. The Georgette was running short of coals, and she decided to leave the Water Police, 8 in number, in their little cutter, but no sooner did the Georgette return to coal than they made tracks and reached the ship as soon as possible; the police coming just near enough to witness their going on board, returned and reported same, upon which the Georgette set out once more. But when they met her next the men were on board, and we know the rest. If the Georgette remained with the Catalpa nothing could save them, and this danger also would be the result of their own shortsightedness.

"I told those fellows those things in presence of some of their friends in New York, and it seems they were not pleased with it, but I care not the dirt of my old boot about either of them. I saw a good deal while in New York, and I tell you candidly I did not feel edified at which I saw—every

The Expedition Wound Up

fore need not be repeated here. He opens his account of the part he personally played by describing how he got to Australia and a movement started there for the rescue of the prisoners. What follows is John King's story:

It is now necessary to go back a little in order to show how I became connected with the movement for the rescue of the prisoners. After the collapse of the Fenian movement in Ireland and the seizure of the Irish People newspaper, matters became decidedly uncomfortable for me in the old country, so I decided to go to Australia and get out of harm's way and at the same time be in a position to render aid to the cause in case any further movement was decided on. I first went to Liverpool and then crossed over to Birkenhead,[233] taking ship from there to Australia. I went to Sydney, New South Wales, and engaged in the grocery business there for some time. From there I went up into the gold fields and remained there for seven years. During all of this time I was actively engaged in building up an organization among Irishmen with the idea of doing something for the release of the prisoners at Fremantle. This was the thought that was ever present in the hearts of Irishmen out there and they responded willingly to efforts on my part and contributed liberally towards a fund which was to be used for that purpose whenever the opportunity might arise.

Irish in Australia at Work

And we had a plan of rescue of our own out there. Our plan was to charter a steamer, man her with our own men, go to Fremantle, rescue the prisoners and take them to the French convict settlement at New Caledonia. We thought we would be well treated there, for only a short time previous Rochefort and three other French newspaper men who were serving a sentence for communism had

---

man there is a Colonel or a General; some of them with their shirts out through the seats of their trousers.

"I believe Rossa to be a good honest man, and many more of them; but I believe Devoy and others to be nothing but factious intriguers. And it is at the beck of such fellows you and Jack would denounce and expel a man, who with all his faults, and he is not free from some, has done more to keep the flag flying than the whole lot put together [J. W. Goff].

"I would request you to be careful to keep to the truth in any statement you may think fit to make. You said here, in reference to the others, that they went wholly unarmed. That is not true, but it is true that they were not sufficiently so.

"Awaiting your reply with address required, and wishing you all the compliments of the season." O'Brien and Ryan, 1, 221–23.

Carroll also wrote Devoy that the "friends at home take umbrage at" Breslin's report. O'Brien and Ryan, 1, 250.

233. A town opposite Liverpool on the Mersey.

145

The Expedition Wound Up

escaped from New Caledonia and came to Sydney going from there to England. We had quite an amount of money at our command and all we were waiting for was the proper time to make the attempt at rescue.

A gentleman who was connected with me in this movement was J. Edward Kelly, who had originally been sentenced to be hanged, drawn and quartered by an English judge for being concerned in the attempted Fenian uprising, a sentence which was subsequently commuted. He regained his liberty under the amnesty decree, came to Sydney and started a newspaper, with Flood[234] as a partner. When the plan of rescue was decided upon some of the released prisoners who had taken up their residence in San Francisco wrote to Breslin and told him that Kelly would be the right man to enlist in the enterprise, as he was on the ground and would be in a good position to give advice as to the proper course to be pursued. It was in this manner that I became identified with the movement, as Kelly seemed to think that my assistance would be necessary and informed Breslin to that effect.

I at once began to devote my energies to a concentration of all the funds which had been contributed by friends of the cause in the different colonies. James McInerney was the treasurer of this fund. He had a brother who was the owner of a stone quarry near Sydney, and so I came back to the city and went to work in this quarry as a laborer. This was merely a blind. I did it to avert any possible suspicion which might attach to my movements, for you didn't know who was an enemy in those days, and the success of the plan of rescue depended entirely on its being kept absolutely secret.

Meeting with Breslin and Desmond

This stone quarry was located at Petersham and we made the trip to and from the city on omnibuses. We had a half holiday in the mines on Saturday, and one afternoon in September McInerney and myself were going home from the quarry on an omnibus a little after twelve. As we passed the bus coming the other way I noticed Kelly seated on the top. There were strangers with him and he signaled for us to get down. We all left the buses and sat down in the shade of a tree by the roadside. Then Kelly introduced me to the stranger and for the first time I had the pleasure of shaking John Breslin by the hand. He was then traveling under the name of Collins and had left America in the summer of 1875 to come down and arrange all the details of the escape. We had a long talk there together and Breslin

234. John Valentine Flood was transported to Australia aboard the *Hougoumont* in 1867. He'd smuggled guns into Ireland and compatriots out and helped plan the ill-fated Chester Castle attack with McCafferty. After his conditional pardon, he remained in Australia, becoming a prominent newspaperman and supporter of Irish independence. Amos, 82–83, 280–81; Ó Broin, 174.

The Expedition Wound Up

seemed very much surprised that we had been active and had a plan of escape under consideration. He showed us that his plan was the very best and urged upon us strongly the necessity of absolute secrecy. Desmond was with him. He was known as Mr. Johnston. Breslin was supposed to be looking for an opening in the country to settle there. Outwardly they were utter strangers to each other.

After learning all the details of their plan Kelly and myself decided that we would co-operate with them. McInerney placed all the money in his possession at their disposal, simply telling that it was urgently needed and that it would be used in a good cause. The people who gave this money asked no questions; they had the utmost confidence in the statement which had been made and they left the matter absolutely in our hands. A large portion of this money was scattered throughout New Zealand.

Shortly afterwards Breslin and Desmond left separately for Fremantle, as the arrival of the Catalpa was expected before long. It was decided that I was to follow in February and bring the money which was to be gathered together in the meantime. It was here that another friend of the cause rendered good service. I will not give you his name, for the reason that he is still living in Sydney, and the fact of his connection with the escape has never become known, and it might do him an injury to have it known even at this late date. The English government never forgets those little things. This friend made a trip through New Zealand, and when he returned he had the money, between $6,000 and $7,000. This and what we collected in the colonies was turned over to me to take to Breslin at Fremantle. It was all in gold and made quite a load. I packed it in a portmanteau and left Sydney in February for Melbourne. I traveled under my own name, for there were many people who knew me who were taking the same trip, although they had no idea of my mission. After my arrival in Melbourne I assumed the name of Jones. I had a sister living there, but not even to her did I confide the secret of my destination, although she was very anxious to find out what brought me to Western Australia.

Started for Western Australia

From Melbourne I took the P. and O. mail steamer China. This boat stops at Albany, the southwestern point of Australia, to receive and leave mail from other points, and that was my destination, for there I could connect with the steamer which came from Fremantle and which made only one trip a month. Another mail steamer from the opposite direction also met the Fremantle boat at Albany. When I left Melbourne the measles were epidemic there and when we reached Albany the passengers found themselves in a fix, for we were all quarantined. This meant a

147

The Expedition Wound Up

great deal to me, for my time was short and I knew that everything depended on my making that Fremantle steamer and getting down to Breslin with the money.

When the other mail steamer from Western Australia came into Albany it was found that there was a case of smallpox on board and the passengers on that boat were also quarantined. We were taken from the steamers that day and sent to Rabbit Island. Here tents were put up for our accommodation. In answer to all inquiries the authorities in charge of the quarantine station said they didn't know how long we would have to stay there. That was a nice outlook, for me especially. Then came the word that all our luggage would have to be fumigated as a precautionary measure. Here again I was in a dilemma. My luggage consisted of the bag in which I had the gold, and I was not overanxious that it should fall into the hands of the authorities, for I had already decided in my own mind that some desperate measure was necessary if I proposed to continue my trip down to Fremantle on the steamer which was scheduled to leave the next day.

To add to my troubles while in quarantine I received a dispatch from Breslin urging haste and saying that everything depended on my getting there in time. When they started to pick up the luggage to fumigate it I threw my portmanteau under a bush, and when questioned concerning my baggage I said that it had already been gathered up. When they returned with the load after fumigation I produced my beloved bag after the luggage had been distributed and in this way kept it in my possession. I must confess that I was willing at that time to have the entire population of Australia stricken down with measles, provided I could catch that Fremantle boat in time.

In the meantime the man who had the smallpox had been taken from the western steamer and made as comfortable as possible in a small boat which was anchored about one hundred yards from the shore. There were no accommodations whatever on the island, and it would not do to expose the passengers in quarantine to the contagion. Matters certainly began to look very dark for me, as it seemed certain that we would all be kept on Rabbit Island for several days at least. There was an awful lot of kicking among the passengers, especially among those who were bound for the west, as to miss the Fremantle boat meant that they would have to wait a month before they could go on. What this delay meant to me you can easily imagine, especially after the receipt of the telegram from Breslin.

Fell in with the Other Men

While I was strolling around Rabbit Island that afternoon, trying to figure out some plan by which I could get away, I fell in with two men who had come in on the mail steamer from the west. I knew by the countenance of one that he was a com-

The Expedition Wound Up

patriot, but the other one puzzled me. He might have been of any nationality—it would depend altogether where you happened to meet him. These men rather seemed to shun the society of the other passengers and I found myself wondering who they were and what they were doing there. The notion came into my mind that they were down in that country on the same mission as myself, and in the course of conversation I had with them I tried to verify my suspicions by what I considered some clever questioning, but it was a case of love's labor lost, for I could learn nothing about them. I took a mental photograph of their faces, though, although I didn't know at the time that I was destined to meet them later under different circumstances.

My one desire now was to devise some scheme by which I could get away from Rabbit Island in time to catch the Fremantle boat. I circulated freely among my fellow-passengers and represented to them that it was all nonsense holding us there simply because they had the measles in Melbourne. This plan worked pretty well among the passengers of the China, and we finally decided that we couldn't stand it and would take our chances in jumping quarantine, quite a serious offense. We put our heads together and formulated a plan of escape. I had found that there was a whale boat on the beach of the island and we decided that we would all come down to the beach that night, take the boat and row across the bay to the jetty where the Fremantle boat lay.

It was ten o'clock that night when we made our way to the beach. The others were there, but at the last moment they all flunked but myself and two others. We tried to get the balance to go with us, but they were afraid to take the chances of the penalty which could be inflicted for jumping quarantine. The pier where the steamer lay was about four miles across King George's sound, as it was called, and two of us had to pull the heavy boat the entire distance, as the other man didn't know how to row. To make matters worse we had to go some distance out of our course to avoid the police patrol boat, which was watching quarantine. It was shortly after ten o'clock when we left the island and it was twelve when we reached the steamer. One of my companions knew the captain of the boat, so that we had no difficulty in getting on board. After I had turned in I overheard a conversation which interested me a good deal. It was the superintendent of police discussing our escape from quarantine, as he seemed particularly anxious to find out all he could about Jones. He said that he would see that we were all brought back from Champion Bay and made to suffer the penalty of law, but as my destination was this side of that port, I lost all interest in the conversation, rolled over and went to sleep.

[XIII]

JOHN KING CONTINUES HIS NARRATIVE
of His Personal Part in the Enterprise—Meeting with the Two Men Sent From the Other Side of the Atlantic on the Same Errand—The Two Parties Arrange to Cooperate

The steamer, which was the Georgette, sailed early the next morning and by Sunday I was in Fremantle, met Breslin and gave him the money, which was a godsend just at that time, the way things had turned out. Breslin told me that he needed my assistance in arranging the final details of the rescue and asked me to remain in Fremantle. A few days later he confided to me the fact that he was worried about the appearance of two men in Fremantle who had come in a sailing vessel from Albany. He said that he was afraid they were spies sent out by the English government, as he had learned from the prisoners that two men were expected from England to take an active part in a plan of rescue which had been formulated by patriotic Irishmen over there. Breslin was suspicious that these were the two men in question, and he was afraid of them, because if the government had gained any inkling of what was going on that would be just what they would do in order to get hold of the ringleaders—send out a couple of spies in the guise of friends to assist in the escape. You must remember that there were fifteen thousand men on the other side of the ocean who knew what we were in Australia for, and the fact that not the slightest knowledge of the movement ever came to the ears of the English government speaks volumes for the patriotism of the men who held the secret.

Still Breslin was anxious. He said he had been advised that these two men were Dennis F. McCarthy, of Cork, and John Walsh, of Durham, England, and that they were all right, but he hesitated to take any chances. Then I told him that I would find out about these two men. I told Breslin about meeting the two strangers on Rabbit Island and said that I felt positive that they were McCarthy and Walsh. I represented to Breslin that it would be better if these men should turn out to be spies that I should be made the scapegoat, in order that the other leaders in the plan of escape might remain free. I said that I would make myself known to these men as the head of the enterprise, and if they turned out false the most they could do with me would be to throw me into prison. Breslin finally consented to this plan.

With this object in view I started out in the evening to meet these men. Fremantle is a small city, nearly all of the inhabitants being convicts—ticket-of-leave men, as they call them. There are few free men there. These convicts all remain under prison discipline, and when the curfew bell rings at ten minutes of nine they are all obliged to be in their houses for the night. This leaves the streets comparatively deserted after this hour. I was strolling up the principal street when I met McCarthy. He was traveling under the name of Dixon, and I at once recognized him as one of the men I had seen in quarantine on Rabbit Island. I spoke to him and called his attention to the fact that we had met only a short time before and stated the circumstances. He did not remember me at first, or at least he pretended not to. We strolled along talking on various subjects until we reached the outskirts of the city.

Put the Question Bluntly

Then I turned to my companion and asked him bluntly what he was doing there. He seemed surprised at my manner of asking the question and finally told me that he had an uncle in Champion Bay and that he was going down there in a few days to engage with him in the business of sheep raising. I let this go for a minute and then I told him flatly that I knew all about his plans and just what he was in Australia for. He seemed thunderstruck and said that I must be dreaming. He tried to make me believe that I had been misinformed, but I insisted and finally told him all his proposed plan, the details of which I had learned from Breslin. I told him furthermore that I was heartily in sympathy with the movement and that I was prepared to give material aid in his enterprise if he could convince me that he was all right. I told him that I was in a position to do him a lot of good in an understanding of that kind. He hesitated and finally said he would meet me on the beach in a half hour and give me his decision.

I felt that he wanted to have a chance to confer with Walsh about the matter, and even then I had not made up my mind whether they would return as friends or come with a posse of police at their back to take me into custody. If it turned out to be the latter I would have been perfectly satisfied, for my arrest would have kept suspicion from Breslin and Desmond and left them free to go on with the good work.

So I went back to the hotel and told Breslin what I had done. He approved of my

John King Continues His Narrative

course and told me to use my own judgment as to whether these men were to be admitted to our confidence. Then I went back to the beach and met McCarthy at the appointed time. He said that he had decided to accept my offer of assistance in his plans, and to prove his sincerity he showed me papers which proved conclusively to my mind that he was all right and was really acting as an agent for Irishmen in England and the old country in a plan of escape for the Irish prisoners in Fremantle. It is certainly remarkable when you come to think of it, how three different bodies of men in widely separated portions of the globe were all working along virtually the same plans for the release of their countrymen, and all of them, too, going right ahead without a knowledge of any other movement, meeting at the same point at about the same time. After McCarthy had shown me his credentials and convinced me that he was all right, I took him down to the hotel and introduced him to Breslin.

There we talked matters over. McCarthy stated his plans, which were somewhat similar to ours, but when he found that we had all arrangements perfected he at once volunteered the services of himself and Walsh. They also insisted on turning over a large sum of money, about $5,000, which they had in their possession and which had been contributed by friends to aid in the proposed escape. We declined their money but took their revolvers. Their offer of assistance was accepted and to them was given the task of cutting the telegraph wires on the day of escape. This was all there was for them to do, as every other contingency had been provided for and there was a constant danger in the presence in Fremantle of so many strangers. In the events which followed the escape they played their part well. They were overhauled by the police after we had got away with the prisoners, but they succeeded in convincing the authorities that they knew nothing of our movements and had no part in the enterprise, so they could not be held and subsequently went on to Sydney, where they took a steamer for San Francisco.

It was only a few days after this incident, on March 29th, that the arrival of the bark Catalpa in Bunbury the day before was posted on the bulletin board in Fremantle. This was good news to us and Breslin immediately telegraphed to Captain Anthony.

"Any news from New Bedford? When can you come to Fremantle?"

That same afternoon Breslin received this reply:

"No news from New Bedford. Shall not come to Fremantle."

Trouble with the Crew

Upon receipt of this message Breslin decided to go to Bunbury at once and see the captain. He left the next morning and upon his arrival put up at the hotel where

John King Continues His Narrative

the captain was staying. He made the acquaintance of the captain in a natural course as a stranger and was invited on board the Catalpa. This was done in order that they might discuss all of the details without any chance of interruption. Breslin told Captain Anthony what we wanted to do with the ship and the latter said he was ready and willing to do everything in his power.

Captain Anthony had a great deal of trouble with his crew at the time of his arrival in Bunbury. The men on the whaler thought it was queer that no attempt was being made to pick up any whales, and as they were in ignorance of the true mission of the ship they became discontented. This feeling culminated upon the arrival of the bark in Bunbury, when four of the crew stole one of the boats, put off in the night and tried to make their escape through the bush. They were soon captured, however, and three of them were brought back to the ship and put in irons. The ringleader of the movement was locked up in the Bunbury jail.

After Breslin had laid all the plans before Captain Anthony it was decided that it would be best for the latter to make a trip along the coast in order to see how the land lay and to get his bearings, so that there could be no possibility of any hitch in the arrangements on the day of the escape. We had decided beforehand that the best place for the boat to land from the whaler would be at Rockingham, a point on the coast about twenty-two miles from Fremantle. It was toward the south and at the head of the sound, with a narrow passage at the head of Garden Island leading out to sea. The plan was to have the Catalpa stand ten or twelve miles out to sea behind Garden Island, while the boat was ashore after our party. She was to cruise around until our arrival, and we figured that we could easily pull out to her in four or five hours. For this reason it was necessary that Captain Anthony should get a good idea of the coast around Rockingham.

In order to accomplish this Breslin and the captain took passage for Fremantle on the Georgette, which left the next day. Captain Anthony as a fellow sailor soon scraped up an acquaintance with the captain of the steamer, and seeing his new friend so eager in the pursuit of knowledge regarding the points of interest concerning the coast, the Englishman went into details and told Captain Anthony everything which he desired to know regarding channels, currents, soundings, etc.

While Breslin and the captain were together it was decided that the attempt to escape would be made on the morning of Thursday, April 6th. This would give the captain time to get back from Fremantle and take his ship to the rendezvous at Rockingham and send a boat ashore to meet our party. But when the Georgette arrived in Fremantle Breslin found a very disagreeable surprise awaiting him. This was nothing less than the presence in the harbor of the British gunboat Conflict carrying two guns and thirty men. She was schooner rigged and a fast sailer, and as

John King Continues His Narrative

the Catalpa was slow unless there was a heavy wind it would have been folly to have attempted the escape with such a dangerous factor against success lying in the harbor ready to start in pursuit at a moment's notice.

Upon this Breslin decided that the escape could not come off on Thursday morning as planned. It was too risky. We found out that the gunboat was in Fremantle on her annual visit of inspection and that she would remain in port for eight or nine days. To make matters worse we also learned that another gunboat was due to arrive about the time of the departure of the Conflict. This latter vessel was coming to take Governor Robinson on a visit to the northwest.

In the face of this dilemma it was deemed the best plan to have Captain Anthony lay up his bark and begin some extensive repairs in order to avert suspicion on account of her long stay in these waters. Breslin told him to overhaul his vessel and paint her, and to be in no hurry in getting his wood and water on board, as it would be absolutely necessary to defer the escape until after the gunboats had sailed away. In the meantime we drove the captain out to Rockingham and marked the place where the boat was to land with some stakes.

Captain Anthony left Fremantle for Bunbury on Thursday, April 6th. Before his departure a system of telegrams was arranged between him and Breslin by means of which the captain was to know just what to do. When the gunboat sailed Breslin was to telegraph:

"Your friend (N. or S., meaning north or south) has gone home. When do you sail?"

This really meant that the gunboat had sailed north or south, that everything was all right and that the Catalpa was to sail at once.

In case the gunboat to take the governor to the northwest should arrive, the telegram was to be:

"Jones is going overland to Champion Bay. When do you clear out of Bunbury?"

And when the coast would be clear and everything all right again, the telegram was to be:

"Jones has gone to Champion Bay; did not receive a letter from you."

The gunboat Conflict remained in the harbor until Tuesday, April 11th, and on that day she sailed for Sydney. Breslin at ten o'clock in the morning sent the telegram agreed upon to Captain Anthony, and Wednesday received the following reply:

"Received your telegram, I sail today. Good-bye. Answer if received."

We had supposed that Captain Anthony would be ready to sail on Tuesday immediately upon the receipt of the telegram and we had fixed upon Thursday as the day for the escape, but when his answer did not come until Wednesday, that meant that it would have to be deferred until the following day, which would be Friday. As

154

John King Continues His Narrative

it happened to be Good Friday and was therefore a government holiday, such a thing was not to be thought of, as the chances of detection would be too great. Breslin thereupon telegraphed Captain Anthony:

"Your telegram received. Friday being Good Friday, I shall remain in Fremantle and start for York on Saturday morning. I wish you may strike oil. Answer if received." That same evening an answer was received from the captain as follows:

"Yours received. Did not start to-day. Wind ahead and raining. Sail in the morning. Good-bye."

The receipt of this telegram from Captain Anthony fixed the start for Saturday morning. We made all arrangements and Breslin, who had previously arranged with Wilson as to the nature of the signal which was to be given when we were ready, wrote a letter to him on Friday morning, giving all the needed instructions and concluding with the words so characteristic of the man: "We have money, arms and clothes; let no man's heart fail him, for this chance can never occur again." On Friday evening Desmond arrived from Perth with a good pair of horses and a four-wheeled wagon. Breslin had also secured a good team, and that night both he and Desmond were out with their teams to see that they acted all right. On his return from his drive Breslin found the following telegram from Captain Anthony awaiting him at his hotel:

"It has blown heavy. Ship dragged both anchors. Can you advance more money if needed? Will telegraph again in the morning."

This news made us feel as if fate were indeed against us, for it indicated that the ship had been caught in a gale, had dragged both anchors and gone on the bar, which would mean another delay of several weeks, until she could be made ready for sea again. By a fortunate chance Cranston was down from the prison with a message to town that evening so Breslin showed him the telegram and told him to notify the others of the delay. Desmond went back to Perth and we prepared to wait patiently for further news from Captain Anthony.

Word came from him a good deal sooner than we expected, for the next morning about half-past ten Breslin received a dispatch from the captain which read:

"I shall certainly sail to-day. Suppose you will leave for York Monday morning. Good-bye."

This news was most welcome and we began to get things in readiness once more. I rode over to Perth and told Desmond to get his team and come to Fremantle on Sunday evening, as we proposed to make the attempt next morning. On Saturday afternoon Breslin walked down to the jetty where Wilson was working and when sure that no one was looking gave him the signal which meant "We start to-morrow morning." He overlooked the fact for a moment that the next day would be Sunday, and seeing that Wilson was puzzled over the same thing managed to get

155

John King Continues His Narrative

near enough to him to say, "Monday morning," without being observed by the warden or any of the prisoners.

The next day was Easter Sunday, and as matters turned out it was a fortunate thing that the day of the escape fell on Easter Monday, which was a holiday, as the majority of the officials were going to Perth to see the regatta on that day. This same fact, however, came near upsetting all our plans, for we found a great deal of difficulty in securing horses for that day, as they had been engaged previously for the use of the officials. Breslin managed to secure a good team, but when Desmond came over from Perth in the afternoon he had a sorry-looking pair of nags. As I was to ride horseback I had secured a good horse some time before and was well mounted.

The distance from Fremantle to Rockingham, then to the point on the coast where we were to meet the whaleboat from the Catalpa, was a little over twenty miles. The first ten miles was a fairly good road for western Australia. The six miles from the Ten Mile Well to the Rockingham Hotel was not so good, being heavy and cut up with sand patches; the four miles from the hotel to the beach was very bad, being nothing but a mere path through the bush. An idea of how we traveled it on that Easter Monday morning may be gained, however, when it is known that we made the entire distance in two hours and twenty minutes.

The culminating point of the anxiety of several months had now been reached and we were all eager for the last desperate venture on the morrow, which we hoped would restore to liberty six of our fellow-countrymen, who were serving out their lives in an English prison. I don't believe there is a man alive to-day who had anything to do with that escape who will ever be able to forget the terrible anxiety of that Easter Sunday and Monday. We were all fully alive to the desperate chances we were taking and the possibility that all our plans would be frustrated at the last moment by the vigilance of the prison authorities, and yet somehow we felt confident of success from the fact that the boldness and daring of the escape was its best protection against discovery.

You may be sure that we did not get a great deal of sleep that Sunday night. We were all in a state of nervousness for fear that something unforeseen would turn up at the last moment. We were all awake and stirring at six o'clock and Thomas Brennan, who had arrived from New York some time before to assist in the escape, was sent on to Rockingham. I got my horse and Breslin and Desmond brought their teams. The rifles and citizens' clothing for the prisoners were placed in the traps, and at half-past seven Desmond left the city by a side street. He was to go out a short distance and then turn into the road to Rockingham, where he was to wait the arrival of Breslin, who drove out High street, as if going to Perth. When he reached the prison he turned into the same road and a short distance further on met Des-

John King Continues His Narrative

mond, where the clothing and the rifles were divided, three of each being put in the two traps.

The convicts were to assemble for parade about eight o'clock and Breslin had arranged that the two traps would be within five minutes' run of the prison at that hour and would wait until nine o'clock. To me had been assigned the position of rear guard. Being on horseback, I was to remain behind in Fremantle for a reasonable time, so as to be in readiness to give the alarm in case the attempt was discovered and any move was made from that direction. After Breslin and Desmond had left I lounged around the hotel, with seemingly nothing more on my mind than the discovery of a pleasant way to spend the holiday, but it is easy to imagine what my true feelings were. As I was passing through the dining—room of the hotel after breakfast I noticed a large loaf of cake on the table. Not knowing what arrangements had been made about provisions, I thought perhaps it might come in handy, so I gathered it in and tied it beneath my coat.

It was after eight o'clock when I mounted my horse and left the hotel. Everything was quiet in the city and I felt that the men had been successful in getting away. After I had passed the prison I turned into the Rockingham road and a short distance further on I came upon Breslin with the team. Darragh, Hogan and Hassett were with him, Wilson, Cranston and Harrington having gone on in Desmond's trap a moment before. There was no time for more than a hasty word of congratulation and greeting, for Breslin was having trouble with his team. They were a little balky and he could not get them to turn around in the narrow road. Darragh took one by the bit and tried to get him to start, but he kicked and struggled so that there was danger of breaking the harness. I then rode on in front of the team, and encouraged by my horse they made a start and when he reached a wider portion of the road Breslin had no difficulty in turning them around. Then he went back and got the three men. All of this consumed several minutes at a time when every second was precious, as we expected that the escape would be discovered every instant and an alarm given, and we still had a long distance to go before we could feel that we were safe. When Breslin finally started he told me to remain about five miles in the rear and in the event of pursuit to overtake the others and give warning of the approach of the police and officials. Breslin was to push rapidly ahead and overtake Desmond, which he did in about half an hour, on account of the superiority of his horses. I remained behind on the alert for any pursuing party until within three miles of the point on the beach where we were to embark. When I reached this point I could see five miles behind me. There was no sign of any pursuit, so I rode rapidly forward and overtook the others and told Breslin that it would be a good idea for me to ride on ahead through the bush and see if everything was clear on the beach, as there was no immediate danger of a pursuit from

157

John King Continues His Narrative

the rear. He said it was a good plan and so I rode on ahead. When I reached the beach I found the whaleboat and Captain Anthony and his men waiting. I told him of our good fortune in getting away with the prisoners and said they would be at the beach in a short time. Then I rode back to Breslin and Desmond and told them that everything was all right.

[XIV]

Conclusion of John King's Narrative

of His Share in the Splendid Work — The Severe Ordeal in the Open Boat and the Race for the Ship Facing British Guns — Safe in the Land of the Free

It was half-past ten when we all reached the beach. There were sixteen of us including the captain's party, and there wasn't any room to spare when we were all stowed away in the boat. We had to crowd ourselves into as small a space as possible so as not to interfere with the work of the men at the oars. These fellows were Malays and Kanakas,[235] and they were pretty badly rattled at the sudden appearance of our party out of the bush, especially as we were all armed with rifles and seemed very much in a hurry to get away. For this reason they did not fall into their stroke at once and the boat acted badly, but under the encouraging voice of their steersman they soon rallied and it was not long before we were moving rapidly out to sea under the impetus of their long and powerful strokes.

After we had got about two miles out to sea our spirits began to rise and we felt for the first time as if the escape which had cost us so much anxiety was really a success at last. Breslin felt so good over it that he could not refrain from a little bit of sarcasm at the expense of the officers. The wind and tide were both setting in shore, so he took a piece of wood and set it afloat, bearing the following characteristic note:

[Here followed the letter to the Governor already given in Breslin's report.]

---

235. "A native of the South Sea Islands." *O.E.D.* "They are called by the whites, all over the Pacific ocean, 'Kanákas,' from a word in their own language which they apply to themselves. . . . This name . . . they answer to, both collectively and individually. . . . Their proper names, in their own language, being difficult to pronounce and remember, they are called by any names which the captains or crew may choose to give them." Dana, 143. (This practice seems to have applied to others, including Malays.)

Conclusion of John King's Narrative

Our joy proved to be short-lived, however, for when we were a little over two miles from the shore we saw some of the mounted police of Fremantle ride up to the point where we had embarked. They were just a little too late, however, and all there was for them to do was to take the horses and traps we had used in our flight and drive them to Rockingham jetty. There was a glass in the boat and through it we could watch the movements of the police quite plainly.

At half-past twelve we were clear of the reefs seaward of Garden island, and hoisting the sail we stood away to the southeast in search of the Catalpa, which Captain Anthony said was cruising off somewhere in that direction. We held on this course until four o'clock in the afternoon, and then seeing no sign of the ship we took in the sail and stood off to the westward. We rowed in that direction until half-past five, when Toby, one of the crew, sighted the ship about fifteen miles ahead of us. We then exerted every effort to get as near to her as possible before dark, and by half-past six we had gained on her so that we could see her topsails quite plainly when our boat was on the crest of a wave. Then we made sail on the boat once more.

Through a Dark and Squally Night

About this time it began to grow dark and the weather became squally. Sixteen people was a big load for our boat and we began to take in water freely as the sea began to rise. The squalls were accompanied by rain and we all got a soaking. The wind kept rising, but we were going ahead at a great rate under sail, every man of us perched on the weather gunwale of the boat as she heeled over under the strong breeze. We were rapidly picking up the ship and our hearts were beating high with hope when we had another stroke of hard luck. Our boat had been bowling gallantly along with the lee scuppers awash, when there was a sharp crash and our mast went by the board, breaking short off at the base. It was growing dark rapidly and by the time we had the wreckage cleared up and the sail stowed away, it had become so dark that we could no longer see the Catalpa. We again took to the oars and pulled in the direction in which the ship had been sailing, hoping that she had seen us and would lie to and that we would be able to find her lights. We pulled until about ten o'clock without success, and then we rigged up a jury mast out of an oar and put the jib on it, which gave us a little better headway. By this time there was an ugly sea running and the weather threatened every moment to become worse. Those who were not at the oars were kept busy in bailing out the boat, as we were shipping water very fast, and we knew in the event of the weather becoming much worse we would surely be swamped.

Toward morning, however, the weather moderated considerably, and this dan-

Conclusion of John King's Narrative

ger was over. Shortly before seven o'clock we raised the ship and at once steered our course to intercept her. She was coming diagonally towards us and her lower sails were plainly visible. We all thought our troubles were over at last, when on looking around we saw the smoke of a steamer and that she was overhauling us rapidly. She was coming along at a great rate and with the aid of a glass we were soon able to make her out as the Georgette. She was evidently in a hurry, as she had all her sails set. It was her day for sailing to Albany with the mails, and we thought she was bound on her regular trip, but in a short time decided that she was too far out of her course for that. After watching her for a few moments we saw that she was bound straight for the Catalpa, which she must have sighted before we did. We were now virtually between the Georgette and the Catalpa and the men at the oars strained every nerve in an effort to reach the bark first. We soon found that the steamer was coming too fast for us and that she would overtake us long before we could reach the Catalpa.

In the Trough of the Sea

The Georgette, the Catalpa and our small boats were now in a triangular position, with the bark at the apex. We saw that we could not make the Catalpa and saw also that the direction in which the steamer was coming would bring her where she could see us plainly if we kept the sail up, so it was lowered and stowed away in the boat and the men took to the oars. The danger of discovery increasing, we soon stopped rowing. While we were lying to the steamer passed without seeing our boat, which was in the trough of the sea most of the time. She was steering direct for the Catalpa, which was now about five miles distant. As soon as the steamer had got far enough ahead, we pulled on in her wake, judging that to be the safest position if she was in search of us. This course also brought us nearer to the ship. Then we saw the Georgette run alongside the Catalpa and after remaining there about ten minutes steam slowly away. The ship held on her course and for a time the steamer kept on in the same direction, but finally sheered off and kept going more and more in the shore. We thought at first that she was shaping her course for Bunbury.

It was now about half past eight in the morning and we made all sail we could and put out every oar and paddle in an effort to overtake the ship. The ship kept going toward the southeast, the steamer in the opposite direction, and both vessels kept increasing their distance from our boat. We kept a close watch on both vessels, and after about three hours we noticed that the Georgette was sailing altogether too close in shore to be on her course for Bunbury. In fact, she turned around a short time afterward and came in our direction, pretty close in short, so

Conclusion of John King's Narrative

that it was plain to all that she was in search of our boat. We were now almost directly in the steamer's course, and if she held out to sea a little more our discovery and capture were certain. In a desperate frame of mind we still continued on in the direction in which the Catalpa was sailing, although she was fast receding from our sight. In view of our past experience she seemed as elusive as the Flying Dutchman, and the boys began to call her the phantom ship.

The Georgette now began to get dangerously close to our boat, so we took down the temporary mast and sail and relied on our oars and paddles. The steamer still continued to come closer and we had abandoned all hope of escape, as it seemed impossible that she could pass us unseen. We took in the oars and all got down in the boat as low as possible. About half-past twelve the steamer passed us, and the fact that we escaped unseen seemed like a special dispensation of providence, for the steamer was so close that we could easily distinguish the men on her decks, while it seemed as if the man on the lookout at the masthead was looking right down into our boat. Even after she had passed we expected every minute to see her turn around and come back to pick us up, but when we found that she continued on her course, we realized that our good fortune had not deserted us.

As soon as the hull of the Georgette dropped below the horizon we got out our sail and made all haste after the Catalpa, and it was not long before we saw her turn around and sail in our direction. It was now about two o'clock and a man was stationed in the bow of the boat with a blue flag to attract the attention of the lookout on the Catalpa. We soon felt certain that we had been seen, for the bark was coming right towards us, although she was edging in shore all the time, as if to screen us from view to landward.

Got Safely Aboard

A few moments later, however, we saw something that again gave us cause for uneasiness. A small boat with all sail set was coming out from the shore toward the Catalpa, and we soon made her out as the police cutter. It now became an exciting race as to which boat would reach the bark first. We had a slight advantage in the wind, and inside of an hour we had come up with the bark on the weather side. There was not an instant to lose, for the cutter was within hailing distance on the lee side. It did not take us long to get on board. As soon as Breslin reached the deck First Mate Smith asked him what to do. Our leader answered:

"Hoist the stars and stripes and stand out to sea."

Never was a manœuver executed quicker or in a more seamanlike manner. Inside of two minutes the emblem of liberty was flying at the peak, the boat had been hoisted aboard, the ship wore round and we were standing out to sea. As we

Conclusion of John King's Narrative

gained headway the captain of police in the cutter saw that he had lost the race. As she dropped behind Breslin stepped to the rail and kissed his hand to the police in token of farewell, and the chief official must have been a good natured man, for he cried out cheerily, "Goodby, captain, goodby."

Then the prisoners felt that they were free at last and they gathered around Breslin and fell on the deck and kissed his feet in token of their gratitude. We were all overwhelmed with thanks and it certainly was a relief to have the long period of nervous strain and tension come to an end. Twenty-eight hours in an open boat, cramped for want of space, with rain and seawater in abundance, was not greatly conductive to personal comfort. Aside from this there was the terrible uncertainty as to whether we would gain freedom or the chain gang. Dry clothes, a glass of New England rum and some hot coffee made us feel all right, and after a hearty supper we walked around the deck, enjoying what we thought was our last glimpse of the shores of Western Australia.

We all went to bed about nine o'clock, for we were greatly in need of rest. During the night the wind, which was light, had shifted a few points, and when we came on deck in the morning we found that the Catalpa was holding a course which would bring her past Fremantle outside of Rottnest island. About half an hour later a sail was reported on the lee bow. It looked like a small coasting vessel, but the first mate quickly pronounced her to be the Georgette. As the daylight advanced we saw that he was right. She was standing directly across our course and was evidently in search of us. About six o'clock we passed her. She was lying to about half a mile to the windward and we saw that she had a vice admiral's flag flying. She turned and followed us after we had passed, but the breeze freshening, we began to drop her astern. The Georgette fired up, however, and came after us, gaining on us rapidly, for the wind soon died away. At eight o'clock the steamer was so close to us that we could see that she had guns, and an artillery force and the water police on board, with their cutter hanging on the davits, ready to be used in boarding.

Ready for a Desperate Fight

Our situation now seemed to be very desperate, for the officials seemed determined upon our capture. There was not a man on the deck of the Catalpa save the lookout and the man at the wheel. We were all in the cabin when Breslin came down and explained the situation. He said that the men on the Georgette had evidently determined to take us back and that they had the advantage of us in every way and would probably succeed. He said that while a prison awaited the men who had been instrumental in helping the prisoners to escape, if any life was lost in an attempt to recapture them, the men who had already been in prison would be

163

Conclusion of John King's Narrative

hanged. He said it was only a question in their case of dying then and there or dying later in prison, and asked them which course they preferred. They answered that they would do whatever he said, so it was determined that he would hold out to the last and sell our lives as dearly as possible. We were all armed with rifles and revolvers and resolved not to be taken alive.

A few moments later the Georgette steamed ahead and fired a round shot across our bows. Breslin and myself were crouching in the companionway, where we could hear all that was going on deck without being seen ourselves. As soon as the Georgette came within hailing distance, her captain shouted through a trumpet:

"Bark ahoy! Heave to!" To which Captain Anthony replied: "What for?"

"You have six crown prisoners on board," then came from the steamer, to which our captain replied, "I have no prisoners here."

"May I come on board?" was the next question from the Georgette, and Captain Anthony quickly settled all doubt upon that point by answering emphatically, "No, sir."

"I see the prisoners on the deck," then came from the steamer, and Captain Anthony ordered his crew to stand up, to show that the prisoners were not there.

Colonel Harvest,[236] the English officer who was in command of the troops, then took up the argument and tried his hand at a little game of bluff. "You are amenable to British laws," he shouted. "Heave to, or I'll blow your masts out!"

"I know no British laws," replied Captain Anthony. "I am sailing under the American flag and am on the high seas; if you fire on my ship you fire on the American flag and must take the consequence."

The threat to fire on the American flag aroused the ire of Mate Smith and he damned Colonel Harvest in good round nautical terms, saying, "We'll sink under that flag before we'll give up."

"I have telegraphed to your government and I find that you are amenable to me," shouted Captain Harvest.

I knew this was a pure bluff, for it was impossible for him to get word in that time to the cable station at Adelaide. I told Breslin so, and he communicated the fact to Captain Anthony, who replied:

"I am bound for sea; I am very sorry, but I really cannot wait."

Anthony Called his Bluff

Then Colonel Harvest got mad because his bluff don't go, so he shouted back: "I'll give you fifteen minutes to surrender. May I come on board, sir?"

---

236. King confuses Harvest probably with Finnerty or Stone (Breslin made the same mistake). Harvest was not on the *Georgette*.

164

Conclusion of John King's Narrative

"No, sir;" said Captain Anthony, so decidedly as not to be mistaken.

In the meantime Mate Smith and the men below had everything in readiness to give the soldiers and police a warm reception in case they should make any attempt to board the Catalpa. The mate secured some short pieces of heavy logs, and these were placed so they could be thrown to sink any boat coming alongside; the whale guns were loaded and harpoons and lances were placed in readiness to be used with good effect. These, with our rifles, made quite a defensive showing.

After steaming alongside for some time Captain Harvest again asked if he could come on board and once more received a decided negative in reply. It became evident that the Georgette was trying to hedge the Catalpa in toward the land, so as to get her in British waters, and Captain Anthony's attention being called to this fact he at once ordered the crew to put the ship about. As the sails filled and she fell off on the other tack, her bow would have struck the Georgette amidships if the steamer had not rapidly backed out of the way. Her captain seemed puzzled at this movement and swung around and followed for a short distance, but she soon gave it up and turned her prow toward the shore, giving up the game of bluff and making the escape of the six Fenian prisoners from Fremantle an accomplished fact.

The homeward trip was without special incident. The Catalpa arrived in New York harbor on Saturday, August 19. We were met off the Scotland lightship[237] by the Herald's marine tug, and our arrival was reported in the shipping news the next morning. As it happened none of the reporters on the tug "tumbled" to the importance of the arrival of the Catalpa as a matter of news, so that newspaper lost a splendid chance for a scoop.[238] Our arrival was made the occasion of a great demonstration by the Fenians and Irishmen in New York. We put up at O'Donovan Rossa's hotel and our first break on Sunday morning was for the Bowery in order to get some clothes, for we had given ours to the prisoners and were certainly a sorry looking lot. We went out during the day and paid a farewell visit to the Catalpa, in common with a large number of other visitors, all of whom were anxious to secure some souvenir of the ship of the escape. The crew reaped quite a harvest from the sale of various articles.

Five days later the Catalpa sailed for New Bedford, where there was another demonstration, John Boyle O'Reilly being the orator of the occasion. The bark was subsequently presented by her owners, the Irish nationalists, to the three men who best deserved her, George S. Anthony, the captain; Henry C. Hathaway, whose fidelity and sagacity had so much to do with the success of the enterprise; and John

237. "[A]bout two and half miles east-southeast of the Sandy Hook Lighthouse and half a mile southwest by southwest of the black buoy that marked the Outer Bar." "Scotland Lightship," New Jersey Lighthouse Society [http://njlhs.burlco.org/scotland.htm], October 2001.

238. Except for the shipping news item, the *Herald* did not have an article on Saturday, August 19, but it did start covering the story on Sunday.

Conclusion of John King's Narrative

T. Richardson, the agent. The crew were also settled with on the most liberal terms, the total expenses of the expedition footing up about $25,000, which had been contributed by friends of the cause all over the world.

[This last installment in the *Gaelic American* (October 22, 1904) ended with "To Be Continued." A search by the editors of subsequent issues failed to locate another installment.]

EDITORS' EPILOGUE

> This day commences with Light breeses from the W. SW
> And clear pleasant weather. Ship heading NW Middle
> And Latter part. Wind from the SW. Steering different
> Courses with the westward. Lat 32 ~ 17 Long 114 ~ 41.
> —*Catalpa Log,* Thursday, April 20, [1876]

Crew member Frank Perry recalled many years later that until the *Georgette* threatened the *Catalpa* there had been an air of mystery among the crew about the whaler's true intentions. Anthony had kept them in the dark so that in the event of their capture, crew members could truthfully state they knew nothing of the mission's purpose. It was only after the crisis had passed that they learned that this had been a humanitarian effort from the start. Now the *Catalpa* was free and the ship's complement had increased by ten (six prisoners, four rescuers) for a total of thirty-three. The initial reaction of the newcomers to their environment was favorable. Perry observed, "The liberated prisoners, to a man wept with joy as they hailed the Captain of the bark as a redeemer."[239]

Except for second mate Antone Farnham's[240] death on May 8 of heart disease, the months of sailing were uneventful. Unknown, of course, to the *Catalpa* was that on May 22, British prime minister Benjamin Disraeli rejected a parliamentary petition to pardon the military Fenians, including those that had, still unknown to the British, just escaped from Fremantle. In the House of Commons floor debate that day, Disraeli ironically said that "these convicts in Western Australia are, in fact, at this moment enjoying . . . comparatively little restraint."[241] Whales were raised for the first

---

239. Frank Farrell, "Frank Perry Only Survivor of Catalpa," *New Bedford Times,* August 30, 1924, 20; Roche, 162.

240. Farnham's given name is spelled differently in various records.

241. Seán McConville, *Irish Political Prisoners, 1848–1922* (London: Routledge, 2003), 212; *Hansard's,* 1604.

Editors' Epilogue

time on July 20 and boats were lowered, but to no avail.[242] A week later, the prisoners demanded that they be put into a U.S. port. Was this ultimatum unreasonable or could the voyage have continued?

Devoy's instructions to Breslin and Anthony had been *to put in at Fernandina,* discharge the prisoners, and resume whaling.[243] In his report to the Clan, Breslin stated that he decided against going to Fernandina, but offered no reason why.[244] The prisoners believed he wanted to experience a whale kill, though no one could recall his ever having said that.[245] When they "mutinied," the ship was at the Tropic of Cancer, just west of the Mid-Atlantic Ridge,[246] and it was a change in course that triggered their demands. According to Pease, Anthony convinced Breslin of the wisdom of staying out:

> Now is just the season for whaling on the Western grounds. We are well enough fitted, excepting that we lack small stores, and we have plenty of money to buy from other vessels. I know the whaling grounds, and by hauling up to the northward we are almost certain to pick up a few hundred barrels of oil, and the voyage can be made as successful financially as it has been in other respects.[247]

It may well have made more sense to stay out than to waste time and resources putting into Fernandina and going out again. But the prisoners had been on board this small bark for over three months. It had taken less time to be transported from England to Fremantle eight years earlier aboard the *Hougoumont,* and at least on that voyage, as Harrington pointed out, they had wine daily. But on the *Catalpa,* they experienced some very rough weather, the boredom and tedium of sailing, and dreadful food, on top of which Darragh told of rations being cut halfway through the voyage.[248] Historian Elmo Hohman's description leaves no doubt on this issue: "One of the greatest evils of whaling life was the food."[249] On the other hand, they had endured poor food for many years. The prisoners told Frank Perry of the inadequate food at the prison.[250] One of their

242. *Catalpa Log,* May 8, July 20, 1876.
243. See chapter 6, "Senator Conover's Services."
244. See chapter 9, "Discontent of the Rescued Men."
245. No doubt all aboard knew that John Boyle O'Reilly joined several hunts launched from the whaler *Gazelle* following his rescue. On one, he was tossed out of the whaleboat and nearly died. Roche, 84–85.
246. *Catalpa Log,* July 27, 1876.
247. Pease, *Catalpa,* 165.
248. "The Catalpa Six," *IW* (supra note 194).
249. Hohman, 126, 130.
250. Farrell, 20 (supra note 239).

Editors' Epilogue

contemporaries, Thomas McCarthy Fennell, who chronicled life at Fremantle, described the wretched and minimal amount of food as a method of slow death.[251] Also, one suspects that army rations, on which they all had once lived, were not very satisfying.

It was a dry environment insofar as alcohol was concerned. If alcoholism did afflict some prisoners, an initial drying-out period would not have allayed subsequent urges for some gratification or relief. Gastrointestinal symptoms, insomnia, moodiness, and emotional complaints are commonly associated with withdrawal.[252] These symptoms were evident to varying degrees in some of the prisoners. At the Clan hearings, Brennan was asked if he thought Wilson was "diseased." Brennan responded, "I believe Wilson is not in his right mind: whiskey aggravates it." The same report reveals that whiskey had been a factor with the others.[253] Even in prison, the relative freedom of movement at Fremantle made it possible to obtain alcohol. Limited funds, though, would have limited consumption, probably causing binge-type drinking. Among nonprisoners, colonial authorities reported extraordinary incidences of drunkenness, in some years ranging at 50 percent of all crime.[254]

The filthy and squalid conditions of the forecastle, common to whalers, also provided no comfort to the prisoners.[255] The future suggested more of the same until more whales could be killed. There is no indication that the prisoners had been told in advance that the ship would continue to whale or that the taking of oil was to pay for the mission. (In one of his letters, Wilson suggested escaping on a whaler, but then promptly transferring to another vessel to get to the United States.)[256] Even had there been foreknowledge, the realities of the hardships to be endured were unimaginable. One modern journalist has written that whaler conditions "would have made prisoners of war balk."[257]

The prisoners were no doubt also feeling a legitimate anxiety about being captured and returned to Fremantle. On the open seas, fear of a British warship bearing down on them—and this time reclaiming them, flag or no flag—was probably very much on their minds.[258] Wilson once

251. Fennell, 239–40.

252. Marc A. Schuckit, *Drug and Alcohol Abuse: A Clinical Guide to Diagnosis and Treatment,* 4th ed. (New York: Plenum Publishing, 1995), 100–103.

253. *Report of the Eighth Annual Convention,* 26 (see appendix B), 53, 54, 55.

254. Hasluck, 99 (supra note 184).

255. Hohman, 69.

256. Letter dated 15 June 1874, to John Devoy.

257. Sebastian Junger, *Fire* (New York: Norton, 2001), 65.

258. The British Law Office later offered the opinion that the *Georgette* would have been within its rights stopping the *Catalpa* on the high seas by whatever means. Amos, 241.

Editors' Epilogue

said, "The horrible thought of being recaptured and carried back to a life worse than my past prison life made me almost crazy."[259] This ruled out any port stops until the ship reached home. Not only would the joys of shore leave remain unknown, but no fresh food would be obtained on the voyage. This eventuality was not foreseen by the planners. It was assumed that following the escape, the ship would be able to find additional food, either purchased through other ships or at stops en route. Also, only two rescuers, Breslin and Desmond, were expected on board. The additional men, King and Brennan, further strained supplies.

At Fremantle, the prisoners had some freedom, certainly more than the deck of a ninety-foot bark provided. And while they had to return to their cells each night, at least those cells afforded protection from the elements, were dry (physically), and didn't roll all the time. Nevertheless, they were hardened men. They had been incarcerated at least ten years. The oldest, Harrington, was forty-eight, and the youngest, Hassett, thirty-six. All had been in the highly disciplined British army and five had experienced combat. The four charged with desertion had had a "D" forcibly branded to their left breast by the military authorities.[260] Only one seemed impulsive (Hassett).

Denis Duggan was simply ill suited for a whaling voyage—which could have been said for most people. He had joined the expedition without any idea of what life was like on board. Duggan and Breslin's past bond (of helping James Stephens escape years before) unfortunately did not hold. Alcohol was also a factor in his behavior. Brennan thought Duggan was not a good choice for this operation, adding that Devoy knew that.[261]

The biggest problem seems to have been Thomas Brennan. He had exhibited extraordinary single-mindedness in getting to Australia to participate in the rescue. He was no mere fame seeker; his determination was sincere and impressive. In the Clan hearings, however, bitterness about his treatment throughout, and particularly about not getting on board the *Catalpa* until the very end, comes through all too clearly. Once aboard, he regrettably applied that same determination to undermining Breslin's authority and even the captain's. Brennan testified that he didn't recognize Breslin's authority and felt he was not a loyal Clan member.[262] While he attributed the change of plan to Breslin wanting to experience a whale kill,

---

259. "The Escaped Fenians," *Post* (supra note 182).

260. Hogan, Harrington, Hassett, and Wilson. Ó Lúing, 177; Amos, 200; Roche, 329.

261. *Report of the Eighth Annual Convention,* 26, 58; in fact, Devoy had observed that Duggan "was noted for his courage and coolness." Devoy, 80.

262. *Report of the Eighth Annual Convention,* 12, 19, 20.

Editors' Epilogue

Brennan seems to have been obsessed with getting to the August 9 Philadelphia Clan meeting, presumably to claim credit for the rescue.

This was the last problem the expedition needed. Perhaps under a single commander the prisoners would have, however reluctantly, agreed to continue the voyage. Darragh had said that he was willing to stay out and maybe the others would have followed his lead. But Brennan successfully preyed on their anxieties and exploited their fears. (King and Desmond's support for the prisoners was later acknowledged to be an effort to avoid bloodshed.)[263] Any change in plans required some tact in dealing with the prisoners. Breslin failed here—even his strongest admirers were aware of his faults.[264] His aloofness was perceived as arrogance by some, which only helped Brennan's strategy.

After the confrontation, Breslin and Anthony wisely concluded to make for land immediately.[265]

On the way to New York, on August 13, the boats were lowered one last time for the chase, but the whales disappeared.[266] On August 19, the *Catalpa* arrived in New York harbor. Reporting for the Boston *Pilot,* Denis Cashman, a former fellow prisoner of the rescued six, went to New York to interview them.[267] Anthony took the night train to New Bedford, arriving Sunday morning. (He went on to Martha's Vineyard to be with his family, who were visiting there.)[268] The ship, under pilot, sailed for home from New York on August 22, arriving at New Bedford the next evening.[269]

This day commences with moderate breezes from the S SE and pleasant weather—Ship still working down the Sound at 8 Am—came to anchor off New London in 7 fathoms of water—give her 30 fathoms of chain and furl the sails—Middle part Much the Same—Latter part—Light breezes from S.S.E.—at 4 Am took our anchors

---

263. Ibid., 60.

264. Of Breslin, John Boyle O'Reilly wrote, "a man of few words, of small acquaintance, earning his bread in unassuming ways—few knew, and to few were shown, the culture and refinement behind the modest exterior. In thought and appearance eminently a gentleman; in demeanor dignified and reserved; in observance, rather distrustful, as if disappointed in his ideal man; somewhat cynical, perhaps, and often stubbornly prejudiced and unjust; a lover of and a successful worker in literature,—such is an outline of a character that may indeed be called extraordinary, of a man, who, if he break down the barrier of reserve that has hitherto hedged him round, has it in his hands to win brilliant distinction in any public career he may select." Roche, 173.

265. Pease makes no reference to the confrontation. He wrote that the prisoners, noting the course change, "pleaded that they might be put ashore without any delay, and after a day or two it was decided to yield to their wishes." Pease, *Catalpa,* 166.

266. *Catalpa Log.*

267. "The Rescued Prisoners," *Pilot,* August 26, 1876, 1.

268. "The Rescued Fenians," *Republican Standard,* August 24, 3.

269. *Catalpa Log.*

Editors' Epilogue

and took a tug and towed through the race[270]—at 12 Noon passed point Judith—At 6 pm took a tug and went to City wharf Made her fast. So Ends this day and pleasant voyage to J. T. Richardson.

Wednesday August 23 [1876][271]

For U.S. Customs, the *Catalpa* passengers gave the following occupations:[272]

Breslin	*Merchant*	*King*	*Gentleman*
Wilson	*Soldier*	*Hassett*	*Carpenter*
Cranston	*Soldier*	*Desmond*	*Wheelwright*
Brennan	*Merchant*	*Hogan*	*Painter*
Darragh	*Soldier*	*Harrington*	*Soldier*

The prisoners made many public appearances to raise funds for themselves and tell the story of the *Catalpa*. Events celebrating the Clan achievement were held throughout the country for years. In 1895, twenty years after the ship departed for Fremantle, the Philadelphia Clan's annual picnic at Rising Sun Park honored the event. Darragh, Cranston, and Hogan attended. Anthony came down from Massachusetts and gave the Clan the *Catalpa*'s flag, which eventually was transferred to the National Museum of Ireland.[273]

George Smith Anthony never returned to sea. He remained in New Bedford with his wife and two children. In 1878, he and Richardson tried to interest Devoy and the Clan in purchasing another whaler, but there were no takers in New York. While Breslin, Carroll, and Devoy were supportive of doing something for Anthony, they were wary of Richardson and let the matter drop. Anthony served for a while with the New Bedford Night Police, a refuge for out-of-work whaling captains. Through the influence of John Boyle O'Reilly, Anthony was appointed New Bedford Port Inspector (U.S. Customs) in 1886 and served in that capacity for many years. He published the first book-length account of the *Catalpa*, written by the New Bedford journalist Z. W. Pease. (He successfully pestered Devoy

270. This race, or channel, lies between Fishers and Long Islands. Ralph Lewis, "Geologic History of Long Island Sound, Connecticut," Geological and Natural History Survey [http://camel2.conncoll.edu/ccrec/greennet/arbo/publications/34/CHP1.HTM], March 2002.

271. In this log entry, the mate has included the afternoon and evening of the 23rd. Normally, that part of the entry would have been recorded the following day, the 24th, but the ship's voyage had come to an end on the 23rd. *Catalpa Log.*

272. National Archives and Records Administration, Microform, *Passenger List,* District of New York, Port of New York, Am. Bark *Catalpa,* August 22, 1876.

273. "The Clan-na-Gael Have a Great Day," *Philadelphia Inquirer,* August 6, 1895, 2.

Editors' Epilogue

The rescued prisoners, from the *Irish World,* September 2, 1876
(Z. W. Pease, *The Catalpa Expedition*)

for the Irishman's photo to be included in the book.) In 1909, the Connecticut Clan raised funds for Anthony to help pay off the mortgage on his new Bay Street home. A ceremony was held in New Bedford at which he was presented with a check for $1,040. Four years later, in 1913, Anthony died. He is buried with his wife, Emma, in New Bedford. His death was widely noted by the press, and representatives of many Irish organizations attended his Masonic funeral. In 1924, some New Bedford businessmen working with Anthony's widow met with Devoy about making a silent film on the rescue, but nothing came of it. On the occasion of the one hundredth anniversary of the rescue, a local group put up a bronze plaque in New Bedford erroneously listing John Boyle O'Reilly as a seventh prisoner rescued by the *Catalpa*.[274]

First Mate SAMUEL SMITH, who was credited by all observers for his exceptional seamanship in picking up the whaleboat, became a master.

---

274. Zephaniah W. Pease, "Fifty Years on the *Morning Mercury,* New Bedford, Mass., 1880–1930: A Reminiscence"; O'Brien and Ryan, 1, 353; O'Brien and Ryan, 2, 334–35; "Captain Anthony of the 'Catalpa' Dead," *GA,* May 31, 1913; "Death of Captain George S. Anthony," *Morning Mercury,* May 23, 1913, 1; "Captain Anthony Has Masonic Funeral," *New Bedford Times,* May 24, 1913, 1; "Connecticut Honors *Catalpa* Captain," *GA,* December 25, 1909, 1; "Rescue of the Fenian Military Prisoners to Be Filmed," *GA,* October 25, 1924, 5.

Editors' Epilogue

Samuel P. Smith, First Mate of the *Catalpa* (Z. W. Pease, *The Catalpa Expedition*)

Until married (and when not at sea) he lived at his parents' hotel in Edgartown. Later he whaled on the West Coast, California having briefly become a whaling center. In 1908, he was honored by the San Francisco Clan chapter, the Knights of the Red Branch, who presented him with a medal inscribed "For Heroic Services as First Officer of the *Catalpa*." He died in 1910 and is buried with his wife in his native Edgartown, Massachusetts.[275]

JOHN BRESLIN continued to be a very active Clan member. In 1877, he was observed inspecting the U.S./Canadian border, causing great concern among British diplomats. (The British believed that arms were buried along the border in preparation for another Fenian incursion.) He was the business manager for John Devoy's first newspaper, *The Irish Nation* (1881–1885), which failed. He stunned some in 1882 when, in response to the Phoenix Park assassinations, he wrote a particularly strong defense of such actions, concluding with, "I have been requested to sign a call for an

---

[275]. "Thomas Desmond Called By Death" [Samuel Smith mentioned], *San Francisco Chronicle*, October 24, 1910, 12; Special Collections, Kendall Institute; Family Search site of the Church of Jesus Christ of Latter-Day Saints (hereafter FSLDS) [http://www.familysearch.org], June 2002: 1880 United States Census, T9, 0526, p. 547D.

Editors' Epilogue

indignation meeting in this connection; but I remember Ireland in the famine years of '47–48 and can feel no indignation at the destruction of the machinery of British rule in Ireland—by any means—in any manner." He was for a period in charge of the Holland submarine project,[276] in which he even intruded on the design elements of the machine, to the annoyance of the inventor. Here again, British agents observed his activities. At age fifty-four, he died at his New York home in 1887 and was buried at Calvary Cemetery, New York City. His wife of eight years and two children survived him. (When in Australia, he apparently had an affair with a woman who bore a child, John Joseph.)[277]

THOMAS DESMOND returned to California. He was elected the twelfth sheriff of San Francisco in 1879 on the Workingmen's ticket, a virulently anti-Chinese party that enjoyed fleeting popularity. He served one term and afterwards remained active in Irish affairs. In the 1880s, British spy reports associated Desmond with the dynamite campaign in England and with a planned raid into Canada.[278] When the Clan experienced great turmoil later that same decade, Desmond sided with the faction that temporarily ousted Devoy, thus causing an estrangement between the two former allies. He died in 1910 at the age of seventy-two and was buried in Holy Cross Cemetery. The Clan's San Francisco branch, Knights of the Red Branch, organized a major tribute to him. The funeral was "like that of an Irish Chief in the days of old," with the principal celebrant intoning, "His heroic figure stands out like Brian at Clontarf, or Shane the Proud or O'Neill at the Yellow Ford, or Owen Roe at Benburb, or Sarsfield at Limerick."[279]

DENIS DUGGAN remained in New York for seven years. When poor health set in, he decided to return to his native Dublin. Shortly before his

276. The Fenian submarine project started in 1876 with financing from the Clan. It went on for some years and while the Fenians were unable to see it through to completion, the inventor John Holland continued to work on it. O'Brien and Ryan, 1, 470–71.

277. D'Arcy, 394–95; "Let the Dead Bury Their Dead," *Irish Nation*, May 13, 1882, 4. The ambivalence other nationalists felt about the murders was best expressed by John Boyle O'Reilly, who wrote, "There is an awful lesson both for Ireland and England in the discovery of these murderers. It is no victory for England to lay bare the abominations of her own misrule. She may use the appalling fact to justify still further coercion. Blind, cruel, and fatuous, will she never learn that such measures cannot have other effect than to increase secret retaliation?" Roche, 224; D'Arcy, 404–5; "Death of John Breslin," *IA*, November 26, 1887, 4; Amos, 249.

278. R. A. Burchell, *San Francisco Irish, 1848–1880* (Manchester: Manchester University Press, 1979), 146–54; Philip J. Ethington, *Public City: The Political Construction of Urban Life in San Francisco, 1850–1890* (New York: Cambridge University Press, 1994), 282–86; Letter from Marquess of Lorne [Governor General of Canada] to the Foreign Office, March 15, 1883, Public Records Office (PRO) 5, 1861; Stanley [British Consulate, San Francisco] to Sackville-West [British Ambassador to the United States], February 16, 1884, PRO 5, 1928.

279. "San Francisco's Last Honors to a Hero," *GA*, November 12, 1910, 1; "Desmond," *San Francisco Chronicle* (supra note 275); O'Brien and Ryan, 2, 232–33.

Editors' Epilogue

1884 death, Duggan's sister wrote Devoy that her brother was anxious to hear from him. (She wisely added, "Any remarks you make about him being so bad, do so on a slip of paper to myself apart from his letter.") His funeral was reportedly attended by twelve thousand persons. In 1938, the National Graves Association decided to erect a memorial to his memory at Glasnevin Cemetery (Dublin). Though he was entitled to some compensation, or his lay, from the *Catalpa* voyage, the final calculations resulted in his receiving only eighteen dollars. He contacted Devoy, who agreed that this was unfair and advised him to appeal to Richardson. Given the difficulties Duggan presented on the voyage, Richardson probably felt he deserved nothing.[280]

JOHN W. GOFF's ambitions in life were realized soon after the *Catalpa* rescue. He was from time to time credited for its success, and he did little to dispel that myth. Admitted to the bar in 1879, he served as an assistant district attorney in New York, was elected the recorder for the city, and then became a state Supreme Court justice. One of his legal achievements was serving as counsel for the Lexow Committee that investigated Tammany corruption in the 1890s. Goff died in 1924 and was survived by his two children. In a lengthy obituary, Devoy observed, "Goff's service to the Irish Cause outweighed his faults, but both are part of the history of the Irish Movement of our time."[281]

THOMAS BRENNAN remained in New York and became a court officer of the New York State Supreme Court (probably through his association with Goff). He was expelled from the Clan for his conduct aboard the *Catalpa*. He married around 1880 and had nine children.[282] In his later years, he suffered from paralysis and died in 1915. Following a well-attended funeral noted by the press, he was buried in St. Raymond's Cemetery in the Bronx. While Devoy's obituary of Brennan was respectful, he later wrote unmercifully that Brennan "took no part whatever in" the rescue.[283]

MICHAEL HARRINGTON, the oldest of the prisoners, whose early yearning for travel was more than satisfied during his life, settled in New York City. He married shortly after arriving there, had two children, and served on the Central Park police force. He was the first prisoner to die, of pneu-

---

280. O'Brien and Ryan, 2, 255–56; O'Brien and Ryan, 1, 180, 268–69; "Duggan," *IW*, September 20, 1884, 11; "Glasnevin Memorial to Be Erected to James Fitzharris and Denis Duggan, I.R.B," *GA*, November 26, 1938, 5.

281. "Ex-Justice Goff Dies of Pneumonia," *NYT*, November 10, 1924, 17; "Goff" *GA* (supra note 93); Theodore D. Rousseau, "Justice Goff's Irish Rescue Party," *Post*, February 1, 1913, Supplement, 1.

282. NA, "Census," 1910, T624, 1003, 191.

283. O'Brien and Ryan, 1, 105; "Thomas Brennan," *NYT*, December 3, 1915, 11; "Thomas Brennan Dead," *GA*, December 11, 1915, 7; "Goff," *NYT* (supra note 281).

Editors' Epilogue

monia, in 1886, and was buried in New York's Calvary Cemetery. Devoy, Brennan, and Clan members attended the funeral. Even the international press noted his passing.[284] While still engaged in boat building in his native Goleen, Harrington had etched his name in a local cave. (In 1964, several researchers located the cave and cleaned the stone for others to admire.)[285]

THOMAS HENRY HASSETT also settled in New York. He married and kept a saloon on Sullivan Street in lower Manhattan. He died in 1893 at his East Harlem home and was survived by his wife Catharine. His funeral was attended by a large number of nationalists. Like Harrington, he was buried in Calvary Cemetery.[286]

JAMES WILSON, whom Devoy considered a great intellect, lived until 1921, his ninetieth year. He resided first in Philadelphia, Pennsylvania, for a number of years (he was reportedly still there at the time of Harrington's passing in 1886) and then went to the Blackstone Valley region of Rhode Island. He settled in Central Falls and worked in one of the many textile mills. In 1877, he wrote Devoy and apologized for "the foolish way that I have acted since my escape." It is believed that he received a small pension for life from the Clan. In 1919, Eamon De Valera, then president of Ireland's Dail, reportedly met Wilson while on a tour of the United States. He was buried by friends, next to his wife, Lucy, in the Patriot's Lot of the (Old) St. Mary's cemetery, Pawtucket, Rhode Island. There were no children.[287]

Daring ROBERT CRANSTON settled in the West Kensington section of Philadelphia. He married and took up police service as a special officer (the predecessor title to detective in the Philadelphia Police Department) and watchman. By 1910, he was widowed.[288]

MARTIN HOGAN, the fine swordsman whose 1871 letter initiated the rescue plan, settled in Chicago, Illinois, and remained active in Fenian activities, so much so that he is mentioned in British reports. He married and

---

284. "Funeral of a Nationalist," *IA,* February 27, 1886, 1. During the latter half of the nineteenth century, New York's Central Park had its own police force. Roy Rosenzweig and Elizabeth Blackmar, *The Park and the People: A History of Central Park* (Ithaca, NY: Cornell University Press, 1992), 241–43. "Burial of a Noted Fenian," *NYT,* February 16, 1886, 8; "Career and Death of a Noted Fenian," *Inquirer and Commercial News,* August 25, 1886, Supplement, 1.

285. Hurley, "In Search of a Forgotten Fenian" (supra note 165).

286. *Herald,* December 16, 1893, 12, col. 2; "A Famous Fenian Dead," *IA,* December 18, 1893, 1; Municipal Archives, City of New York, microform, *Police Census Records* [1890], Roll 97; FSLDS 1880 Census, T9, 0872, 236C.

287. "James Wilson, Aged Irish Leader, Dead," [Rhode Island] *Providence Journal,* November 7, 1921; O'Brien and Ryan, 1, 263–64; W. J. Laubenstein letter of November 19, 1964 to Walter McGrath; NA, "Census," 1910, T624, 1438, 5.

288. FSLDS 1880 Census, T9, 1178, 7B; NA, "Census," 1900, T623, 1461; Philadelphia City Directory, microform, 1915 (Philadelphia: C. E. Howe, 1915); "Career and Death," *Inquirer* (supra note 284).

had a daughter. He resumed his trade as a painter, moving often around the Near West Side, a slum area of the city. By 1900, he was a widower and long-term patient at Cook County Hospital, where he died the following year. The brief accounts of his passing noted he had been "in straightened circumstances for a long time."[289]

THOMAS DARRAGH, who might have become a British officer, settled in Philadelphia with Cranston. He worked initially as a wool merchant and lived in rooming houses in the Center City and south Philadelphia. He too remained active in Clan activities, holding the position of "Junior Guardian" for one of the Philadelphia camps.[290]

JOHN DEVOY lived for another fifty-two years. He held to his convictions through thick and thin: with the Clan, Davitt, the Land League, Parnell, De Valera, and virtually every dimension, principal, and party of the independence movement in that half-century. In 1903 he founded his second and more successful newspaper, the *Gaelic American,* to which he devoted the rest of his life. (According to Devoy's biographer, "the paper existed to propagate the gospel according to Clan-na-Gael.") Devoy died in September 1928 while visiting Atlantic City, New Jersey. His death received international attention and his funeral mass in New York had an overflowing crowd. However, his burial was deferred until June 1929, when his body was transported to Dublin and, after a state funeral, interred at the Patriot's Plot in Glasnevin Cemetery.[291]

HENRY CLAY HATHAWAY, whose English forebears, like Anthony's, had arrived in America in the 1630s, rose to be chief of the New Bedford Police Department. He left to return to the sea, though this time as captain of a packet. For four years (fourteen voyages) he sailed to and from the Azores. He lived in New Bedford with his wife and son and dabbled in real estate and auctioneering until being appointed a U.S. shipping commissioner in 1884. He held that and a similar post for many years, dying in 1931, his ninetieth year.[292]

---

289. "Martin Hogan's Death," [Western Australia] *Western Mail,* February 8, 1902; "Was Convict in British Penal Colony," *Tribune,* November 26, 1901, 4; FSLDS, 1880 Census, T9, 0194, 282D; NA, "Census," 1900, T623, 259, 90; Letter from British Consul Crump (Philadelphia) to Thornton, June 12, 1878, Foreign Office (FO) 5, 1707.

290. FSLDS, 1880 Census, T9, 1179, 137B; *Gopsill's Philadelphia City Directory, 1896* (Philadelphia: James Gopsill's Sons, 1896); Letter from Crump to Thornton, December 16, 1877, FO 5, 1559.

291. Terry Golway, *Irish Rebel: John Devoy and America's Fight for Ireland's Freedom* (New York: St. Martin's Press, 1998), 183, 318–19.

292. "Henry Clay Hathaway," *Representative Men and Old Families of Southern Massachusetts,* 2 (Chicago: J. H. Beers, 1916), 624–27; "Captain H. C. Hathaway," *NYT,* May 4, 1931, 26; FSLDS, 1880 Census, T9, 0525, 72A.

Editors' Epilogue

John Devoy, Captain of the *Catalpa* (Z. W. Pease, *The Catalpa Expedition*)

JOHN T. RICHARDSON continued in the outfitting business, living in New Bedford with his wife and son. For a period, his daughter Emma and now famous son-in-law George also lived with them.[293]

The two IRB agents, JOHN STEPHEN WALSH and DENIS FLORENCE MCCARTHY, didn't leave Fremantle until two weeks after the *Catalpa* sailed with the prisoners. They were questioned and closely watched by the police but not arrested. They sailed to California and soon returned to Ireland. McCarthy, a Cork native, resumed his nationalist activities for a few years and then emigrated to the United States. He settled in Chicago and died there in 1909. Though also from Cork, Walsh had had his organizing base in northern England. He was later associated with the Invincibles, a militant movement that assassinated Lord Cavendish and his aide in

293. FSLDS, 1880 Census, T9, 0525, 198D.

179

Editors' Epilogue

Phoenix Park, Dublin, in 1882. Walsh fled to France and then went to New York where he died in 1891.[294]

JOHN BOYLE O'REILLY took over ownership of the *Pilot* in 1876 and was a prolific writer and public figure for the rest of his life. He married and had three daughters. O'Reilly continued his interest in Irish affairs and also became a strong advocate for the rights of the American Indian and Negro. Upon his death, he had achieved considerable prominence in this country leading the *New York Times* to comment, "In the death of Mr. O'Reilly, the Irish race in America loses one of its brightest representatives, and the literary world one of its most thoughtful and active poets." Years later, the first sitting president of the United States to visit Ireland, John Fitzgerald Kennedy, quoted O'Reilly in his address to the country's Parliament.[295]

O'Reilly's associate and friend DENIS BAMBRICK CASHMAN left the *Pilot* in 1876 and held positions with the City of Boston and the federal government for many years. His wife, whom he had married before being transported to Fremantle, joined him in Boston, where they raised a family. He also wrote about Irish matters and completed a biography of Michael Davitt. He died in 1897, and large numbers attended his funeral. Both Cashman and O'Reilly were buried in Holyhood Cemetery, Boston.[296]

FR. PATRICK MCCABE left Western Australia more than a year before the *Catalpa* rescue and journeyed to South Australia, serving as a priest in the Adelaide diocese.[297] His connection with the earlier O'Reilly escape had brought him unwanted attention from the authorities, and his willingness to serve as an intermediary for prisoners' mail resulted in the revocation of his visiting privileges to Fremantle Prison.[298] In 1882, he emigrated to the United States, taking a pastoral assignment in the diocese of St. Paul,

---

294. Amos, 248, 265; McGrath, "The Great *Catalpa* Rescue of 1876" [Part 2] (supra note 229); "John Walsh Is Dead," *NYT,* March 7, 1891, 5.

295. "John Boyle O'Reilly Dead," *NYT,* August 11, 1890, 1; "Kennedy's Address to Irish Parliament," *NYT,* June 29, 1963, 2. The poem quoted was "Distance," Roche, 452. Kennedy often cited this poem in his 1960 presidential campaign and as president.

296. "John Boyle O'Reilly Dead," *Herald,* August 11, 1890, 1; Ryan, "Cashman" (supra note 104); "Obituary, Cashman—Dennis [*sic*] B.," *IW,* January 16, 1897, 5.

297. Erickson, 1930.

298. While both Laubenstein and Keneally offer similar accounts of McCabe being present at Fremantle throughout the *Catalpa* rescue, no other credible accounts do, and according to church records, McCabe was attached to the Adelaide diocese at the time (1875–1877), over one thousand miles from Fremantle. Laubenstein, 121–27, 132–38, 169, 172, 174, 213; Keneally, 536–37, 548, 558; "Funeral of a Famous Priest," [Minnesota] *Winona Daily Herald,* October 25, 1899; "Aided John Boyle O'Reilly to Escape," *Tribune,* October 24, 1899, 4; Amos, 222–23; Peggy O'Reilly, 211; Byrne, 20–21; Bourke, 72–74, 93; "Catholic Priests in South Australia, 1841—1906" [Adelaide Archdiocesan Archives] [http://homepages.picknowl.com.au/mjfitzgerald/Priests.htm], May 2002; Sr. M. T. Foale, RSJ, Adelaide Archdiocesan archivist, to Fennell, email, July 31, 2002.

Editors' Epilogue

Minnesota. He saw his good friend John Boyle O'Reilly several times, the last being in St. Paul in 1890. McCabe died in 1899 from Bright's disease at St. Mary's parish in Waseca, Minnesota.[299]

THOMAS MCCARTHY FENNELL settled in Elmira, New York, where he lived until his death in 1914. An active Republican, he owned and operated a hotel, held several public offices, and raised a family.[300]

JOHN KENEALY, a prominent Democrat, lived out his life in Los Angeles, California, operating a prosperous dry goods business. He also had an interest in an insurance business and was a city official. He died in 1908.[301]

JAMES REYNOLDS, "Catalpa Jim," continued his Connecticut manufacturing business, served as New Haven town agent, and remained very active in the Clan. He had five children, four of whom tragically died early in life. He died in 1897 but his contributions to Irish independence were long remembered. He was buried in St. Lawrence Cemetery in New Haven. (Devoy's account opened with a reference to the 1904 service and monument established in his memory.)[302]

Judge MICHAEL COONEY continued to practice law and live with his family for many more decades in San Francisco. He was president of various fraternal insurance societies. The local British consul noted his activities, and, in one example, Cooney is named in a complaint to the American government about his mischievous intentions in Canada. During the Boer War, the "Transvaal committee of California" operated from his office. At the end of the century, he was prominently involved in establishing what is now San Francisco State University.[303]

U.S. senator SIMON B. CONOVER continued to be active in Clan affairs. He arranged for a Fenian delegation to meet with the Russian ambassador to the United States in 1876. In 1886, he was the owner of record of the Holland test submarines. He did not stand for reelection for a second Senate term but returned to Florida, held a variety of appointed posts, eventually moved west, and practiced medicine until his death in 1908.[304]

Fellow physician and Conover's good friend WILLIAM CARROLL was

---

299. "Personal," *Irish Nation* (supra note 61); File Notes, Department of Records Management, Archdiocese of Saint Paul and Minneapolis; Peggy O'Reilly, 206–12; "Famous Priest," *Winona Daily Herald* (supra note 298); Roche, 344.

300. Fennell, 280–82.

301. Keneally, 599–600.

302. "Monument Unveiled," *GA* (supra note 55).

303. Shuck; Hamilton Fish, *Papers of Hamilton Fish, 1732–1914* [microfilm], diary entry, January 13, 1877, Archival Manuscript Material, Library of Congress, Microfilm 17,634-6N-6P (diaries, 1869–1876).

304. "Conover," *Biographical Directory*; O'Brien and Ryan, 1, 209, II, 306.

Editors' Epilogue

chairman of the Clan from 1875 to 1880. His relations with Devoy were sometimes stormy (as were most relations with Devoy), but they remained friends. (In his 1890 public testimony about spying on the Clan, Le Caron spoke highly of Carroll, who returned the compliment by wondering who this spy, or "ruffian," was. Apparently they had never met.) One observer wrote of Carroll, "he had the fierce longing for revenge and wanted not only to benefit Ireland but to injure England." He continued his medical practice for many years and kept active in Irish-American affairs. He died in 1926 at his home in Philadelphia, where he had lived for over half a century.[305]

Miles M. O'Brien, who, with Goff, harassed Devoy during and after the *Catalpa* rescue, became a prominent citizen in New York City. He was a successful dry goods merchant and banker. He was also a member of the city's Board of Education for many years, serving as its first Irish-American president.[306]

John A. Tobin, the young naval officer who surveyed the *Catalpa* for the Clan, never became an admiral as Devoy had hoped. He retired after twenty years of service with the rank of lieutenant. He invented "Tobin bronze," a frictionless brass alloy used to cover ship bottoms (including the *Vigilant,* which won the 1893 America's Cup). Today, various ship parts such as shafts are still made of "Tobin bronze."[307]

After escaping from Ireland in 1866, Peter Curran, in whose Dublin house the Fenians had often gathered, settled in New York. He married and resumed a spirits business. He died in 1881 and was buried in Calvary Cemetery.[308]

The Australian and British authorities held several inquiries about the escape. Britain's Home Office decided to dismiss Acting Comptroller Fauntleroy, Assistant Superintendent Doonan, and Warder Booler. (Fauntleroy no doubt would forever regret his words in March, as recalled by Doonan, when he was considering the possibility of the military Fenians escaping: "in fact the most trustworthy men we have.") John Stone, the superintendent of Water Police, became the new convict superintendent.

Governor Robinson left his post in 1877 and subsequently served as governor of South Australia, the Straits Settlements (Singapore), Prince

---

305. O'Brien and Ryan, 1, 125–26, 2, 309; "Dr. William Carroll, Once Head of Clan-na-Gael, Dead," *GA*, May 15, 1926, 1.

306. "Miles M. O'Brien Dead," *NYT*, December 23, 1910, 13.

307. "Tobin," *NYT* (supra note 129); "Vigilant Again the Victor," *NYT*, October 10, 1893, 1; "Marine Shafts," Machine Works at Essex, Inc. [http://www.machineworksatessex.com], August 2002.

308. "Peter Curran, an Old Dublin Nationalist," *Irish Nation*, January 7, 1882, 5.

Editors' Epilogue

Edward Island, and the Leeward Islands; he was also, briefly, acting governor of Victoria and returned to Western Australia, twice serving again as governor. A practical official, he responded to the Colonial Office inquiries about the escape, acknowledging the lapses in the police pursuit but also expressing himself as "patently glad that the Fenians had quitted the shores of Western Australia to become the problem of some other nation."[309]

Major CHARLES FINNERTY, who commanded the pensioner guard aboard the *Georgette,* was so enraged at one local newspaper's criticism of the authorities that he reportedly went, saber in hand, to confront the publisher, but he was no more successful in this endeavor than in the *Catalpa* pursuit. The publisher, James Pearce, temporarily dispatched him with one punch. (The Irish Catholic community cheered the news because Finnerty was also a magistrate considered anti-Catholic.)[310]

PATRICK MOLONEY, who had put the *Catalpa* rescuers up at his hotel and was suspected of being an accessory by the authorities, went through quite a life change: he ended up as governor of Wagga Gaol in New South Wales. He died in 1892.[311]

Of Fenians MICHAEL CODY and JOHN EDWARD KELLY, who rendered financial and technical assistance to the rescuers, Cody is believed to have remained in Australia and continued organizing. Kelly came to the United States and died in Boston in 1884 at age forty-three. A monument was established at his grave in Mt. Hope Cemetery, and John Boyle O'Reilly spoke at the dedication.[312]

JAMES KEILLEY, known as the "seventh prisoner" or the "Fenian left behind," remained in Australia after his conditional pardon in 1878. Upon learning of his harsh living conditions, other Fenians raised funds in 1904 to care for him. In 1906 he was honored with Thomas Duggan[313] at Maylands, Western Australia, by the Irish community. He died in a nursing home in 1918 at age eighty-two.[314]

The round-trip voyage of the *Catalpa* took fifteen and half months. Its outbound crew totaled twenty-four persons. During the voyage, there

---

309. Amos, 229, 236, 250–52; *Australian Dictionary,* 6, 50–51; Hasluck, 78 (supra note 184).

310. [Western Australia] *Sunday Times,* June 21, 1925, August 7, 1927; Amos, 263.

311. Amos, 266.

312. Ibid., 289–90; O'Brien and Ryan, 1, 212, 230; Roche, 236.

313. Thomas Duggan (1822–1913) was a Cork teacher who became a Fenian center early in the movement's history. He was arrested in 1865, tried, and found guilty. He was transported aboard the *Hougoumont.* He spent his final free years teaching in Australia. [Western Australia] *Kalgoorlie Miner,* January 1, 1914, 1.

314. Amos, 279–80, 290; "The Ex-Fenian Prisoners," [Western Australia] *Western Mail,* February 17, 1906.

Editors' Epilogue

The Anthony house at 14 Bay Street, New Bedford, still stands. The mortgage on this house was paid off by the Clan-na-Gael to ensure George and Emma's future. (Courtesy Philip Fennell)

were two deaths, five successful desertions, and three discharges. With eight replacements, the return complement of officers and seamen was twenty-two, and there were ten passengers. Based on negotiations with the Clan, the ship was reregistered on April 24, 1877, to Richardson (nine-sixteenths), Anthony (three-sixteenths), and Ariel E. Chase (four-sixteenths). She continued whaling until 1879, when she was sold to new owners. The British, ever vigilant since the rescue, kept an eye on the vessel. For instance, responding to rumors of more mischief in 1881, the New York consul reported to London the *Catalpa* "to be still at New Bedford, and to be dismantled and unfit for sea."[315] The shipping news of a newspaper last reported her at London in 1882.[316]

315. Edwards to Principal Secretary of State for Foreign Affairs, July 20, 1881, FO 5, 1778.
316. "New Bedford Whaling Fleet," *NYT*, August 14, 1878, 5; "Whaling Intelligence," *NYT*, May 19, 1879, 5; "Marine Intelligence," *NYT*, November 27, 1879, 8; "Marine Intelligence," *NYT*, March 3, 1882, 8.

APPENDIX A: LETTERS FROM
JAMES WILSON

Fremantle,
West Australia,

4 September, 1873

To Mr. John Devoy.

Dear Friend,

I sit down to write to you with the liveliest feelings of satisfaction; I was delited to find that Martin Hogan had opened up a communication with you. It was the thing of all others that we most wanted, for we are under the impression that you have divised some scheme to get us out of this if you had have known the real position of affairs with regard to us; now there is not the least thing in the world to prevent us getting away from this place if it was managed properly, the whole amount of the population of this country is only twenty-four thousand.

There are some good ports where whalers are in the habit of calling and several other towns in the interior of the country. You perceive at a glance that the number of inhabitants in any of those places are not very great. The greater portion of the people are in and about the capital, Perth, and the great seaport, Fremantle, where is situated the convict establishment. There is a guard of pensioners at Fremantle and also Perth. They are about three hundred strong all told. This forms the whole disposable force of the colony; with a few police. So you see that it would not be much risk for any vessel, whaler or otherwise, to run in on some pretence or other. And if we had the means of purchasing horses could make through the bush to the coast where the vessel might be and so clear out, or there is another way that we might try; that is the way that Thomas Hassett tried. And he would have succeeded if he had the means of paying a skipper that offered to take him away for thirty pounds. If we had sufficient in our own hands we would not be long without at least trying to clear out of this.

Now there are some things that it is my duty to acquaint you with that are occurring out here. Things of so base a nature that it would be wrong to hide them; I

Letters from James Wilson

allude to the acts of a Mr. Nunan,[317] one of the civilians who, together with Mr. Brophy,[318] was left in charge of the money that was sent from the other Australian colonies at the time that the first batch of the prisoners was released. The amount, I believe, was somewhere about 500 £, and should amount, according to the statement of the Reverend Father McCabe to 82 £, eighty-two pounds per man if divided fairly; now I was told by Mick Cody when he came to bid me farewell on his leaving this Colony that on the division of the money at the release of the last batch of prisoners that John, with a nobleness that does him honour, said that we should receive the same amount as they did, and that if the British Government made a distinction between us by a harsher mode of treatment and by retaining us in prison it was not for their own countrymen and compatriots to imitate that conduct. And so I believe that the money was equally divided. There is the testimony of Con Kane,[319] James O'Reilly,[320] John Flood and Mick Cody to the effect that there was sixty-four pounds, 64 £ left to each of the military men.

It was arranged by the released men that we all should all be got out of the country, and this Mr. Nunan was left behind to carry out the intention. This he could the more readily effect as he, with Mr. Brophy, had gone into business as builders and contractors and so they were in a position to carry the scheme into effect without attracting much notice; well, the first of the released men went away, and I was assured positively by Jerry O'Donovan[321] that we would be got away and that I was

---

317. Joseph Noonan (or Nunan) (1842–1885) was a Fenian from Kerry. He fought near Killarney but avoided arrest. He was later seized near London, escaped, and was recaptured. Sentenced to seven years, he was transported on the *Hougoumont*. Following his 1869 pardon, he established, initially with Hugh Brophy, a building business. Later he married into an established Catholic family in Perth and became a successful architect as well as builder. Amos, 187, 267 290; "An exchange . . . ," *West Australian,* November 16, 1885. Supporting Noonan, Australian Gillian O'Mara describes this conflict with Wilson in her article, "Joseph Noonan, Fenian Success Story," Bob Reece, ed., *The Irish in Western Australia,* Studies in Western Australia Series, 20 (Nedlands, WA: University of Western Australia, 2000), 59–66.

318. Hugh Francis Brophy (1829–1919) was a Dublin building contractor and center for a large Fenian circle. He was arrested with Stephens, for whom he served as a right-hand man. Transported on the *Hougoumont,* he was pardoned in 1869. He remained in Australia, married, started a contracting business, and remained active in Irish activities. Amos, 84, 187, 281–82, 289.

319. Cornelius Dwyer Keane (1839–1891) had been a law clerk and center from Skibbereen. Transported aboard the *Hougoumont,* he was conditionally pardoned in 1871. Forbidden from returning to Ireland, he never reunited with his wife and children there. He settled in Queensland, where he became a civil servant. Amos, 84, 280, 290; McGrath, "The Fenians in Australia," 51–52.

320. James Reilly (also known as O'Reilly) was a Kerry Fenian. Transported on the *Hougoumont,* he was pardoned in 1869, remained in Australia for about five years, and then returned to Ireland. (Some scholars believe that Reilly, and not John Boyle O'Reilly, is the one who had an affair with a warder's daughter in Bunbury.) Amos, 151, 188, 290; Walter McGrath, "The Fenian Riddle of Seamus Raol/James O'Reilly/The Major," photocopy, June 1988 (editors' files).

321. Jeremiah O'Donovan was from Cork. He had been charged with Thomas Duggan for administering the Fenian oath. Transported aboard the *Hougoumont,* he was fully pardoned in 1869 and returned to Ireland. Amos, 185, 290; McGrath, "The Fenians in Australia," 50.

Letters from James Wilson

not to attempt anything on my own account, but to wait patiently and Joe Nunan would make all right, there could not be a failure in Joe's hands, and if any of us made a move it would only spoil all. They departed and time wore on, and still we were told to keep quiet and not spoil Joe's plans; the remaining men went out and they before they left the Colony repeated the same old cry to wait patiently.

It was about this time that Hassett made his attempt. He was stationed in a gang on one of the roads in the interior of the country at a place called Newcastle, and he went into the bush and made his way to Perth, where the two Fulhams were living. A man, a stranger to most of us but a thoro' Irishman, got him a place of shelter for a few days. When he started for Bunbury, a port where whalers call, and the same place where J. B. O'Reilly made his exit from amongst us. On his leaving Perth the men who were living there made a collection to assist him on the road. The collection amounted to twenty shillings, although at this time he should not have stood in need of assistance as the money had arrived more than twelve months previous. However, it was arranged with Nunan that his money should be sent after him to Bunbury. He went and encountered the greatest hardships that could be imagined. He found friends, but, alas! Times had changed since O'Reilly was there; money was then in abundance but now gaunt poverty stalked across the land, but still the warm Irish heart was there, and they did what they could. They found him employment at a low rate of wages, his food in fact, until he might get a chance of escape. A chance soon presented itself and a skipper of a vessel offered to take him away for thirty pounds. He wrote to Nunan to send the money. He sent back answer that he would do so as soon as possible. Hassett waited for some time and not seeing the money forthcoming, he spoke to the "Soggarth,"[322] and he wrote three separate times to Nunan, but without success. Hassett was then forced to stow himself away on board another ship that was bound for London. He was discovered on board and made prisoner by the water police which has been established here since O'Reilly's escape. He received three years as a punishment for his attempt. If Nunan had sent his money as he should have done he would now be a free man. The case of William Foley is also very bad. He was, you may remember, one of the Clare Lane men. He belonged to my regiment. His sentence was five years. He got out on his ticket of leave about the same time that the first batch of men were released. He was forced to have a master according to convict law, so he got employment with a farmer of the name of McManus and so he kept working until his time had expired. He then thought he would get to a port and see if he could get out of the country. He went to Champion Bay. He worked there for some time until, employment failing, he was left without any means to get away. He then bethought himself of sending for his portion of the money, which would enable

322. Rev. Patrick McCabe. O'Brien and Ryan, 2, 563.

Letters from James Wilson

him to pay his passage to some other place. Again, as in the case of Hassett, there were plenty of excuses but no money, and my poor but true and brave comrade—he who had spurned the offer of a release, if he would inform on Hogan and myself— was left not only to remain in this land of tears and toil, but was reduced to a state of starvation and forced to sleep at night in a horse's manger with scarcely a rag to hide his nakedness or a bit to satisfy the cravings of hunger. I will not cite any more cases but I will content myself with stating that not one of all the military who have been released on ticket have received their money in a lump but a few pounds now and again just as it suited him. I can't forbear to mention Patrick Keating[323] who had been sick in hospital for eighteen months, and was on the point of death when the clergy interfered and the governor gave him ticket of leave to try as a last resource to save his life. He went out of here on a cold black day in the midst of winter, and, only for the exertions of our own men inside the prison, he would have had nothing to cover him except the regulation blue shirt and pants which was all unfit for the covering of a sick man in cold and stormy weather. He, Mr. Nunan, could not say that he was not aware of the circumstances as we made it our business to acquaint him with the facts. Keating had to return to hospital after he got the district that he was allotted to. After witnessing the conduct of Mr. Nunan to the other men, and after he had broke all his promise to myself, it would not do for me to trust him any longer with our fate, so I resolved, in conjunction with Hogan and Hassett to try fortune once more on our own account. With this object in view, I wrote to Nunan to ask him if he would give us the sum that was allotted to us and we would try and shift for ourselves. This seems to have highly offended him as his reply was not very courteous. To this I replied that if he did not give me an answer to the question if he would give me my share of the money that he held in trust for us that I would take other steps in the matter. He replied in the following words which I copy from his letter as they are written: "Sir, To reply to you in plain and candid terms; I will not comply with your request, in sending you the money that I hold in trust for you." And this after keeping us on the tiptoe of expectation for four years. This money you see he will not part with only by "dribs and drabs" and that is of no use to us. He sometimes sends small [illegible] to us if we want it. In this way the money is nearly all exhausted. I believe that some of the men have drawn largely in this way; I anyway have not drawn so much. The full extent of the money that I have drawn is about £8, eight pounds—but some have drawn three times that amount. But Mr. Nunan, since I asked him for the full amount, will not answer any of my letters so that this source of supply is cut off,

323. Patrick Keating (1826–1874) was a military Fenian from Clare. He had been in the same regiment as Delaney, Foley, Hogan, and Wilson and was transported on the *Hougoumont*. Amos, 85, 290.

Letters from James Wilson

even although I have written to him stating the fact of my not being in good health and that I required a little extra nourishment that I could not get without money, still up to the date of this letter he had made no reply; in the letter of his that I refer to and that I have quoted from he says that he is ready to give an account of the trust reposed in him and to hand over the balance into any respectable person's hand that may be appointed for the purpose; that each man was to receive thirty £ one and eight pence, £30-1-8d. You will thus perceive that either him or the other men whose names I have mentioned above must have told a gross untruth; I am inclined to think that such a man as John Flood would not make a willful misstatement or pervert the facts of the case. However that may be, Mr. Nunan says that there is only £30-1-8 for each man and that he will not give without an order from those who placed it in his hands. These parties I don't know but I have reason to believe that the Editor of the *Melbourne Advocate*[324] was the chief man, and I think all the money passed thro' his hands, please to see some of the released men who may be in New York and ask them about this money. If you could take any steps in the matter I would thank you. In closing this account, I may say that since the departure of Mr. Brophy we have been treated with the greatest contempt imaginable. The cool indifference to our fate that this man displays would sicken you. All our hopes of honourable or fair treatment vanished with Mr. Brophy.

Now, dear friend, let me pass to something more pleasant. Let me tell you that Martin [Hogan] and I expect you to do something for us, we look upon you as our leader and chief, and as such we expect that you will not forget your humble followers but that you will try to get us out of this mare's nest that we have got into. I must tell you that we are much altered in appearance, that from young men we have become old ones, that our hair is now of a nice grey colour, truly if ever we get out, we shall want to make the acquaintance of Madam Rachel.[325] It is now seven years last month since we were tried, a pretty good apprenticeship to the trade of a lag, and yet you know that John Bull has not succeeded in reforming us. I am afraid he never will.

You said in your letter to Martin [Hogan] that you would begin to work for us at once and that you would write again and let us know some further particulars, pray do, for we have been in great anxiety ever since. Month after month we were waiting with eager eyes and beating hearts the arrival of the mail, expecting to hear from you what we were sure would be glad tidings; but we were doomed to disappointment. Now I hope that on receipt of this you will write in return and let us

324. Samuel Winter. Amos, 177.
325. Madame Rachel Levison was a notorious nineteenth-century cosmetics entrepreneur in London. Joe McLaughlin, associate professor, Ohio University, email to Philip Fennell, May 10, 2002.

Letters from James Wilson

know what we have to expect. I hope that your message will be a good one. I must tell you that Hogan and I are together once more after a separation of many years. Shortly after our arrival in this colony, he received a sentence of six months separate confinement for going to kill a warder that spoke slightingly of Ireland and he was eventually sent to Champion Bay, where he received many kindnesses from Mr. Brophy. It is his opinion that if Mr. Brophy had remained we would be treated differently than what we have been treated; and that is my feeling on the subject also. Martin wishes me to say that he has sent you three letters and he has only received one from you in all; but about two of his letters he has some doubts if they ever were posted. We are both very anxious to hear from you because it is only the want of money that keeps us here this moment. If you knew the real facts connected with the chances of getting away, you would see in a moment that it is only money that is required to set us free. Will you be so kind as to let Jack O'Reilly know that we are still alive please to convey to him our best wishes for his happiness and also that we would like to hear from him. We both send our respects to Mr. And Mrs. Curran and also to all those friends and wellwishers that may be near you. I may state for the information of the Currans that neither Hogan nor myself have ever altered in our feeling or principles from what we were when you last saw us. We have just heard a piece of news that fills us with the most unbounded delight. We hear that "Nagle"[326] of accursed memory is shot, let us know if the news is true. In directing your letter please to avoid putting my name on the outside, but use two envelopes; on the outside one direct to Mr. Francis O'Callaghan, Victoria Hotel, Fremantle, Western Australia, and on the inner one put the simple name Red Hugh. This letter is written with the approval of Hogan, who has seen it and sends his best wishes for your welfare, and I also beg to send you a blessing on your future career and remain with every feeling of respect.

Yours, etc.
J. Wilson

Fremantle,
Western Australia

15 June, 1874

Dear Friend,

It is now over 12 months since I wrote to you before, and ever since I have been waiting and watching every mail expecting and hoping that you would answer my

---

326. Pierce Nagle worked at the offices of the *Irish People* and gave evidence against a number of Fenians, including Thomas Clarke Luby, John O'Leary, O'Donovan Rossa, and Charles Kickham. Ó Broin, 4. He was later shot in London. [London] *Times,* July 7, 1873, 8 (col. d).

Letters from James Wilson

letter, but concluding that it never reached your hand or else that you have been waiting to see the result of the appeals made at home for our release. I have decided now that these efforts have failed to appeal to you once more.

I think it my duty to make this appeal to you; my duty to my comrades as well as to myself because no man should surrender himself to death and despair without making some effort to save himself; it is to enable us to make this effort that I now appeal to you. It is most certain that the British Government will never release one of the soldiers. This is as true Holy Writ; most of us are beginning to show symptoms of disease, in fact, we are all ailing to a greater or less extent, and cannot expect to hold out much longer, and one of our number, the finest man amongst us named Patrick Keating, is dead. This will also be our position if we do not get some assistance soon, assistance that will enable us not only to get a little extra nourishment but also to enable us to make some attempt to break our chains. And what a death is staring us in the face, the death of a felon in a British dungeon, and a grave amongst Britton's ruffians. I am not ashamed to speak the truth and it is the simple truth, viz., that it is a disgrace to have us in prison to-day. A little money judiciously expended would have sufficed to release every man that is now in West Australia, and our country would not have to suffer the repeated insults at the hands of the Brittish officials that she has done. Besides it would be more agreeable to our own feelings to be our own liberators; but our own liberators we cannot be or attempt to be without some means. This country is so thinly populated that it would be impossible to hide for even a day in any of the little towns without being discovered, and if you took to the bush the whole of the inhabitants will give chase or a civilian will arrest you at sight if he is able to, if not able he will at once go or send to the police and place them on your track, and the police will follow you with one or more natives and trackers until you are utterly worn out and will have to give in for want of food. The only way that can be managed in the bush is to have a supply of money, and you could then purchase clothes and food. A man who can pay for everything is never suspected; but the best way to get out of this is to have a ship to call at a certain place and go there at speed and embark at once. This can be readily done thro' a whaler. There could be a whaler spoken to in Boston or any other port that they sail from and for a trifle she would call here for water and provisions, and if we could know the name of the captain and also of the ship, we could be ready to start as soon as she was ready for sea. Even then we would require a little money to get us clothes and to enable us to get to the ship as quick as possible; and if there is sufficient sum sent for the purpose we could have a small vessel that would take us to the other colonies or to the "Java Islands," where we could get on board of some American vessel and so to the States.

With money you can do anything, without it nothing; this remark applies to this

Letters from James Wilson

country in an especial manner. Here is to be found man in his most degraded form. Men that would sell your body and soul for a shilling. Every man has his price in this land of Cain. One can get anything done for money.

I have now to state a melancholy fact, viz., the death of Patrick Keating of the 5th Dragoon Guards. He died of aneurism of the main artery brought on by hardships and long imprisonment. He had been bad for about 2 years in the convict hospital. At length, the priest, the Rev. Father Burke,[327] interfered and addressed the Governor on the subject, stating it to be his opinion that if Keating had a change of scene and a change of diet and friendly faces around him that he would recover. He underwent a medical examination and they allowed him out to die. I was permitted to attend him in his last moments. The Rev. Father Gibney[328] attended to his spiritual welfare and he was also visited by the Bishop and the Sisters of Charity. He is buried by the side of the Brothers Fulham.[329] My space will not permit me to say more of Keating at present than that a truer son of our dear Motherland was never reared on her green bosom. May the Lord have mercy on his soul!!![330]

Now, dear Friend, you see our position and we want you to let our case be known to O'Donovan Rossa and the Council and tell them that in the hour of trial we flinched not and that we expect to be assisted out of our difficulty like men that have been true to the cause in the most trying circumstances that men could be placed in. We expect great aid from you yourself who know us perhaps better than any other men in the organisation. We ask you to aid us with your tongue and pen, with your brain and intellect, with your ability and influence, and God will bless your efforts, and we will repay you with all the gratitude of our natures. If you will aid us in the way I speak of we will soon be in the Land of Freedom. You could also write to Dublin and let them know at home how we are situated and that a little money would secure our liberty, and also to the different Australian colonies and they could forward the amount they wished to send direct here. But I am sure if this case of ours is explained in its true colours to our countrymen in the United

327. Rev. Anselm Bourke. Bourke, 74.

328. Rev. Matthew Gibney (1837–1925) was stationed at Perth before the 1868 arrival of the *Hougoumont*. He remained in the area for many years, rising to the rank of bishop in 1887. Throughout his career he was helpful to the Fenians, including being involved with the *Catalpa* rescuers. The authorities were aware of his sympathies, and one governor, Sir Frederick Weld, even wrote Rome to complain of his fellow Catholic's activities. Amos, 98, 133, 222–23; "The Diocese of Kilmore" [http://www.cavannet.ie/kilmore/histmisn.htm], January 2002; Russo, 32.

329. Lawrence Fulham (1830–187[?]) and his brother Luke (1822–1870) were both Fenians from Louth. They were each sentenced to five years and transported on the *Hougoumont*. Pardoned in 1869, they remained in Australia for the brief time before their deaths from tuberculosis. Amos, 130, 290.

330. Wilson was given permission to stay with Keating at the Guildford hospital, and later at Joseph Noonan's Perth house, where Keating died. On one of the daily inspections, a warder found Wilson drunk at the house. Wilson was reprimanded. Amos, 207.

Letters from James Wilson

States that they will soon subscribe as much as would hire a whaler to call for us and also to supply us with an outfit.

Now, dear Friend, remember, this is a voice from the tomb. For is not this [a] living tomb? In the tomb it is only a man's body that is good for worms but in this living tomb the canker worm of care enters the very soul. Think that we have been nearly 9 years in this living tomb since our first arrest and that it is impossible for mind or body to withstand the continual strain that is upon them. One or the other must give way. It is to aid us in this sad strait that I now, in the name of my comrades and myself, ask you to aid us in the manner pointed out. We think that you can do it if you will. There ought to be a sufficient sum raised in the States in one day for the purpose, but at all hazards make our position known and ask a little assistance for us of those who enjoy the blessing of liberty, and let us know the result. If there were any other way of getting out of this difficulty, I would not apply to you, but our faith in you is unbounded. We think that if you forsake us then we are friendless indeed.

There are now in prison in this col[ony] 7 life sentence men. The other man who received the sentence of life is now dead. The remaining 8 are on ticket of leave. The names of the 7 men who are actually in prison out here are as follows:— Martin Hogan, Thomas Hassett, Robert Cranston, James Keilly, Thomas Darragh, Michael Harrington, James Wilson.

So you see there are not many of us and it would not take a very great amount to get us all away. So, dear Friend, I will trust this matter to your kindness and will now conclude by assuring you that whether this appeal succeeds or not that the greenest spot in our memory is connected with you, and that we never forget that we are still Soldiers of Liberty.

With respects to all friends, believe me to be,
Ever fraternally yours,
James Wilson

Mr. John Devoy, Cor. Sec.
Irish Confederation, New York City, U.S.

APPENDIX B: FROM THE REPORT OF THE EIGHTH ANNUAL [CLAN-NA-GAEL] CONVENTION, CLEVELAND, OHIO, SEPTEMBER 4, 1877

Friday September 7th—Morning Session.

On the re-assembling of the Convention a statement was made that Bro. Bridgman of Troy had revealed the time and place of the Convention. The matter was referred to the Judiciary Committee.

The report of District D was then read and referred to the appropriate committees.

A motion to re-consider the action by which it had been decided to admit Thomas Brennan to the floor was lost, and, on motion, it was ordered that his statement, together with the questions put to him and his answers be taken down in writing. It was then voted that any member of the Convention who became demonstrative during the hearing of Brennan's case should be censured. Bro. John Walsh of New Britain offered his services as stenographer which were accepted. Mr. Brennan was then introduced and made his statement.

Thomas Brennan's Statement.

The first thing I heard about going to Australia was from the S G of D 1. He sent me to Eighth Street where I saw A of the F C, Goff, who asked me if any person was speaking to me—this was about half-past 9—I said no. He asked me if I would go to Australia, I said yes. He asked me if I was ready, I said yes. He asked me if I was ready to go to-morrow, I said yes. I left him and went to my work. About 10 o'clock next day he came to me again and told me to prepare to go. I left my employment, and I left directions to get my wages, and he and I went to New Bedford; there I met

From the Report of the Eighth Annual [Clan-na-Gael] Convention

Devoy and Denny Duggan. Bro Goff showed me a telegram in New York, before I went down, from Devoy, telling him to bring me along. If I could not get on board the ship in the capacity of steward, that I would go for the Vigilence Committee to see the ship sail, and that she was properly provisioned. I never sought to go to Australia—I never looked to go. I saw Richardson the agent of the ship when I went down, and I partly thought he came to the conclusion that I was not a fit person to go on board the ship. They had a steward for the ship engaged. O'Connor and Mulledy were asked; I said I knew as much about being a steward as they did; however they refused to let me go. I then asked if I could go in any capacity at all—I made up my mind to go if I had to stow away or go before the mast. The captain told me that he would call at St. Michael's and take me; Devoy told me the same; Richardson told me the same. I returned to New York and remained at my business, and was told shortly after the last meeting of the F C in D 1 that I was to go to Australia—that I was to go to the Azores to get on board the ship; that the F C felt satisfied that I was to go, and that I would get further instructions from Mr. Goff. Bro Goff gave me a check for $300 to pay my passage to the Azores to meet the vessel. I was then elected by D 54 a delegate to the Providence Convention, I went to the Convention, this check was handed into the Convention and passed upon by the Committee on Foreign Relations; I saw all the members of the F C that were there, they understood that I was to go to the Azores. I saw—

Bro W. Carroll. I positively knew nothing about it—the incoming F C knew nothing about it.

Bro Brennan. Is Bro Mahon in the room? I ask Bro Mahon if he knew I was going?

Bro Mahon. Yes, sir; I knew you were going to Australia.

Bro Brennan. Did Devoy know?

Bro Devoy. If the brother will confine himself to the outgoing F C, they were aware of it.

Bro Carroll. I must say that the incoming F C did not know anything about the matter.

Bro Brennan. This I know, that my receipt for the money went into the Convention and was passed upon by the Committee on Foreign Affairs, my receipt was there and I was there myself. I was not told not to go, and I went from that Convention with the understanding that I was to go.

Richardson told me that a vessel would leave Boston to take me to the Azores and I would land about the 1st of October. I returned to New York. I could not find any vessel going, as I was there told, in New Bedford. Bro

From the Report of the Eighth Annual [Clan-na-Gael] Convention

Goff telegraphed to the Portuguese consul in New Bedford and said there was a small schooner of 62 tons going to the Azores. I went to the hotel where Devoy was stopping but could not find him. I went to New Bedford, and was four weeks in going to the Azores. When I got to the Island of Fayal I saw an old Irishwoman who kept a hotel there. Hearing that a number of vessels had put into Fayal I left a letter for Duggan on the ship, in case he called, told him that I was there and went on to St. Michaels; remained in St. Michaels two months; in about six weeks got a letter from him that the captain was at that island, and that he would not take any person on board his ship. The vessel, instead of going to the island to meet me, went to an island 180 miles away; was told that the vessel would go to St. Michaels by the captain, the agent, Devoy and Goff. Had to wait for a return steamer to take me to Fayal. When I got there it was only to be disappointed, for the captain had sailed twenty-four hours before. Went to the hotel and the keeper told me that he believed the captain went to that island to avoid me. They left without taking water on board. I came to the conclusion I was sold—that I was treacherously deceived by the men who claim now I had no right to go. Was determined to go to Australia, and came to the conclusion that I would stow away in the cargo of the boat as the boats would not take passengers at any cost. Met an Irishman and he told me that he thought he could get me a passage on board a ship to London by spending a little money among the sailors. He conveyed my luggage and revolvers on board. In the morning the captain saw me on deck and he asked me what I was doing on board the ship, and he said he would not have any person come on board his ship. When he was going away he saw three other stowaways. He read the act of parliament that we were liable to three months imprisonment and a fine of twenty pounds. That was hard on me. I had close on twenty pounds. When he got to London he hoist the signal for the police boat, but he did not wait for it. Going into the dock I jumped from the vessel to a boat and was rowed ashore for a little money, and went round to the dock and got my clothes and revolver from the crew.

I remained in London trying to get a chance to work my way to Australia as a stoker on board one of the Australian vessels. Went to Liverpool and got work at my trade, wrote a letter to New York that I was there, and that the vessel had not put in at the island as she promised; in answer received a letter from Goff, enclosing twenty-eight pounds. The letter I wrote was calling for funds; this letter enclosed twenty-eight pounds all the money he could then raise for me. He told me I was then going to a

From the Report of the Eighth Annual [Clan-na-Gael] Convention

strange place where I would meet friends if they had not already got away before I got there; that if I did not meet them I would be without money or friends in a strange land; in his concluding words he said: "I would advise you to think well of what you are doing. My advice would be for you to return, I leave it to yourself, do what is right, and, if you intend to go, God speed you." Paid fifteen guineas for a third class steerage passage; in two months got to Melbourne, and remained in Melbourne ten days, got a passage on a vessel calling at Adelaide for eight pounds, at Adelaide got a passage on the "*Georgette*" for Freemantle,[331] when I got into Bunbury saw the whaler "*Catalpa*." Previous to this it was alleged I received orders to return. Never received orders to return from any person.

When I got into Bunbury saw the vessel, went ashore and got aboard of her. The first man I met was Captain Anthony made myself known to him and asked if there were any friends on board; met Duggan, he was surprised to see me, went to the hotel and saw Breslin, went up to him after a while and asked him if he knew me, said that my name was Brennan and was from New York, asked him outside how he was situated for funds, for at that time I had only about four pounds, he had plenty of funds, told him how I was situated but he never gave any money; met Duggan and asked him how he was getting along, he said he got along badly—he had no shoes, no money, had been on a twelve month's voyage and was without tobacco—and out of my few shillings I was obliged to give some to Duggan, for Breslin, who had hundreds of pounds in his possession, could not give him any; remained in Moloney's hotel and came away without paying my board. Breslin knew that and he never gave me a cent.

On the morning of the rescue, or the night before, Breslin had horses for himself and the rest of the party, I had to go shift for myself, had to go to Perth, a distance of twelve miles, alone, after walking around could only get a sorry looking excuse for a horse to carry me thirty-six miles, such as it was I came to Freemantle and saw Breslin who told me I was to start in the morning at four o'clock to take the baggage, started before four with the animal I had, twenty three miles, on a bad road, through the bush, I was to go to bed and he was to remain up and call me in the morning. In the morning he did not call me, awakened myself, went around the house and could not see any person. There were revolvers and rifles lying around in his room and four hundred pounds in a bag on the bed in that open room. Went into another room and there was a man there drunk, he

331. Here again, the name of the town, Fremantle, is misspelled.

From the Report of the Eighth Annual [Clan-na-Gael] Convention

belonged to the hotel, I became uneasy at this, did not know who the man was until a light was struck, my suspicions were aroused at the open door and no person there. Breslin came up stairs and after him the proprietor of the hotel, Mr. Maloney. I have been charged with saying that Breslin was drunk on the morning of the rescue, I did not; I say Moloney, the proprietor of the hotel, had liquor in him. Was to have been called at four and this was six. Asked Breslin what he intended to do, he got very angry. Was not satisfied the way I saw things. There was a scene near ensuing in the place. Rode twenty-three miles on a road I had never been on before, did not know the way, got lost and was lost for an hour until I got on a hill and saw the sea, saw no person, a ship, a boat or anything else, then saw two men, the captain of the vessel, and the crew, and the boat on the beach. The captain told me there was a strange man there and he did not know what to do. I asked the man if he would have something to drink and he refused; he asked what way the captain got his boat unto the beach, he pointed across a reef of rocks, he said a boat never got in the same way before. He seemed to be satisfied we could get out by pulling along shore to Garden Island, that if he went out the same way as he came in he would be swamped—the bottom would be ripped out of the boat.

When we came to the vessel we got on board, Breslin went into the cabin. The six prisoners were in a bad state—without any bed and sleeping on the bare boards—there were three of them that I would not be surprised if they were found dead any morning—Harrington had diarrhoea, he had to go the bows of the vessel six or seven times a day, he was kept constantly going all the time, Hassett was spitting blood, Wilson was also sick, and, on one occasion, when Wilson went to Breslin, he said, "God damn you, you are always sick." I will read—

Bro Breslin. I ask a question, if he heard me make that statement?

Bro Brennan. I have been told so by those that heard him.

Bro Griffin of D 14. I will ask if all Brennan has stated is of his own knowledge?

Bro Brennan. The men were lying on deck, on bare boards, without anything in shape of a bed, and Breslin in the state room of the cabin: that is all right.

Bro Burns of D 2. Does Brennan know, of his own knowledge, that there were four hundred pounds in the bag he spoke of?

Bro Brennan. I believe, to the best of my knowledge, there was about four hundred pounds in gold in it, had it in my hand did not open it to look at it.

From the Report of the Eighth Annual [Clan-na-Gael] Convention

Bro Burns. How do you form that conclusion?

Bro Brennan. I was told by Desmond and King, Desmond said so.

Bro ———. Are we to take evidence here?

President. We are not.

Bro Desmond. Do you say that I told you how much money was in the gentleman's bag?

Bro Brennan. I did not.

Bro Desmond. I said I knew there was money it.

Bro. Brennan. With your permission I will read a little of the evidence given by the prisoners.

Bro Breslin. If any portion of the proceedings of the trial committee be read I ask that all the proceedings be read. I understand the District Member has a very brief synopsis of the evidence. I ask that I get fair play and be allowed to produce the evidence on the other side also.

The President. That will be allowed.

Bro Taaffe of D 22. We ought not to receive one-half of the evidence— it would be unjust to receive part of the evidence.

Bro Brennan here read extracts from the evidence taken on his trial, and, after reading a portion of the evidence, said—"I acknowledge that I called Breslin a scoundrel, I called it to him in the room of D 1 after the D was out of session." After which he continued to read the other portions of the evidence.

Bro Brennan (continuing). Now, Mr. Chairman, I understand that I have been charged with being the cause of mutiny on board the ship, if that is mutiny I don't know what mutiny is. The vessel was to put into Fernandina in Florida, she was out nearly four months, said to be whaling, but had caught nothing.

Bro Breslin. How does he know what the captain's orders were?

Bro Brennan. Devoy told me that she was to put into Fernandina, and preparations were made to receive them, when the vessel was not putting into Fernandina but was going to gratify Breslin to see a whale caught; he had the captain's state-room and the captain's office, he had no consideration for those six men; the vessel was sent out for the prisoners not for whales, and the organization would rather see the vessel home than taking two thousand dollars worth of oil. When we saw the vessel was not going into port, but was going to keep the men out an indefinite period; Desmond, Duggan and I came to the conclusion that it would be best to put the vessel into port, we went to Breslin and made known the wishes of the men to him. He asked me what was the matter, I told him I was told

From the Report of the Eighth Annual [Clan-na-Gael] Convention

that the men were wanted on shore better than getting oil, and that they were sick of the confinement on the vessel; he said I came there as a pimp and a spy, I said the man who called me a pimp and a spy was a liar, that was nice language to use to a man who went out to Australia, to be called a pimp and a spy; I told him the men were uneasy about getting into port. The prisoners and we drew up a document saying: "We the undersigned, hereby request you to bring the vessel into port, owing to the innutritious quality of the food; second, owing to ill health we deem it dangerous to prolong the voyage; that the prisoners are not actually free men until placed on American soil. By complying with the above we believe it will be satisfactory to all concerned."

That document was signed by Desmond, King, Duggan, I and the six prisoners. I leave it to any one whether that was mutiny or not. After that document was signed, we said we claimed all responsibility for bringing the vessel into port.

Bro McCarthy. Are you a navigator?

Bro Brennan. No, sir. She was steering east then. When we got to New York a tugboat brought us up the bay. I live in New York; my friend and relations are there. I asked the captain of the tugboat to take me ashore. Breslin told the captain to order me back. The captain of the tugboat would not give me leave; I had to go back on the ship. In the morning Breslin went ashore, himself and the captain. I got off on the first boat that came alongside. The prisoners were so fairly disgusted with their treatment that not one of them would go ashore with Breslin; they refused to go with him?

Bro Breslin. Did I at any time ask the prisoners to go ashore with me?

Bro Brennan. I say they all told me so; some of them swore it on the trial. There was a disagreement when we should go ashore.

I met several of the members of the F.C. afterwards at Sweeney's [*sic*] Hotel,[332] the prisoners, Desmond, King and I were there; we were there to make complaint of the treatment at the hands of Breslin on board. Breslin was sent for, but he would not put in an appearance before that meeting to hear the complaints. When I came to New York men went around to watch my movements. Where is the man that if he was watched could not be caught; I may have said hard words and hard things; in New York they go so far as to strike a brother in open D.

---

332. A prominent hotel that existed for over half a century in downtown New York City, Sweeny's was known as a meeting place for Roman Catholics, Irish nationalists, politicians, and journalists. Various Irish exiles stayed there over the years, including those who arrived on the *Cuba* in 1871. "Old Landmark to Be Sold," *NYT,* December 31, 1895, 13.

From the Report of the Eighth Annual [Clan-na-Gael] Convention

Bro O'Sullivan of D 42. Do you recollect when I met Martin Hogan, after their return, in the city of New York. I was then introduced to Wilson: Do you recollect that I asked Martin Hogan in your presence what kind of treatment he got?

Bro Brennan. I don't.

Bro Langdon of D 125. He stated he had but four pounds when he reached Australia, and gave some of this amount to other parties; did he have any money when he left?

Bro Brennan. I paid two pounds two shillings for one week's board, that was the last of the money; to pay for washing on board I had to borrow four shillings.

Bro ———. Were you ever refused the privilege of oil on that ship?

Bro Brennan. Yes, sir, we were; we had to burn blackfish oil.

Bro 4 of D 200. Is this statement you made in regard to that mutiny all that you had to do in the so-called mutiny?

Bro Brennan. That is the only thing. There is the document we had.

Bro Cannon of D 19. Who told you where this Convention was held?

Bro Brennan. It is well known all around New York. Several brothers of D 13, one member of D 1 told me, his name is Nolan. He told me the Convention was to be held in Cleveland; Sheehy of D 1 told me it was to be held in the same place. I was told two weeks ago it was to be held in Cleveland.

Bro ———. After they got on board at Freemantle, Brennan states they were put into bunks without any clothing. I ask if he supposed that the reason they were put in the hold was because the weather was rough?

Bro Brennan. The weather was not rough; the first night we had to sleep around like dogs wherever we could lay our heads. Hogan was five, six or seven days without a blanket; some of the blankets were a piece of a horse blanket.

Bro. Smythe, D 189. You say you were sent by authority of the F.C. to be one of the men on board that ship?

Bro Brennan. Yes, sir.

Bro Smythe. Did you know that Breslin was in charge of that expedition?

Bro Brennan. I went there as an equal, inferior to no man. I never was told to look to Breslin for authority. I went on the understanding that there was to be no failure.

Bro Smythe. Who gave you your orders to go on the ship to Australia?

Bro Brennan. Goff.

From the Report of the Eighth Annual [Clan-na-Gael] Convention

Bro Smythe. Did Goff tell you that you were on equal terms with Breslin?

Bro Brennan. He did not tell me; I wanted no one to tell me I was—I knew it.

Bro Devoy. Do you remember sitting with Goff and me in the Stevens House in New Bedford?

Bro Brennan. I remember.

Bro Devoy. Do you remember the day on which the instructions were written?

Bro Brennan. I remember.

Bro Devoy. What were those instructions?

Bro Brennan. My instructions were given to see the man that would be sent, in case you could not go I would be recognized.

Bro Devoy. Will you undertake to swear that you were not told that that man would not be the chief of the expedition?

Bro Brennan. I positively swear you never told me anything of the kind.

Bro Devoy. I say I did. Did I ever charge you with actually receiving orders to come back?

Bro Brennan. I went as one of the rescuing party, that I had nothing to do with.

Bro Devoy. Did I ever charge you with receiving orders to return, and you made a statement that Goff only received it?

Bro Brennan. You charged me with not coming back; when that money was given to Goff I was on my way to Australia.

Bro Devoy. In that letter of Goff's do you remember was there a statement that the F.C. had decided to recall you on account of failing to get on the ship?

Bro Brennan. I recollect I received a letter from Goff with twenty-eight pounds; he advised me to return; I have also heard of being ordered to return by the F.C., but I am sure I never received the order to return.

Bro Devoy. When you got on board the ship state whether you informed the prisoners that the rest of the rescuers were on equal terms with Breslin?

Bro Brennan. I believe I did.

Bro Devoy. Do you think that had anything to do with their hostility?

Bro Brennan. I don't know.

Bro Devoy. Did you ever tell them that he was only initiated by a kind of a fraud?

Bro Brennan. I never told them anything of the kind.

From the Report of the Eighth Annual [Clan-na-Gael] Convention

Bro Devoy. Did you ever tell them that you were a more important man in the organization than Breslin?

Bro Brennan. No.

Bro Devoy. And that you had more say in the property of the ship than he had?

Bro Brennan. I did not; the conversation at the time occurred between Duggan, Desmond and I.

Bro Devoy. Did you state that you were prosecuted for your honest convictions, in stating that he was a dangerous man to the organization, is that true?

Bro Brennan. I did say he was a dangerous man to the organization; I am in this organization seven years, Breslin was then in the organization, he came to D 1 to clear it out, Jerome J. Collins[333] was the leader, they seceded and formed the U I B, Breslin was high in that organization in Boston, that organization is virtually opposed to this, men in New York and Boston know it; after I came to New York from Ireland and was in this organization a short time, I was asked to join the U I B, they brought me down, I saw Breslin's brother and several other members there, was asked if I belonged to any other secret society working for Ireland, I refused to answer—would not answer the question—was taken blindfolded and put out of the room. Breslin was a member of that organization, they are bitterly opposed to this organization, they are men who seceded from this organization.

Q. Do you know that there is any such organization in existence at the present time?

A. I do not to my own knowledge.

Bro ———. In the year 1868, I believe it was, you were present at the time there was trouble in a New York D, I want to know how you know Breslin had anything to do with it?

A. I did not say he had anything to do with it, he belonged to the organization that seceded.

Bro Devoy. Q. I ask Brennan, through you, about that telegram Goff received from me, are you sure it was a telegram?

A. I believe it was a telegram—it said "Brennan will go along. If he cannot go in the capacity of steward he can act for the Committee of Safety."

Q. Do you know that Goff wrote a telegram to me saying, "Brennan must go on the ship"?

333. Jerome J. Collins in fact founded the Clan-na-Gael in 1867. He was the science editor for the (New York) *Herald* in the 1870s and perished in 1881 on the ill-fated *Jeannette* Arctic expedition. O'Brien and Ryan, 1, 3, 339; "To Honor Jerome Collins," *NYT*, February 14, 1884, 3.

From the Report of the Eighth Annual [Clan-na-Gael] Convention

A. No, sir; the first thing I heard of being asked to go was at a meeting in Fourth Street; this telegram had passed between you and him.

Bro Devoy. Did you make any representations to the men on board that the accommodations were not what was intended for them?

Bro Brennan. Yes, sir.

Bro Devoy. What did you know about it?

Bro Brennan. I knew in New Bedford there were boards put on for bunks, that there were plenty of clothes, salt beef, salt pork. I knew the money was given for that purpose; I know they were badly treated.

Bro Devoy. They could not get any rum. Did you ever incite the prisoners to make a raid on the store?

Bro Brennan. No, sir.

Bro Devoy. Do you know that any of the prisoners said you did?

Bro Brennan. They would swear an untruth.

Bro Devoy. Are you aware the captain ordered them something for a bed?

Bro Brennan. I am aware that Hogan picked oakum to make a bed; the captain ordered Hogan, like a dog, to leave it; Breslin did not provide a bed for him.

Bro Devoy. Did you ever know of these men making frivolous demands?

Bro Brennan. As a joke; they were only humbugging Martin Hogan, because he has not the best sense.

Q. Did you know them to demand fresh meat and vegetables?

A. They would be very foolish to ask it.

Q. Do you think that, on board a whaler sent out to catch whales and her provisions subject to inspection of the custom house people, it would be prudent to put luxuries on board?

A. You could put anything on board; there was money sufficient to fit out that vessel for a two years' voyage.

Q. Did you ever come into the knowledge of the fact that the reason the captain put away from the port he was to meet you was in consequence of being caught smuggling tobacco?

A. Yes, sir; he was smuggling.

Q. About the meeting in Sweeney's hotel, do you know for a fact that Bro Breslin was asked to appear?

A. I could not say; he was not in the hotel.

Q. Is that a refusal?

A. It was an evasion, he knew the thing was to be settled.

Q. Did you agree to give evidence?

A. I was asked to make charges, I believe.

From the Report of the Eighth Annual [Clan-na-Gael] Convention

Q. You stated that certain members of the F C were there. Dr. Carroll was there. Did you positively refuse to give evidence unless Goff was present?

A. I did; all the members of the out-going F C—Goff had a right to be there.

Bro Egan of Elizabeth, N.J.:

Q. Do you swear that there was any dereliction on the part of any of the rescuers?

A. I do not, sir.

Q. Was there a time fixed when the men were to make their escape, and a communication came and there was nobody there to receive it?

A. That was in the shape of a telegram; Cranston was down in the town, and a person from the hotel called him over to tell him that the vessel could not keep her appointment and he brought the news to the men in the prison.

Q. The time was fixed for the escape and the information that the ship had slipped her anchor came and no one to receive it?

A. Yes.

Q. Whose fault was that?

A. It was the fault of no person being there to receive it.

Q. Do you believe that the men would have then been retaken again?

A. I believe they would.

Q. Did you ever refuse to obey the orders of Breslin or any one in command?

A. I never did.

Q. How do you know the ship had changed her course?

A. From the way she was going.

Q. Were you informed the ship was to put in at the nearest port?

A. I was informed that the ship was to put in at Florida.

Q. Something was said that Breslin would like to see a whale caught?

A. I said that Breslin would like to see a whale caught.

Q. Did you ever hear him express an opinion on that?

A. No, sir.

Q. Do you know, of your own knowledge, that Breslin wanted to see a whale caught?

A. No, sir.

Q. Are you aware when Breslin was initiated into the organization?

A. He acknowledged himself he was initiated some years ago.

Q. You do not know, of your own knowledge, the time he was initiated?

A. No, sir.

From the Report of the Eighth Annual [Clan-na-Gael] Convention

Q. Something was said about gold, where did it come from?

A. It came from Sydney by King.

Q. Were you told by any person the amount?

A. I was told there were £400 in the bag; I carried it on board the ship.

Q. When on board the ship it has been charged that you incited those men to mutiny?

A. I did not.

Q. Did you advise them to mutiny?

A. No, sir.

Q. Did you advise those men to sign this request to change the voyage to New York?

A. No, sir; they were most anxious to sign it. I stated I should not be surprised to see one of these men dead.

Q. Any other reason?

A. On the high seas they were liable to capture by British vessels.

Q. You said you were never ordered to report to any particular person, but when you arrived did you refuse to obey the person who assumed command?

A. I never refused to obey him. I done everything I was told.

Q. Did you know that Breslin was in authority?

A. No, sir.

Q. You then considered Breslin a mere individual on board that ship?

A. I considered we were all equal.

Q. Who had the money?

A. Breslin.

Q. Why did Breslin take the cabin?

A. He had the money.

Bro ———. Is it a fair question—was Breslin the party that had the control of the expedition?

A. He was.

Q. If it is true you knew that Breslin was in command why did you refuse to obey him?

A. I never refused any order.

Q. Were you in search of the ship all the way?

A. Yes, sir; I chased her around the world and caught her in Bunbury.

Q. Why did not you obey your superior officer?

A. I did not recognize him as a superior officer.

Bro Boland of D 59:

Q. By whom was Brennan sent?

From the Report of the Eighth Annual [Clan-na-Gael] Convention

A. By the F C. Bro Devoy knew I was going and told me to go; I got $300 and gave a receipt for it.

Q. I would ask if he had a written authority to go on that expedition?

A. The check was passed on by the Providence Convention.

Q. Who was he ordered to report to?

A. Report to where?

Q. Anywhere?

A. This document was made out in New Bedford; Devoy, Goff, Duggan and I were present when it was arranged that I was to go, and he gave me a hailing sign.

Bro Breslin. Q. Was Brennan tried by a trial committee for false accusations?

A. Yes, sir.

Q. How long did the trial last?

A. It lasted a couple of months—about two months.

Q. Did he state to the trial committee that he was under the influence of drink when he used some of the language?

A. No, sir.

Bro Breslin. He made a plea that he was under the influence of drink.

Q. Did he admit that my statement, written in my journal was correct?

A. I do not recollect that I did admit anything of the kind.

Bro Breslin. I state now you did.

Q. Did you know that the captain's orders were to put into Fernandina?

A. I had heard of it.

Q. Were you aware that, while the captain was instructed to go into Fernandina, he had a certain discretion in case of any accident?

A. I don't know.

Q. Did you know that he had any instructions to land the men in Fernandina?

A. Yes.

Q. Did you know that it was necessary—that it was desirable—that the men should be brought in on the coast?

A. In conversation with Desmond and Duggan I said there would not be any of this trouble if the vessel had been in time for the Convention, it would be so much better for the organization. You had such a high opinion of the Convention you said it would be better to have $2,000 than what a lot of green Micks could do for them.

Bro ———. Did you understand them to dictate a course to go into port for the Convention, or there would be trouble?

From the Report of the Eighth Annual [Clan-na-Gael] Convention

A. I do not understand it, only the document that was signed.

Bro Devoy. Was there any fear of revolvers?

A. They had no revolvers.

Q. Will you swear that they did not say that, if Breslin did not do this there would be trouble?

A. Wilson told me.

Q. Do you believe Wilson is diseased?

A. I believe Wilson is not in his right mind: whisky aggravates it.

Q. At the meeting in the cabin would you swear positively that there were not remarks made there, that if Breslin refused to bring the vessel into port you would take her in by force?

A. No, sir, it would be the last thing to do, it would be impossible.

Q. You say you never refused to obey any orders from Breslin; if you were on equal terms why did you obey them.

A. He assumed the responsibility, I did not think it would be right to do anything against him.

Q. At personal interviews with you, after your arrival, did I take any trouble to make you change your course?

A. Yes.

Bro ———. You made a statement that $2,000 was of more value than the combined wisdom of this or any other Convention—that Breslin designated this or a similar Convention as a pack of green Micks?

A. When he was reminded that the Convention would be in session early in August, he said it would be better to make a couple of thousand dollars in oil than any pack of green Micks could do for them.

Bro Breslin. I never used any such words with regard to the Convention; I said it would be better to make $10,000 or 14,000 by staying out six weeks than to bring the men home—I said that $10,000 or 14,000 would be of greater use to the Irish cause than to bring these green men home for parading, and it could easily have been made if the vessel had stayed out six weeks longer.

Bro Meehan. Do you think that John Devoy, in his official capacity, used his influence in prosecuting you since your return?

A. Yes, of course he did.

Q. Do you know that John Devoy used his influence against you?

A. I know that John Devoy brought Dr. Carroll from Philadelphia, and, after the adjournment of the trial committee, he was giving evidence when I was not there.

Dr. Carroll. Were you in the room when I gave my testimony?

208

From the Report of the Eighth Annual [Clan-na-Gael] Convention

A. I was told to go back to Military Hall; the committee adjourned for a specified time; when I went to Military Hall the case for the defense was in progress.

Dr. Carroll. I beg to state, on oath, that the thing is absolutely false: I was summoned to New York before the trial committee, where my report, which was read at the last Convention, was brought up. In his evidence Goff swore that that report never had been read to the Convention. You were in the room all the time I was giving my evidence.

Dr. Carroll. Are you aware that I was summoned by the committee?

A. I am not aware.

Bro Morrissey. Were you recompensed for your services in Australia?

A. I spent $150 of my own money.

Q. Did you get any money after coming back?

A. I did.

Q. How much?

A. $150.

Q. Who did you get it from?

A. Some from Devoy, Denny Duggan and Rossa.

Q. Did you give a receipt for it?

A. I did not.

Bro Devoy. Will you swear how much money you got from me personally?

A. I will swear I did not get over $150 entirely.

Q. Did you keep an account of it?

A. No; I got $50 from Denny Duggan.

Q. You got $50 from me personally?

A. Yes.

Q. You got $20 also?

A. I got $20, and I got $20 from Rossa.

Q. Did you get another $20 from me in the Herald office?

A. I did.

Q. How much did the clothes cost?

A. I don't know what the clothes cost; I have been informed by a brother they cost $25. Breslin got an outfit at a Broadway store and we were brought to a sailor's slop-shop on the docks.

Q. Will you swear it was a sailor's slop-shop?

A. I will swear it is a sailor's slop-shop where we got our outfit.

Q. Who brought you to the place?

A. You did.

From the Report of the Eighth Annual [Clan-na-Gael] Convention

Q. Had I any money then?

A. I don't know.

Q. Had I seen Breslin then?

A. I believe you had.

Q. Will you swear that; what day was it?

A. Saturday night.

Q. The day the Catalpa arrived?

A. Yes.

Q. Did I tell you I had just arrived from Philadelphia without any money and that I could not get the clothes without getting them on credit?

A. I won't swear you did not.

Q. Will you swear that I did?

A. One party went to one place and the other to another.

Q. Will you swear I had seen Breslin then?

A. I will not.

Q. Did you ever see the bill for these clothes?

A. I did not.

Q. How much did you pay for your board in Rossa's?

A. I paid for it.

Q. If a bill was furnished to me then, will you swear it was fraudulent?

A. I paid over the counter for my meals for the first couple of days.

Q. How much did it all amount to—the money you got in cash, the clothes and board?

A. It appeared in the newspaper as being paid to Thomas Brennan, when I did not get any such amount in money.

Q. You admit receiving two sums of $50 and three of $20?

A. I do.

[Q.] That makes more than the amount you said, without taking any account of your clothes, board and lodging, and yet you have the audacity to insinuate that there was dishonesty somewhere.

Bro Breslin. Were not you wearing a new suit of clothes at Rossa's while I was still wearing the old clothes I had on board?

A. That is true. I left my portmanteau and everything I had behind me.

Q. Do you wish to convey to this Convention that there was no mutiny on board that ship?

A. Of course I will say that there was no mutiny.

Bro ———. You said you considered yourself equal to Breslin on board, bearing in mind, you felt you were not bound to obey him?

A. If an order came from Desmond I would obey.

APPENDIX C: DRAMATIS PERSONAE

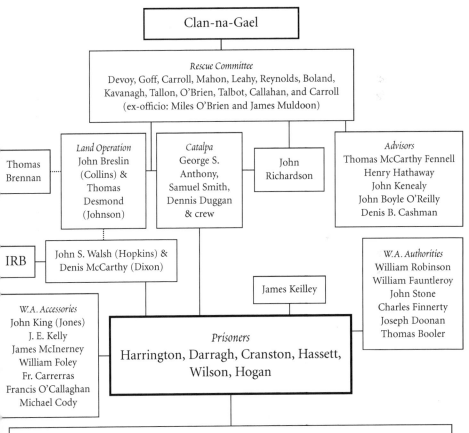

Reception Committee: John O'Conor, Richard Murphy, Bernard O'Reilly, Martin Hanley, Timothy Plunket, Thos. Kane, John Conway, Pat'k. Lennon, Thos. Fennell, Thomas Bolger, J. Crowley, Patrick Sheridan, Thomas Taaffe, Pat'k Cullen, John Madden, Michael Boland, John Coughlan, Col., R. O'S. Burke, Maj. Richard Dillon, M. A. Foran, S. B. Conover, William C. McClure, George Flemming, James O'Neill, Jeremiah Sheenhan, Thomas MaGuire, Capt. Lawrence O'Brien, William Cannon, Edward Byrne, Edward Moolic, Capt. James R. Curran, Thomas McCarthy, Capt. Wm. Cusack, Wm. F. Roantree, John K. Forde, C. V. Gallagher, Thomas Tallon, James L. White, William Collins, Jeremiah Kavanagh, John C. Talbot, Barth. Colgan, Wm. M. Stackpoole, Judge M. Cooney, Francis Foley, John Kenealy.

John Devoy, *Chairman,* Jer. O'Donovan Rossa, *Secretary,* Patrick Mahan, *Treasurer.*

SOURCES

Amos, Keith. *The Fenians in Australia, 1865–1880.* Kensington, N.S.W.: New South Wales University Press, 1988.

Anthony, Charles L. *Genealogy of the Anthony Family from 1495 to 1904.* Sterling, IL: Charles L. Anthony, 1904.

Anthony, Captain George S. *Logbook of Bark Catalpa of New Bedford, Mass., April 29, 1875 to August 23, 1876.* The Kendall Institute, New Bedford Whaling Museum: microform, Log #557.

Australian Dictionary of Biography. Vol. 6. Melbourne: Melbourne University Press, 1976.

Battye, J. S. *Western Australia: A History from Its Discovery to the Inauguration of the Commonwealth.* Nedlands, W.A.: University of Western Australia Press [facsimile edition], 1978.

Bayor, Ronald H., and Timothy J. Meagher, eds. *The New York Irish.* Baltimore, MD: Johns Hopkins University Press, 1996.

Beck, Horace. *Folklore and the Sea, American Maritime Library.* Vol. 6. Middletown, CT: Wesleyan University Press, 1973.

Biographical Directory of the U.S. Congress. [http://bioguide.congress.gov].

Bourke, D. F. *History of the Catholic Church in Western Australia.* Perth, W.A.: Archdiocese of Perth, 1979.

Breslin, John J. *The Cruise of the Catalpa.* Boston: Rockwell and Churchill, 1876.

Burchell, R. A. *San Francisco Irish, 1848–1880.* Manchester: Manchester University Press, 1979.

Burrows, Edwin G., and Mike Wallace. *Gotham: A History of New York City to 1898.* New York: Oxford University Press, 1999.

Byrne, Geraldine. *A Basilica in the Making: The Centenary of St. Patrick's, Fremantle.* Fremantle, W.A.: Mazenod Press, [2000].

Caron, Henri Le. *Twenty-five Years in the Secret Service: The Recollections of a Spy.* London: Heinemann, 1892.

Casey, John S. *Journal of a Voyage from Portland to Fremantle on Board the Convict Ship "Hougoumont."* Martin Kevin Cusack, ed. Bryn Mawr, PA: Dorrance, 1988.

Cashman, Denis. *Fenian Diary.* C. W. Sullivan, ed. Dublin: Wolfhound Press, 2001.

Church, Albert Cook. *Whale Ships and Whaling.* New York: Norton, 1960.

CIS US Serial Set Index, Part II, 35–45th Congresses, 1857–1879, Sub-indexes A–K, L–Z. Washington, DC: Congressional Information Service, 1977.

Clark, C. M. H., ed. *Select Documents in Australian History, 1851–1900.* Sydney: Angus and Robertson, 1969.

Sources

Connolly, S. J., ed. *The Oxford Companion to Irish History.* New York: Oxford University Press, 1998.

Dana, R. H. J. *Two Years before the Mast and Twenty-four Years After,* 61st printing (New York: Collier, 1937), 16.

D'Arcy, William. *The Fenian Movement in the United States: 1858–1886.* New York: Russell and Russell, 1971.

Davitt, Michael. *Life and Progress in Australasia.* London: Methuen, 1898.

Devoy, John. *Recollections of an Irish Rebel.* New York: Chas. D. Young, 1929.

Ellis, Leonard Bolles. *History of New Bedford and Its Vicinity, 1602–1892.* Syracuse, NY: D. Mason, 1892.

Encyclopedia Britannica. 15th ed. Chicago, 1993. Volumes 1, 2, 4, 14, 29.

Erickson, Rica, ed. *Bicentennial Dictionary of Western Australians.* Nedlands, W.A.: University of Western Australia Press, 1988.

Erickson, Rica, and Gillian O'Mara. *Convicts in Western Australia, 1850–1887.* Nedlands, W.A.: University of Western Australia Press, 1994.

Ethington, Philip J. *Public City: The Political Construction of Urban Life in San Francisco, 1850–1890.* New York: Cambridge University Press, 1994.

Evans, A. G. *Fanatic Heart: A Life of John Boyle O'Reilly.* Boston: Northeastern University Press, 1997.

Fenian Rescue! A Graphic Account of the Escape of Six Fenian Prisoners from Penal Servitude in Australia. By a Friend of the Oppressed [Anonymous]. New York: Published by the Author, 1876.

Fennell, Thomas McCarthy. *Voyage of the Hougoumont and Life at Fremantle.* Philadelphia: Xlibris, 2000.

Golway, Terry. *For the Cause of Liberty: A Thousand Years of Ireland's Heroes.* New York: Touchstone, 2000.

———. *Irish Rebel: John Devoy and America's Fight for Ireland's Freedom.* New York: St. Martin's, 1998.

Gopsill's Philadelphia City Directory, 1896. Philadelphia: James Gopsill's Sons, 1896.

Hansard's Parliamentary Debates (microform), Third Series, Vol. 229. London: Cornelius Buck, 1876.

Henderson, G., and K. J. Henderson. *Unfinished Voyages.* Vol. 2, *Western Australian Shipwrecks: 1851–1880.* Nedlands, W.A.: University of Western Australia Press, 1988.

Hitchcock, J. K. *History of Fremantle, the Front Gate of Australia, 1829–1929.* Fremantle, W.A.: Fremantle City Council, [1929].

Hohman, Elmo P. *The American Whaleman: A Study of Life and Labor in the Whaling Industry.* Clifton, NJ: Augustus M. Kelley, 1972.

Hughes, Robert. "The Real Australia," *Time,* September 11, 2000.

———. *The Fatal Shore: The Epic of Australia's Founding.* New York: Knopf, 1987.

Jackson, Kenneth T., ed. *The Encyclopedia of New York City.* New Haven, CT: Yale University Press, 1995.

Junger, Sebastian. *Fire.* New York: Norton, 2001.

Sources

Kane, Michael H. "American Soldiers in Ireland, 1865–1867." *Irish Sword* 90 (Winter 2002).

Keneally, Thomas. *The Great Shame and the Triumph of the Irish in the English-Speaking World.* New York: Nan A. Talese, 1999.

Kemp, Peter, ed. *The Oxford Companion to Ships and the Sea.* New York: Oxford University Press, 1976.

Laubenstein, William. *The Emerald Whaler.* London: Andre Deutsch, 1961.

Lloyd's Register of British and Foreign Shipping, July 1, 1875–June 30, 1876. London: Wyman and Sons, 1875.

Mawer, Granville Allen. *Ahab's Trade: The Saga of South Seas Whaling.* St. Leonards, N.S.W.: Allen and Unwin, 1999.

McConville, Seán. *Irish Political Prisoners, 1848–1922.* London: Routledge, 2003.

———. *A History of English Prison Administration.* Vol. 1. London: Routledge & Kegan Paul, 1981.

McGrath, Walter. "The Fenians in Australia." *Journal of the Cork Historical and Archaeological Society* 95 (1990).

———. "The Fenian Rising in Cork." *Irish Sword* 33 (Winter 1968).

McKissack, Patricia C., and Fredrick L. McKissack. *Black Hands, White Sails: The Story of African-American Whalers.* New York: Scholastic Press, 1999.

McManamin, Francis G. *The American Years of John Boyle O'Reilly, 1870–1890.* New York: Arno Press, 1976.

Morison, Samuel Eliot. *The Oxford History of the American People.* New York: Oxford University Press, 1965.

National Archives and Records Administration. "Despatches from U.S. Ministers to Great Britain, 1790–1906" (Microfilm Publication M30, rolls 125–26).

———. "Diplomatic Instructions of the Department of State, 1801–1906" (Microfilm Publication M77, roll 83).

———. "Notes from the British Legation in the United States to the Department of State, 1791–1906" (Microfilm Publication M50, roll 100).

———. "Notes to Foreign Legations in the United States from the Department of State, 1834–1906" (Microfilm Publication M99, roll 46).

———. Federal Population Census Schedules, 1880 (Microfilm Publication T9), 1900 (Microfilm Publication T623), and 1910 (Microfilm Publication T624).

O'Brien, William, and Desmond Ryan, eds. *Devoy's Post Bag, 1871–1928.* Vols. 1 and 2. Dublin: C. J. Fallon, 1948.

Ó Broin, Leon. *Fenian Fever: An Anglo American Dilemma.* New York: New York University Press, 1971.

Ó Lúing, Seán. *Fremantle Mission.* Tralee, Cork: Anvil Books, 1965. (Reprinted as *The Catalpa Rescue* in 1985 by Anvil.)

O'Mara, Gillian. "Joseph Noonan, Fenian Success Story." Bob Reece, ed., *The Irish in Western Australia,* Studies in Western Australia Series, 20. Nedlands, W.A.: University of Western Australia, 2000.

Sources

O'Reilly, John Boyle. *Moondyne Joe: A Story from the Underworld.* New York: P. J. Kenedy and Sons, 1879.

O'Reilly, Peggy. "Fr. Patrick McCabe." *Journal of the Old Drogheda Society* (2000).

Pease, Z. W. *The Catalpa Expedition.* New Bedford, MA: George S. Anthony, 1897.

———. "Fifty Years on *The Morning Mercury,* New Bedford, Mass., 1880–1930: A Reminiscence." New York Public Library, microform.

———, ed. *History of New Bedford.* New York: Lewis Historical Publishing, 1918.

Philbrick, Nathaniel. *In the Heart of the Sea: The Tragedy of the Whaleship Essex.* New York: Penguin Putnam, 2000.

Public Record Office (U.K.), Foreign Office, Series 5. General Correspondence with the United States of America.

Report of the Eighth Annual Convention, "V.C." [Clan-na-Gael], Cleveland, Ohio, September 4–8, 1877. "The Fenian Brotherhood Records and O'Donovan Rossa Personal Papers," The American Catholic History Research Center and University Archives, Catholic University of America, Washington, D.C.

Representative Men and Old Families of Southern Massachusetts. Vol. 2. Chicago: J. H. Beers, 1916.

Roche, James Jeffrey. *Life of John Boyle O'Reilly.* New York: Cassell Publishing, 1891.

Rosen, Bruce. "The 'Catalpa' Rescue." *Journal of the Royal Australian Historical Society* 65, pt. 2 (September 1979).

Russo, George. *Race for the Catalpa.* Perth, W.A.: Lynward Enterprises, 1986.

Ryan, George E. "Dennis [*sic*] B. Cashman, Warmly Devoted to His Native Land," *Bulletin* (March 1983), The Eire Society of Boston.

Schofield, William. *Seek for a Hero: The Story of John Boyle O'Reilly.* New York: P. J. Kenedy, 1956.

Schuckit, Mark A. *Drug and Alcohol Abuse: A Clinical Guide to Diagnosis and Treatment.* 4th ed. New York: Plenum Publishing, 1995.

Ship Registers of New Bedford, Massachusetts. Vol. 3. Boston: National Archives Project, 1940.

Shuck, Oscar T., ed. *History of the Bench and Bar of California.* Los Angeles: Commercial Printing House, 1901.

Stackpole, Edouard A. *The Sea-Hunters: The New England Whaleman during Two Centuries, 1635–1835.* Philadelphia: Lippincott, [1953].

Story of Yankee Whaling. New York: American Heritage Publishing, 1959.

Sullivan, T. D, A. M. Sullivan, and D. B. Sullivan, eds. *Speeches from the Dock; or, Protests from the Dock.* Providence, RI: Murphy and McCarthy, 1881.

U. S. House Executive Documents, 1868, 40th Cong., 2nd sess., 167.

———. 1870, 41st Cong., 2nd sess., 170.

Vital Records of New Bedford, Massachusetts to the Year 1850. Volume—Births. Boston: New England Historic Genealogical Society, 1932.

Sources

NEWSPAPERS

Echo [Cork]
Evening Post [New York]
Gaelic American [New York]
Herald [Western Australia]
Inquirer and Commercial News [Western Australia]
Irish-American [New York]
Irish Nation [New York]
Irish World/Irish World and American Liberator [New York]
Kalgoorlie Miner [Western Australia]
Morning Mercury [New Bedford]
New Bedford Evening Standard
New Bedford Times
New York Daily Tribune/New York Tribune
New York Herald
New York Times
Philadelphia Inquirer
Providence Journal [Rhode Island]
Republican Standard [New Bedford]
San Francisco Chronicle
Times [London]
W. A. Times [Western Australia]
West Australian
Western Mail [Western Australia]
Winona Daily Herald [Minnesota]
World [New York]

INDEX

Alabama claims. *See* Civil War (American)

Albert's (Fremantle stables), 92

Alcohol, problems and effects, 21, 38, 115–118, 169, 192f

Anthony family, 17–20; Emma Richardson, 18; George Smith, 17–20, 172; Humphrey, 17; Sophie, 18

Arbor Hill Prison (Dublin), 33

Australia, 24–25

Azores, 20, 21; Fayal, 69, 74; Flores, 21; St. Michael's, 69, 74f

Baines, Thomas, 37f

Beach, Thomas W. *See* Le Caron, Henri

Bell, John, 95, 121, 144f

Biggar, Joseph, 143

Boland, Michael, 54

Boland, Michael C., 41

Booler, Thomas, 94, 182

Boucicault, Dion, 53

Bourke. *See also* Burke

Bourke, Rev. Anselm, 192

Bourke, Thomas F., 33f, 35f

Branding prisoners, 170

Brennan, Thomas, 66, 170–171, 176; account of the rescue, 68f; arrival at Fayal, 74, Breslin's report, 119–121; Fremantle, 89. *See also* Appendix B, 194–210

Breslin, John J., 27, 43, 72, 73, 174; arrival at Sydney, 84; confrontation with Hogan in N.Y.C., 131f–132f; Fremantle, 84; letter to His Excellency, 95–96;

meets IRB agents, 152; meets John King, 146; O'Reilly's description of, 171; visits Fremantle Prison, 86. *See also* Appendix B, 194–210

Brophy, Hugh Francis, 186

Brown, George, 34f

Bunbury, 86f, 90

Burke, Ricard O'Sullivan, 52

Butt, Isaac, 30

Buzzards Bay, 15, 69

Byrne, Michael. *See* Cody, Michael

Cable (Java), 104, 123f. *See also* Telegraph

Callahan, Felix, 41

Calvary Cemetery (N.Y.C.), 174, 176, 177, 182

Canada. *See* Fenians

Canary Islands, Santa Cuz, Tenerife, 22, 23

Canton, 87

Cape Bouvard, 100

Cape Naturaliste, 101

Cape Verde, 21, 23

Carrerras, Rev. J., 117f

Carroll, Dr. William, 42, 181

Casey, Richard, 39

Cashman, Denis, 43, 45, 74, 171, 180

Catalpa: albacores, 22f; arrival at Bunbury, 88, 152; chronometers, 26f; crew list, 137; deaths at sea, 21, 167, 184; desertions, 21–22, 88, 118, 119, 184; final disposition, 184; finances, 29, 65, 133–138, 152; gams, 21; *Georgette*, first encounter,

Index

Catalpa (continued)
98, 161; *Georgette*, second encounter, 103–108, 163–165; log references, 15, 24, 98f, 106f, 167, 171; measurements, 29f; official response to escape, 107f; prisoners' protest, 109–113, 199–201; race to the ship, 94–100; settlement disagreement, 131–132, 139–142; smuggling tobacco, 74, 140. *See also* Appendix B, 194–210
Catalpa Jim. *See* Reynolds, James
Celtic Club (Boston), 44
Chambers, Thomas, 30
Chase, Ariel, 184
China, 147
Civil War (American): "Stone Fleet", 16; *Alabama* claims, 16
Clan-na-Gael: Baltimore Convention 1874, 37, 39, 56, 120; Cleveland Convention 1877, 124, 277; Philadelphia picnic, 172; Providence Convention 1875, 55; reception committee, 124, 211. *See also* Appendix B, 194–210
Cody, Michael, 84, 111, 183
Cohannet, 18
Collins, James (alias). *See* Breslin, John J.
Collins, Jerome L., 203
Collins, Patrick, 44
Condon, Edward O'Meagher, 53
Conflict, H.M.S., 89, 90,104, 144f, 153
Conover, Simon Barclay, 74, 181
Cook, Captain James, 24
Cooney, John M., 83, 86f, 181
Costello, Augustine E., 68
Coughlin, John, 50f
Cozens, Captain William, 23f
Cranston, Robert, 82, 177; letter about funds, 131f–132f
Crowley, Peter O'Neill, 75
Cuba Five, 33f, 34p
Curran, Peter, 35, 128, 182, 190
Curry, William, 32

Darragh, Thomas, 82, 100f, 178
Davitt, Michael, 178, 180
Delaney, Thomas, 116
Desmond, Thomas, 73, 84, 175
De Valera, Eamon, 177
Devoy, John, 35, 178, 220f
Dixon, Alfred (alias). *See* McCarthy, Denis Florence
Donahoe, Patrick, 45
Doonan, Joseph, 86, 182
Doran, Charles Guilfoyle, 142f
Draco, 18
Duffy, Edward, 76
Duggan, Denis, 20, 22, 170, 175
Duggan, Thomas, 183
Dunn, James. See Cody, Michael

Emerald Isle Hotel. *See* Moloney, Patrick

Farnham, Antone, 167
Fauntleroy, William Robert, 93, 182
Fayal. *See* Azores
Fenians: Canadian invasions, 31f; Holland submarine project, 175; military members, 30–33; transported to Australia, 25. *See also* O'Mahony, John; Roberts, William
Fennell, Thomas McCarthy, 37, 43, 169, 181
Fernandina, Florida, 73
Finnerty, Charles, 97, 183
Fitzgerald, Anthony, 70
Fitzgerald, James, 51
Fitzgerald, John E., 44
Flood, John Valentine, 146, 189
Florence, 79
Flores. *See* Azores
Foley, William, 85, 117, 123, 187
Fremantle Prison, 24
Fulham, Lawrence and Luke, 192

Garden Island, 89, 96, 153, 160

Index

Gazelle, 28, 168f, 188f

Georgette, 84, 87, 89, 93, 103

Gibney, Rev. Matthew, 192

Gifford, Captain David, 118

Giles, Ernest, 86

Gladstone, William E., 30, 41

Glasnevin Cemetery, 39, 176, 178

Goff, John W., 41, 43, 67–68, 176

Hall (alias). *See* Brennan, Thomas

Halpin, William, 68f

Harrington, Michael, 82, 176

Harvest, Edward Douglas, 105

Harwood's Hotel (Fremantle), 120

Hassett, Thomas Henry, 82, 177, 187

Hathaway, Henry C., 28, 56–57, 63–65, 80, 178

Henry Curtis, 18

Herald (Fremantle), 94–95, 96–97, 98–99, 100–101, 102, 106–108

Hitch, James C., 29

Hogan, Martin Joseph, 81, 131f, 132f, 177, 189; confrontation with Breslin in N.Y.C., 131f; letter to Peter Curran (1871), 35–36; letters to Ireland 1875, 143

Hogan, Mike, 69

Holden, Thomas M., 36f

Holland submarine project. *See* Fenians

Homan, F. W., 29

Hopkins, Henry (alias). *See* Walsh, John S.

Hougoumont, 23, 25, 168

Howell (Perth solicitor), 105f

Hue-and-Cry, 76

Invincibles, 179

Irish Republican Brotherhood (IRB), 40, 104,142–143. *See also* McCarthy, Denis Florence; Walsh, John Stephen

Johnston, Thomas (alias). *See* Desmond, Thomas

Jones, T. (alias). *See* King, John

Joyce, Dr. Robert Dwyer, 44

Kanaka, Robert, 21

Kanakas, 159

Kavanagh, Jeremiah, 39, 41

Keane, Cornelius Dwyer, 186

Keating, Patrick, 188, 191

Keilley, James, 30, 183

Kelly, John Edward, 84, 146, 183

Kelly, Thomas J., 77

Kenealy, John, 43, 181

Kennedy, John Fitzgerald, 180

Kentuckian, 110

Kickham, Charles, 190f

King, John, 84, 87, 126; arrival at Fremantle, 87, 150; meets Walsh and McCarthy, 148–151; his account, 144–166

Knights of the Red Branch, 174, 175

Leahy, Michael W., 41

Le Caron, Henri, 40

Lennon, Patrick, 34f, 67, 111, 125–126

Lomasney, William Mackey, 50

Loughlin, 39

Luby, Thomas Clarke, 50, 190f

Mackey, William. *See* Lomasney, William Mackey

Mahon, Patrick, 41, 78

Manchester Martyrs, 70

Maughan, Peter, 34f

McCabe, Rev. Patrick, 36, 39, 180, 187

McCafferty, John, 35

McCarthy, Charles, 30

McCarthy, Denis Florence, 104f, 117f, 142, 150, 179

McCleery, John, 97

McClure, John, 33f, 75

McGee, Darcy, 42

McInerney, James, 84, 146

Index

McManus (settler), 187
McManus, Terence Bellew, 39
McNally, James. *See* Wilson, James
Meledy, Patrick, 53f
Mid-Atlantic Ridge, 168
Mills, Coxswain, 97
Mitchel, John, 47, 56
Moloney, Patrick (Emerald Isle Hotel), 85, 121, 183
Moore, George Henry, 30
Mulcahy, Denis Dowling, 34f
Muldoon, James, 59
Mulleda, Harry S., 33f, 66
Murphy, Michael F., 142f
Murray Head(s), 97, 100

Nagle, Pierce, 190
Napper Tandy Club, 121
Nicholson, W. J., 38
Nolan, John, 30
Noman's Land, 18
Noonan, Joseph, 186
Nunan, Joseph. *See* Noonan, Joseph

O'Brien, James F. X., 50
O'Brien, John Patrick, 30
O'Brien, Larry, 52
O'Brien, Miles M., 59, 70, 182
O'Callaghan, Frank, 104, 117f, 190
Ocean Beauty, 23
O'Connell, Charles Underwood, 33f
O'Connor, Edward. *See* Tierney, Patrick
O'Connor, James, 66f
O'Connor, John, 66, 79
O'Connor, Patrick, 39
O'Donovan, Denis, 124
O'Donovan, Jeremiah, 186
O'Gorman, Richard, 51
O'Kelly, James J., 53, 127
O'Leary, Patrick "Pagan," 36
O'Mahoney, Cornelius, 117
O'Mahony, John, 34

O'Malley, P., 37
O'Neill, James, 39
O'Reilly, James. *See* Reilly, James
O'Reilly, John Boyle, 25, 28, 31, 43, 127, 165, 180

Panic of 1873, 17
Papal Brigade, 37f, 83f
Parker House (New Bedford), 45
Pearce, Captain, 23
Pease, Zephaniah W., 19
Perron Point, 97
Perry, Frank, 167, 168
Pilot (Boston), 45
Portland Prison, 25
Power, Edmund, 33f
Power, John O'Connor, 71

Rabbit Island, 148
Reilly, James, 186
Reynolds, James, 27, 29–30, 41, 181
Richardson, John T., 17, 27, 81, 178, 184
Roantree, William Francis, 34f, 35, 37, 76
Roberts, William, 31f
Robinson, William C. F., 89, 182
Rockingham, 88
Rockingham Hotel, 94, 156
Rockingham Jarrah Timber Company, 95
Ronayne, Joseph, 143
Rossa, Jeremiah O'Donovan, 36f, 70, 123, 145f
Rosser (guest at Moloney's Hotel), 121
Rossiter, John J., 121
Rottnest Island, 89, 98, 102
Russia, 33
Rynd, James, 37

Santa Cruz. *See* Canary Islands, Santa Cruz, Tenerife
Searle (guest at Moloney's Hotel), 121
Sloan, William, 87
Smith, Samuel (Mate), 22, 173

Index

Somers (hotelier), 94
Spencer's Hotel (Bunbury), 117
St. Clair, Edward Pilsworth, 33f
St. Michael's. *See* Azores
St. Raymond's Cemetery (NYC), 176
Stackpoole, M. W., 83
Stephens, James, 30, 32, 37, 76
Stevens House (New Bedford), 202
Stewart, A. T., 41f
Stone, John F., 92, 97, 107, 182
Sulphur Bay, 97
Sweeny's Hotel (NYC), 200

Talbot, John C., 41, 73, 83
Tallon, Thomas, 41
Telegraph, 102, 104f, 123f. *See also* Cable
    (Java)
Tenerife. *See* Canary Islands, Santa Cruz,
    Tenerife
Ten Mile Well, 156
Thompson, 92
Tierney, Patrick, 32

Tobin, John A., 60, 62, 182
Tropic of Cancer, 23, 168

United Brotherhood of Ireland, 72

Walsh, John Bennett, 116
Walsh, John Stephen, 104f, 117f, 142,
    143f–145f, 150, 179
Walsh, Patrick, 34f, 39
Warner, John, 32
Warren, John, 68f
Weld, Sir Frederick, 192
"Whaleman's Shipping Paper," 37f
Whaling, 15–17; Artic fleet, 16; crew
    turnover, 21, 22; food, 168; forecastle
    conditions, 169; gams, 21; lay, 18–19,
    137–138
Whelan, Captain, 33
Williams, Archbishop John Joseph, 45f
Wilson, James, 37, 40, 81f, 177. *See also*
    Appendix A, 185–193
Winter, Samuel, 189

ABOUT THE EDITORS

Marie King, holder of two degrees from New York University, is an elementary school teacher. Her husband, Philip Fennell, is an accountant. Their first editing collaboration resulted in the publication of an ancestor's recollection, *Voyage of the Hougoumont and Life at Fremantle: The Life of an Irish Rebel.* They live in Pawling, New York, with their two children.

Printed in the United States
By Bookmasters